Starting Strong 2017

KEY OECD INDICATORS ON EARLY CHILDHOOD EDUCATION AND CARE

OECD
BETTER POLICIES FOR BETTER LIVES

Please cite this publication as:
OECD (2017), *Starting Strong 2017: Key OECD Indicators on Early Childhood Education and Care*, OECD Publishing, Paris.
http://dx.doi.org/10.1787/9789264276116-en

ISBN 978-92-64-27610-9 (print)
ISBN 978-92-64-27611-6 (PDF)

Photo credits: Cover © Wavebreakmedia/Shutterstock.com; © Goodmoments/Shutterstock.com

Corrigenda to OECD publications may be found on line at: *www.oecd.org/about/publishing/corrigenda.htm*.

Foreword

A consolidated body of research in recent years, in particular from neuroscience, shows that early childhood education and care (ECEC) provides a crucial foundation for future learning by fostering the development of cognitive and non-cognitive skills that are important for success later in life. Research also suggests that much of the benefit of ECEC for children's future learning and development depends on the quality of ECEC services. Therefore, governments are also increasingly looking to international comparisons of ECEC's opportunities and outcomes as they develop policies to mobilise resources to meet rising demands.

For over 15 years, the OECD's Directorate for Education and Skills has contributed to these efforts by conducting policy analysis and developing new data on ECEC to provide valid, timely and comparable international information to help support countries review and redesign policies to improve their early childhood services and systems. The publication **"Starting Strong 2017: Key OECD indicators on early childhood education and care"** is a first attempt to bring together all of the key OECD ECEC indicators. The report addresses the needs and interests of a wide audience, including national and local policy makers and researchers interested in better understanding what is happening in the ECEC sector, as well as national statisticians who collect and report education data to international organisations. Together with OECD country policy reviews, the indicators published in this report can be used to help governments build more effective and equitable ECEC systems.

The publication is a comprehensive and catalogued data source for international ECEC data. The policy relevance, the adherence to quality standards and the interpretability of indicators were the three main criteria for selection. Some recent reforms are also highlighted in this volume when they are useful for the interpretation of the data. The indicators are organised in five chapters:

- **Chapter 1:** An overview chapter with the main findings and challenges for improving the ECEC sector.
- **Chapter 2:** Focusing on contextual information, this chapter provides a general review of a range of socio-economic and other factors that may determine the need for ECEC, policy on ECEC, the kinds of ECEC provided and uptake of what is on offer.
- **Chapter 3:** This chapter on policy inputs presents indicators of the resources invested in a system, such as the level and type of ECEC financing, the regulations of staff-child ratios, and some indicators on the teaching workforce at the ECEC level (e.g. level of qualification, teacher salary, and working time of teachers).
- **Chapter 4:** This chapter on policy outputs includes indicators that are the result of the policy inputs put in place, such as enrolment rates by age and type of

institution, duration of early childhood education, and content areas of curriculum frameworks.

- **Chapter 5:** This chapter on policy outcomes includes indicators on the outcomes of children associated with both policy inputs and policy outputs. For example, it includes indicators on student performance, health, well-being and labour market outcomes.

While much progress has been accomplished in recent years, member countries and the OECD continue to strive to strengthen the link between policy needs and the best available internationally comparable data. Thus, additional efforts are needed to fill in remaining gaps in system-level indicators, for instance: by collecting more robust and comparable indicators on ECEC settings that enrol children under the age of 3; by improving the definitions of public and private funding; and by improving the country coverage, time series and quality of the key ECEC indicators related to actual child-to-staff ratios, content areas of the curriculum, public support to families, and average time children spend on intentional pedagogical or educational activities.

The OECD will continue to address these challenges vigorously and develop ECEC indicators where it is feasible and promising to develop data; it will also advance in areas where considerable investment still needs to be made in conceptual work. However, international efforts are also necessary to develop new indicators, especially on child outcomes and process quality (e.g. on the quality of pedagogical interactions between ECEC staff and children, the quality of communications between staff and parents, and, most importantly, the quality of interactions among children, as well as the quality of interaction of children with space and materials). Therefore, the OECD programme of work over the period 2017-2020 includes a series of projects to develop the scope of available data on ECEC. These include:

- The **Teaching and Learning International Survey (TALIS), Starting Strong,** is the first international survey of ECEC staff and the quality of the learning and well-being environment in different ECEC settings across OECD member and non-member economies. This will contribute to a better understanding of the quality of the learning and well-being environment that children experience (instrument development and pilot study in 2015/16, main study in 2018 and reporting in 2019).

- The **Policy Review on Quality in ECEC** is a project that aims to influence how to interpret quality dimensions, in particular, quality beyond regulations, for which a common understanding is yet to be established at the international level. The project will enable countries to draw on the most recent available international evidence on the effectiveness of both structural and process quality standards, and to learn from other countries' experiences and challenges in this regard. The project started in 2017 and will undertake different steps until 2020.

- The **International Early Learning and Child Well-being Study** is an international study to measure the non-cognitive and cognitive learning outcomes of children. The results of this pilot study will show what is possible in children's early learning in various socio-emotional and cognitive domains, and will help countries monitor progress at a system level. The conceptual framework for the assessment of children's learning was developed in 2015, with a scoping exercise conducted in 2016 and reporting scheduled for 2020.

Acknowledgements

The publication was drafted by Eric Charbonnier, with contributions from Guillaume Bousquet, Arno Engel, Maria Huerta and Victoria Liberatore of the Directorate for Education and Skills. Mernie Graziotin, Sophie Limoges, Rachel Linden, Anne-Lise Prigent, Margaret Simmons and Elizabeth Zachary (external editor) provided valuable support in the editorial and production process. Members of the OECD Network on Early Childhood Education and Care provided valuable input, case studies, country information and data, and helped guide the development of this publication. The ECEC Thematic Working Group on Data provided useful guidance to select the indicators included in the report (see the Annex B for a list of contributing members). In addition, the publication also received valuable input from our OECD colleague Olivier Thevenon of the Directorate for Employment, Labour and Social Affairs, and from Cristina Stringher (researcher from the Italian National Institute for the Educational Evaluation of Instruction and Training - INVALSI). Overall guidance was provided by Yuri Belfali, head of the OECD Early Childhood and Schools Division, Directorate for Education and Skills and Miho Taguma (OECD ECEC project manager).

Table of contents

Figures

Tables

Boxes

Executive summary

The first years of life lay the foundations for future skills development, well-being and learning.

Early childhood education and care (ECEC) can improve children's cognitive abilities and socio-emotional development, help create a foundation for lifelong learning, make children's learning outcomes more equitable, reduce poverty, and improve social mobility from generation to generation.

The number of years spent in early childhood education and care (ISCED 0) is also a strong predictor of the level of performance reached at later stages, both in and out of school. Programme for International Student Assessment (PISA) 2015 data show that children who attended early childhood education for at least two years perform, on average, better than others at age 15. After accounting for student and school-level socio-economic status, the difference is still statistically significant in half of the 57 countries with available data.

The benefits of ECEC are not limited to learning outcomes.

Affordable and high-quality ECEC with an adequate number of hours per week contribute to an increase in the participation of women in the labour force. The relationship between a mother's labour market participation and enrolment rates in formal childcare is strong, especially for mothers with their youngest child under the age of 3.

Thus, in countries where mothers' labour market participation rates are highest, such as Denmark, Luxembourg, the Netherlands, Portugal, Slovenia and Switzerland (above 70% employment among women aged 15 to 64 with their youngest child under the age of 3), the proportions of young children enrolled in formal childcare are also the highest.

In recent decades, governments have recognised the importance of public investment in ECEC and have delegated responsibility for ECEC public funding to local authorities.

ECEC has experienced a surge of policy attention in OECD countries in recent decades. In 2013, expenditure on ECEC (ISCED 0) accounted for an average of 0.8% of GDP, of which around three quarters went to pre-primary education (ISCED 02).

In most OECD countries, there is substantial public investment in ECEC, and parental fees are often publicly subsidised. In early childhood educational development (ISCED 01), public sources account for an average of 69% of total expenditure, while in pre-primary education (ISCED 02), it amounts to 83%.

Many governments delegate responsibility for ECEC public funding to local authorities. Therefore, public funding is also more decentralised in early childhood education (ISCED 0) than at any other level of education. On average across OECD countries, only 34% of public funds for early childhood education came from the central government, after transfers to regional and local levels of government.

The level of qualification required to be a teacher in pre-primary education has increased. However, their salaries are still below those of other tertiary-educated workers.

Prospective teachers should be provided with high-quality initial training. In 27 out of the 37 countries with available data, an individual can teach at the pre-primary level of education after earning a bachelor's degree or equivalent (ISCED level 6) at the end of initial teacher education. Despite this increase in the level of qualification required for being a teacher in pre-primary education, teachers' salaries remain below those of other tertiary-educated workers in most countries. On average, pre-primary teachers in OECD countries earn only 74% of the average salary of a tertiary-educated, 25-64 year-old full-time, full-year worker.

Universal or quasi-universal access to at least one year of ECEC has become the norm. However, ECEC provision for children under the age of 3 takes different forms across OECD countries.

Access to ECEC is on the rise in all countries, partly because of increased public spending to extend legal entitlements to a place in ECEC, as well as efforts to ensure free access, at least for some ages and selected population groups. In 2015, most OECD countries provided free access to ECEC to all children for at least the last year before entering primary school.

High enrolment rates are also observed for lower age groups: among 4-year-olds, 90% or more are already enrolled in pre-primary (or primary education) in two-thirds of the 37 countries with available data, while 70% of 3-year-olds are already enrolled in ECEC.

The share of children under the age of 3 enrolled in ECEC settings is also on the rise in most countries. On average across OECD countries, around one third of children under the age of 3 were enrolled in formal childcare in 2014. This percentage increased by over eight percentage points between 2005 and 2014. However, enrolment rates and intensity of participation at these ages vary significantly across countries. For instance, ECEC settings in some countries, such as Estonia, Finland, Greece, Hungary, Latvia and Poland, provide long hours per week to a small proportion of children under the age of 3. By contrast, fewer hours per week are provided to an above-average proportion of children under the age of 3 in a small group of other countries.

Universal access is not a guarantee for high-quality ECEC. A move towards an integrated ECEC system regarding curricula and governing authority is observed in several OECD countries.

Recent international trends show that an increasing number of countries with split systems are moving towards integrated ECEC settings regarding curricula and/or governing authority. The integration of ECEC systems administered under the responsibility of one ministry (or agency) is associated with better ECEC quality and can help enhance universal entitlement, more affordable access, better qualified staff and smoother transitions.

Today, more than half of OECD countries have an integrated ECEC system. The other countries have a split system, where the settings enrolling most children under the age of 3 are often under the authority of the Ministry of Social Affairs, while the settings providing ECEC for older children are under the authority of the Ministry of Education. In these countries, different standards are often set for different ECEC settings or for different age groups of children. In contrast, in all countries and jurisdictions with an integrated system, the same standards are applied to any ECEC setting.

Some challenges remain for improving the ECEC sector.

- **Financing**: Developing clear and consistent strategies for efficiently allocating public resources to ECEC priority areas.
- **Teaching workforce**: Improving the working conditions and professional education of ECEC staff.
- **Parents**: Engaging parents, especially in ensuring high-quality learning at home and communicating between ECEC staff and parents.
- **Curriculum**: Developing broad guidelines and curricular standards for all ECEC services.
- **Access and governance:** Increasing public provision for children under 3 and facilitating the transition from childcare to early education are two key challenges, especially for countries with split systems.
- **Equity in access to ECEC**: Ensuring equitable access for all children to attend quality ECEC, with a focus on children under the age of 3.
- **Knowledge gaps:** Filling in the knowledge gaps of child outcomes with longitudinal designs would allow the study of developmental trajectories and the ECEC process quality's long-term effects on particular groups of children.

Chapter 1.

Overview: Why we need indicators on early childhood education and care

Early childhood education and care (ECEC) has experienced an increase in policy attention globally over the two past decades, with major initiatives recently launched at the international level. ECEC is one of the 10 targets Sustainable Development Goals (SDGs), while the International Standard Classification of Education (ISCED 2011) was implemented in 2011 and better captures programmes for very young children. For more than 15 years, the OECD has conducted analysis and developed new data on ECEC to provide valid, timely and comparable international information to help support countries review and redesign policies to improve their early childhood services and systems. This publication brings together for the first time all the key indicators in one volume dedicated to ECEC. This overview chapter includes the main findings of the publication and the challenges for improving the ECEC sector. The scoreboard at the end shows the data underlying some key indicators on ECEC.

The statistical data for Israel are supplied by and are under the responsibility of the relevant Israeli authorities. The use of such data by the OECD is without prejudice to the status of the Golan Heights, East Jerusalem and Israeli settlements in the West Bank under the terms of international law.

Why a full volume dedicated to OECD indicators on early childhood education and care?

Early childhood education and care (ECEC) has experienced an increase in policy attention across the world over the two past decades.

Early childhood education and care has experienced a surge of policy attention in OECD countries in recent decades, at the national as well as international level. However, this increasing attention is not the only change; the nature of the public debate has also significantly evolved over this period. Policy makers have recognised that equitable access to quality ECEC can strengthen the foundations of lifelong learning for all children and support the broad educational and social needs of families, and they have therefore increased the resources allocated to this sector over the last decade. With this trend, governments have taken recent initiatives that aim to enhance the quality of ECEC services and improve the equity of access to ECEC settings. This is in contrast to the public debates of the past, which were limited to quantitative issues, and public spending was mainly concentrated on measures to expand access to affordable ECEC.

This new policy direction is a positive step and is supported by several international studies, programme evaluations and quality measurements that have repeatedly shown that access to ECEC programmes has positive effects on children's well-being, learning and development. However, to ensure that children can access ECEC services is not enough; positive results for children can only be achieved if the level of quality of these services is high. Otherwise, children may even be harmed by low quality care and education.

Major initiatives have been recently launched at the international level: ECEC is one of the 10 targets in the Sustainable Development Goals (SDGs)…

At the international level, there is the same increasing policy attention on early childhood education issues. For instance, when world leaders in 2015 defined the global ambitions for the next 15 years by adopting 17 Sustainable Development Goals (SDGs) at the United Nations Summit in New York, they first considered "Education" as a cornerstone of the sustainable development agenda. This was in recognition of the relevance of the topic for envisaging living in a more inclusive world. Second, they decided that the aim of one the 10 main education-related goals was to "ensure by 2030 that all girls and boys have access to quality early childhood development, care and pre-primary education so that they are ready for primary education" (Target 4.2 of the SDG project). This initiative is a supplementary incentive to develop policy relevant, comparable and robust indicators to assess in the next decade if this goal is achieved or not across the world.

…while the revised International Standard Classification of Education (ISCED 2011) better captures programmes for very young children that provide ECEC (ISCED 01).

Major changes are not limited to an increase of the policy relevance of ECEC in public debate; technical improvements of ECEC indicators have also been implemented to produce internationally comparable education statistics (OECD/Eurostat/UNESCO Institute for Statistics, 2015). For instance, the International Standard Classification of Education (ISCED) - the reference classification for organising education programmes by education levels - was revised in 2011, and programmes for very young children (i.e. under the age of 3) were included for the first time in the nomenclature if they adhered to several criteria (e.g. duration and intensity of participation, staff qualification, governance, curriculum content).

The first level (ISCED 0) previously encompassed only pre-primary education programmes designed for children from the age of 3 to the official primary school entrance age. In the new version, this level has been expanded to include an additional sub-category of educational or pedagogical programmes designed for children below the age of 3. Acknowledging that learning starts at birth, and that quality in care and support for the youngest children's development and learning is important, these types of educational and pedagogical programmes for very young children are becoming increasingly important and prevalent. This new provision will therefore make it possible to compare data on this sub-level for the first time.

This classification is significant progress and was implemented in international data collection in 2015. However, further progress is still needed as ISCED 2011 is not yet capturing some ECEC programmes that are an integral part of countries' ECEC systems, but that are not in adherence with one or several of the ISCED criteria. Therefore, this publication will go beyond the ISCED 2011 classification and will also present indicators on participation in ECEC, including the other registered ECEC settings outside the scope of ISCED 2011 (see mapping of ECEC programmes in Table 2.1 and Figure 4.2).

This publication is a first attempt to bring together all of the key OECD ECEC indicators. The policy relevance, the adherence to quality standards and the interpretability of indicators were the three main criteria for selection.

For more than 15 years, the OECD has conducted policy analysis and developed new data on ECEC to provide valid, timely and comparable international information to help support countries review and redesign policies to improve their early childhood services and systems. This publication brings together for the first time all the key existing ECEC indicators in one volume.

The indicators volume of Starting Strong is a comprehensive and catalogued data source for international ECEC data. Each chapter covers around 10 indicators, and this overview chapter includes the main findings and challenges for improving the ECEC sector. There were three main criteria for the selection of the indicators: 1) policy relevance; 2) adherence to quality standards (e.g. adequacy of the concepts and definitions that set out what the indicator seeks to measure; adequacy of the calculation methods used to implement the indicators; quality/availability of the data); and 3) an easy understanding of the indicator (for example, an indicator may be difficult to interpret in the national institutional context where international standards deviate from national ones).

Some recent reforms are also highlighted in this volume when they are useful for the interpretation of the data. This publication will be useful for policy makers and researchers interested in better understanding what is happening in the ECEC sector, as well as for national statisticians collecting and reporting data on education to international organisations.

The scoreboard at the end of this chapter (Table 1.1) shows all the data underlying some key indicators on ECEC. Six main themes on ECEC are covered in the scoreboard (access and intensity of participation, financing, governance, legal entitlement to place, teaching workforce and equity). These are all taken from the analytical work presented in this publication, and each ECEC dimension includes several indicators. Countries are ranked according to the indicators underlying each dimension. The scoreboard highlights (using colour coding) countries in the bottom 25%, countries in the top 25% and those around the OECD average (in the remaining part of the distribution). A sharp threshold has been applied, which means that some countries can be classified in one group (e.g. the bottom 25%) but be close to the other group (e.g. average).

OECD indicators on ECEC: What do the data reveal and what are the main trends?

The indicators are organised in four chapters (contextual information, policy inputs, policy outputs and policy outcomes). The **first chapter on contextual information** provides an overview of the main contextual factors influencing ECEC policies, such as the legal entitlements to access ECEC, the nature of the programmes, and the earliest starting age. It also includes indicators illustrating the socio-economic context, some recent demographic patterns, and some changes in family structure. The **second chapter on policy inputs** presents indicators of the resources invested in a system, such as the level and type of ECEC financing, the regulations of staff-child ratios, and some indicators on the teaching workforce at the ECEC level (e.g. level of qualification, teacher's salary or working time of teachers). The **third chapter on policy outputs** includes indicators that are the result of the policy inputs put in place, such as enrolment rates by age and type of institution, duration of early childhood education, and content areas of curriculum frameworks. Finally, the **fourth chapter on policy outcomes** includes indicators on the outcomes of children associated with both policy inputs and policy outputs. For example, it will include indicators analysing the relationship between attendance in ECEC and performance reached at later stages, mainly drawn from the Programme for International Student Assessment (PISA) 2015 data (OECD, 2017a). The next sections include the main findings by theme underlying the indicators.

Governance

More than half of OECD countries have an integrated ECEC system regarding curricula and governing authority.

Findings from the literature show that having integrated ECEC systems administered under the responsibility of one ministry (or agency) are associated with better ECEC quality and help to enhance universal entitlement, more affordable access, better qualified staff and smoother transitions (Bennett, 2008). A study conducted by Kaga, Bennett and Moss (2010) on five countries (Brazil, Jamaica, New Zealand, Slovenia, and Sweden) suggested that the integration of ECEC systems from age 1 until entry into compulsory education had several positive effects: 1) it increased access and enrolment (particularly for programmes designed for children under the age of 3; 2) it improved staff working conditions and status; 3) it increased staff recruitment levels and training; and 4) it had a positive impact on pedagogical practices and curriculum development.

A move towards integrated ECEC settings is observed in several OECD countries. Today, in more than half of the countries with available data - Australia, Estonia, Finland, Germany, Kazakhstan, New Zealand, Norway, Slovenia and Sweden - the ECEC settings enrolling most children under and above the age of 3 are administered under the responsibility of one ministry, or have integrated curricula. The main advantage of integrated systems is that they provide a continuum in learning and services. Whether or not to have education or social affairs ministries responsible for all ECEC settings is ultimately a decision for countries, and both strategies have pros and cons.

In the other countries, including, for example, Belgium, France, Israel, Italy, Korea, Japan, the Netherlands, Portugal, Switzerland, Turkey and the United States, some ECEC settings for children under 3 are officially registered but provided in distinct settings and under the responsibility of different ministries (split model). Among these countries, Italy and Korea are moving towards integrated ECEC settings regarding curricula or/and governing authority (see Box 2.1 for Italy). In split systems, the settings enrolling most children under the age of 3 are often under the authority of the Ministry of Social Affairs, while the settings providing ECEC for older children are under the authority of the Ministry of Education. In these countries, different standards are often set for different ECEC settings or for different age groups of children. In contrast, in all countries and jurisdictions with an integrated system, the same standards are applied to any ECEC setting.

In early childhood education and care, many governments delegate responsibilities of ECEC to local authorities. As a result, public funding is more decentralised in early childhood education than at any other level of education.

The devolution of tasks in the early childhood field can be needed as the concrete acknowledgement of the rights of local communities, but also for reasons of practical management. A shift towards more devolution can also be motivated by the desire to bring decision making and delivery closer to the families being served, and to adapt services to meet local needs and circumstances. Thus, central authorities can delegate responsibility to centres and school-based settings to manage a variety of tasks, including implementation, monitoring, evaluation and reporting. Local authorities can better co-ordinate with parents and communities to determine the appropriateness of national ECEC goals (Mahon, 2011).

Public funding is more decentralised in early childhood education (ISCED 0) than at any other level of education. In 2013, on average across OECD countries, only 41% of public funds for early childhood education came from central government, before transfers to regional and local authorities. After transfers, this share drops to 34%, and the share of local funds rises from 45% to 54%. Central government is the source of over 80% of funds after transfers only in Australia, Colombia, Ireland and New Zealand. Local government is the source of over 90% of funds after transfers in 11 countries: Brazil, Estonia, Finland, Iceland, Latvia, Lithuania, Norway, Poland, the Slovak Republic, Slovenia and the United Kingdom (Figure 3.5).

The devolution of powers had also some disadvantages, and may widen differences of access and quality between regions. In the devolution process, it seems important to ensure that early childhood services are part of a well-conceptualised national policy, with devolved powers to local authorities on the one hand, and a national approach to goal setting, legislation and regulation, financing, staffing criteria, and programme standards on the other.

The proportions of children enrolled in private early childhood educational development settings (ISCED 01) are considerably larger than for pre-primary education (ISCED 02), and exceed 50% in two thirds of OECD countries.

As countries continue to expand their early childhood education programmes, it will be important to consider parents' needs and expectations regarding accessibility, cost, programme and staff quality, and accountability. When these needs are not met in public settings, some parents may be more inclined to send their children to private pre-primary settings.

When analysing private settings, a distinction needs to be made between government-dependent and independent-private settings: (1) **independent-private ECEC settings** are controlled by a non-government organisation or with a governing board not selected by a government agency that receive less than 50% of their core funding from government agencies, (2) **government-dependent private ECEC settings** are controlled by a non-government organisation or with a governing board not selected by a government agency that receive more than 50% of their core funding from government agencies.

Some 10% of children in pre-primary education (ISCED 02) are enrolled in independent-private settings on average across OECD countries. When considering government-dependent private schools or ECEC institutions, 32% of children are enrolled in private pre-primary programmes. This proportion exceeds 45% in Australia, Belgium, Chile, Germany, Japan, Korea, Norway, New Zealand and Portugal. The proportions of children enrolled in private early childhood educational institutions (ISCED 01) are considerably larger compared to pre-primary education. In two thirds of the countries with available data on early childhood development programmes, more than 50% of children are enrolled in private institutions (Figure 4.6).

Financing of ECEC

Expenditure on ECEC (ISCED 0) accounts for an average of 0.8% of GDP. However, significant variations are observed across countries, mainly because of significant differences across countries in the number of years children spend in ECEC.

Expenditure on all ECEC (ISCED 0) accounts for an average of 0.8% of the collective GDP, of which 0.2% goes to early childhood educational development (ISCED 01) and 0.6% to pre-primary education (ISCED 02). Differences between countries are significant. For example, while 0.2% or less of GDP is spent on ECEC (ISCED 0) in Japan, Ireland and Switzerland, more than 1.0% of GDP is spent in Chile, Denmark, Finland, Iceland, Israel, Norway, the Russian Federation, Slovenia and Sweden (Figure 3.2).

These large variations are mainly explained by significant differences across countries in the participation in ECEC services, the mode of enrolment (full-time versus part-time), teaching working conditions (e.g. teacher's salary and working time), child-to-staff ratios, the fees requested, and public support provided to families to enrol their children in ECEC settings and in the number of years children spend in ECEC. In some countries, such as Ireland and the United Kingdom, children typically enter primary education at age 5, while in Estonia, Finland Latvia, Poland and Sweden, they typically enter this level at age 7. In all other countries, children typically enter primary education at age 6.

Governments have recognised the importance of public investment in ECEC, especially for pre-primary education.

Public spending on ECEC is an important guarantee for equity. Without sufficient public spending, there is a greater risk that access to ECEC programmes will be restricted to affluent families, and that the quality of programmes will vary. In most OECD countries, there is substantial public investment in ECEC. Publicly-funded ECEC tends to be more prevalent in the European OECD countries than in the non-European.

However, a distinction should be drawn between pre-primary education (ISCED 02) and a programme typically designed to enrol younger children. Thus, in most countries with data for both categories, the share of public spending tends to be smaller in early childhood educational development (ISCED 01) than in pre-primary education (ISCED 02). On average, in early childhood educational development (ISCED 01), public sources account for 69% of total expenditure, while in pre-primary education (ISCED 02), the share of public expenditure is 83% (Figure 3.4; OECD, 2016).

The annual expenditure per child enrolled in early childhood educational development programmes (ISCED 01) is significantly higher than in pre-primary education (ISCED 02) in most countries.

In pre-primary education, annual expenditure per child for both public and private institutions is an average of USD 8 070 in OECD countries. Expenditure ranges from USD 4 000 or less in Turkey, to more than USD 14 000 in Luxembourg and Norway. Annual expenditure per child enrolled in early childhood educational development programmes (ISCED 01) is significantly higher than in pre-primary education (ISCED 02) in 10 out of the 13 OECD countries with available data for both programmes, with an average of USD 12 501 (Figure 3.1; OECD, 2016).

Smaller child-to-teacher ratios observed in early childhood development programmes is the main factor influencing this pattern. On average across the 12 OECD countries with available data for both programmes, there are 14 children per pre-primary teacher working in pre-primary education, while the ratio is only 9 children per teacher in early childhood development programmes (Figure 3.10; OECD, 2016).

Similar levels of expenditure among countries can mask a variety of contrasting policy choices. This helps to explain why there is no simple relationship between overall spending on education and quality of ECEC settings.

Four main factors influence the salary cost of teachers per child enrolled in pre-primary education (ISCED 02): 1) time children spend on intentional pedagogical or educational activities; 2) contact time of teachers with children; 3) teachers' salaries; and 4) estimated group size. Specific levels of the salary cost of teachers per child may result from different combinations of these four factors.

Higher levels of expenditure on education cannot automatically be equated with better performance at later stages. This is not surprising, as countries spending similar amounts on ECEC do not necessarily have similar education policies and practices. For example, at the pre-primary level, the Netherlands and Norway had very similar levels of teacher salary costs per child in 2014, both slightly above the OECD average.

In Norway, this can be explained by an above OECD average time children spent on intentional pedagogical or educational activities, above-average contact time of teachers with children, average level of teacher salaries, and below-average estimated group size. In the Netherlands, there were above-average teacher salaries, average contact time of teachers with children, and small estimated group size compared to the average, however, these were more than offset by a significant below-average amount of time children spent on intentional pedagogical or educational activities (Figure 1.1).

Figure 1.1. Contribution of various factors to salary cost of teachers per child, pre-primary education (2014)

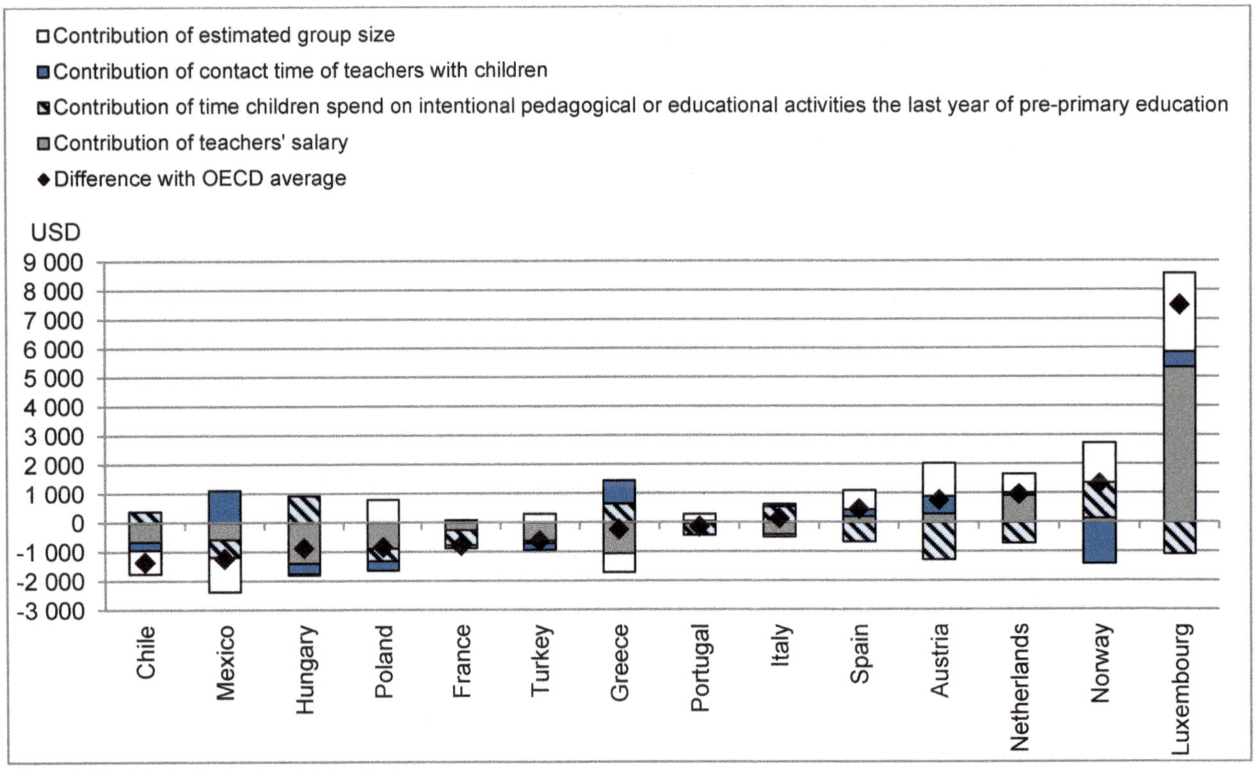

Notes: This chart shows the contribution (in USD) of the factors influencing the difference between salary cost of teachers per child in the country and the OECD average. For example, in Hungary, the salary cost of teachers per child is USD 877 lower than the OECD average. This is because Hungary has lower teachers' salaries (- USD 1 392) than the OECD average, above-average time children spend on intentional pedagogical or educational activities the last year of pre-primary education (+ USD 921), above-average contact time of teachers with children (- USD 357), and slightly above-average estimated group size (- USD 49).

Countries are ranked in ascending order of the difference between the salary cost of teachers per student and the OECD average.

Source: OECD (2017b), OECD Online education database, OECD, Paris, www.oecd.org/education/database.htm.

StatLink http://dx.doi.org/10.1787/888933487130

Comparing the relative salary cost of teachers per child using this analysis affects the ranking of some countries when compared to measuring in USD. For example, because of Luxembourg's high USD salaries, it has by far the highest salary cost in pre-primary education: at USD 9 729, it is over triple many countries shown in Figure 1.1. However, when differences in countries' wealth are considered, Luxembourg is still in first position, but the differences with other countries are significantly smaller.

Teaching workforce

There are few teachers from minority and ethnic communities, and women represent the overwhelming majority of ECEC teachers in OECD countries.

The diversity of staff is particularly beneficial to open the minds of disadvantaged children and to ease their integration. It is also important for children – particularly boys – to have a strong male role model in the classroom or centre. However, teachers in ECEC are mainly women. A reinforced male presence is critical to counter traditional views of women in childrearing positions, and to ensure that school and learning remain gender neutral. Among the predominantly female workforce, there are few teachers from minority and ethnic communities.

The age distribution of teachers varies widely across OECD countries. However, a common pattern emerges when the gender of teachers is analysed. The highest proportions of women teachers are concentrated in the earlier years of schooling, and shrink at each successive level of education. On average across OECD countries, around 97% of teachers in pre-primary education are women. While women represent 97% of the teaching workforce in pre-primary education on average across OECD countries, the average drops to 43% at the tertiary level.

In 35 out of the 39 OECD and partner countries with available data, 93% or more of pre-primary teachers are women. The exceptions are France, where 92% of pre-primary teachers are women, the Netherlands (87%), Norway (91%) and Spain (93%) (Figure 3.6).

A bachelor degree has become the minimum qualification required in most countries to be a teacher at the pre-primary level of education. However, the duration and pedagogical component of initial teacher training vary significantly across countries.

Better educated ECEC staff with specialised training are more likely to improve children's cognitive outcomes through larger vocabularies, increased ability to solve problems, and increased ability to develop targeted lesson plans (NIEER, 2004). However, it is not only qualifications that affect outcomes; it is the ability of staff members to create a better pedagogic environment that makes a real difference.

In 2014, almost all teachers were awarded a tertiary qualification upon completion of a teacher training programme. In 27 out of the 37 countries with available data, an individual can teach at the pre-primary level of education after earning at least a bachelor's degree or equivalent (ISCED level 6) at the end of initial teacher education. However, the duration of initial teacher training for pre-primary teachers ranges widely among the 37 countries with relevant data: from two years for basic certification in Japan and two years of college for kindergarten teachers and high school graduates and one year training for childcare teachers in Korea, to five years in Austria, Chile, France, Iceland and Italy.

There are two models of teacher education: concurrent and consecutive (OECD, 2014). In 23 out of the 35 countries with available data, initial teacher training for pre-primary teachers is organised according to the concurrent model, in which pedagogical and practical training is provided at the same time as courses in subject matter (Chapter 3). In the other countries, pedagogical and practical training follow courses in subject matter (Consecutive model).

Teachers' salaries in pre-primary education vary widely across countries, and remain below those of other tertiary-educated workers in most countries.

Competitive salaries and good working conditions may attract young people to teaching in some countries and, in others, help to retain effective teachers in the profession (Huntsman, 2008). Teachers' salaries in pre-primary education (ISCED 02) also vary widely across countries. For instance, the annual statutory salaries of pre-primary school teachers with 15 years of experience (before taxes and converted into USD using purchasing power parity) range from under USD 20 000 in the

Czech Republic, Hungary and the Slovak Republic, to more than USD 50 000 in Australia, the Netherlands and the United States, and exceed USD 100 000 in Luxembourg (Figure 3.7).

ECEC systems differ not only in how much they pay teachers, but in the structure of their pay scales. Salaries at the top of the scale for teachers with typical qualifications are, on average, 65% higher than starting salaries in pre-primary education. In 2014, teachers' salaries in pre-primary education remained below those of other tertiary-educated workers in most countries. On average, pre-primary teachers in OECD countries earn only 74% of the average salary of a tertiary-educated, 25-64 year-old full-time, full-year worker (Chapter 3).

At the pre-primary level, 83% of teachers' statutory working time is spent, on average, on teaching, and the rest on non-teaching tasks.

In most countries, teachers are formally required to work a specific number of hours per year. This may be specified as the number of hours that teachers must be available at school for teaching and non-teaching activities. It corresponds to official working hours as specified in contractual agreements. On average across countries with data, for both teaching and total working time at school for pre-primary teachers, 83% of teachers' working time is spent on contact with children, with the proportion ranging from less than 65% in Colombia, Chile, England (UK) and Greece, to more than 90% in France, Hungary, Israel and Turkey.

Translated into salary per hour for pre-primary school teachers, the average statutory salary per teaching hour and for working hour after 15 years of experience is USD 44, compared to USD 33. Salaries per teaching hour at the pre-primary level are USD 65 or more in Australia, the Flemish Community of Belgium, Luxembourg and Korea (Chapter 3).

Both teacher salaries and the number of teaching hours per year in pre-primary education vary considerably across countries.

Teachers' salaries are only one part of the equation for improving teacher quality. In order to attract the best candidates to the teaching workforce, countries need to offer adequate pay, which is evidence that teachers are valued by society, but also provide an environment in which teachers are given the autonomy to work as professionals and are given a direct role in school improvement.

Teacher salaries and working time are not strongly correlated. However, as with teacher salaries, countries vary considerably in the number of teaching hours per year required of the average public school teacher in pre-primary education. Required teaching time at the pre-primary level in public schools varies more across countries than it does at any other level.

The number of teaching days ranges from 162 days in France to more than 220 days in Iceland and Norway. Annual contact time with children ranges from less than 700 hours in Greece, Korea and Mexico to more than 1 450 hours in Iceland and Norway. On average across OECD countries, teachers at this level of education are required to be in contact with children 1 005 hours per year, spread over 40 weeks or 190 days of teaching (Figure 1.2). Translated into hours per day, teachers are required to be in contact with children between four and six hours a day in 17 out of 25 countries with available data.

Figure 1.2. Organisation of teachers' teaching time over the year in pre-primary education (2014)

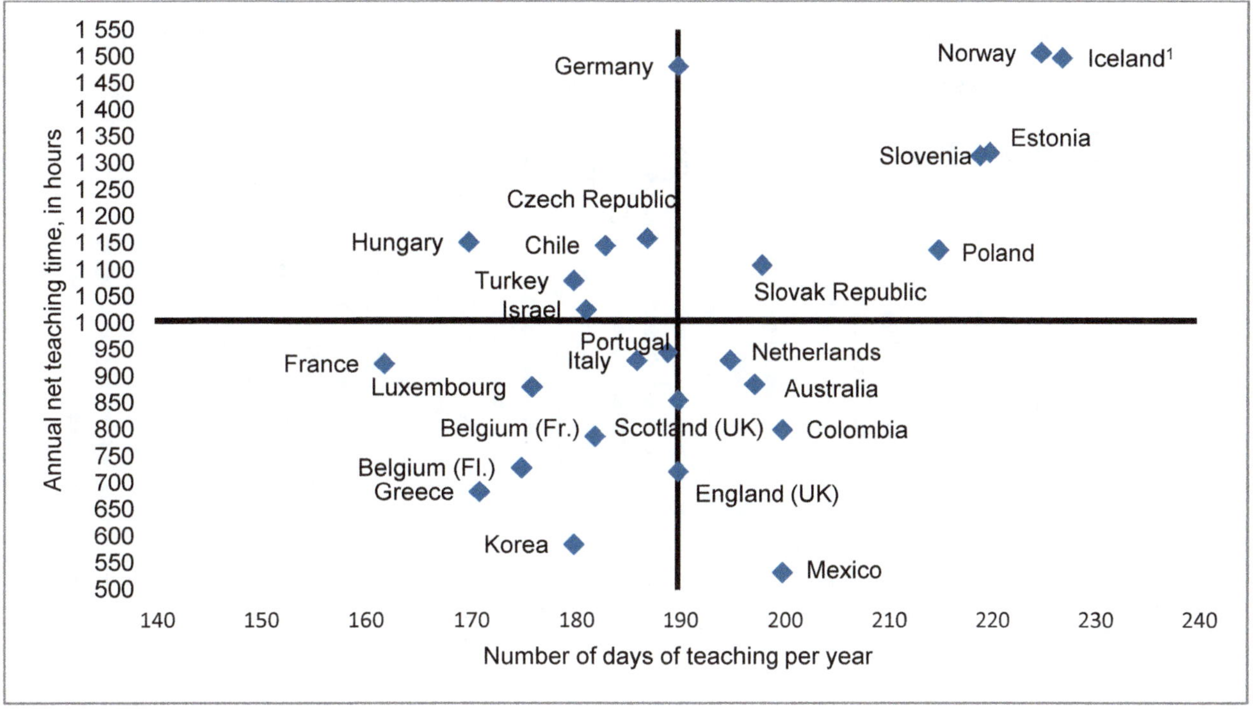

1. Year of reference 2013.

Source: OECD (2017b), OECD Online education database, OECD, Paris, http://www.oecd.org/education/database.htm.

StatLink http://dx.doi.org/10.1787/888933487141

Access to early childhood education and care

Universal or quasi-universal access to at least one year of ECEC is now a reality in most countries, which is significant progress towards the Sustainable Development Goals education targets.

In most countries, more than 90% of children are already enrolled in pre-primary education (or in primary education in some countries) at age 5. These countries are already close or have reached the SDGs target recommending the universal participation in organised learning one year before official primary entry age. High enrolment rates are also observed for lower age groups. Therefore, among 4-year-olds, 90% or more are already enrolled in pre-primary (or primary education) in two-thirds of the 37 countries with available data (Figure 1.3).

Figure 1.3. Enrolment rates in early childhood education and primary education, by age (2014)[1]

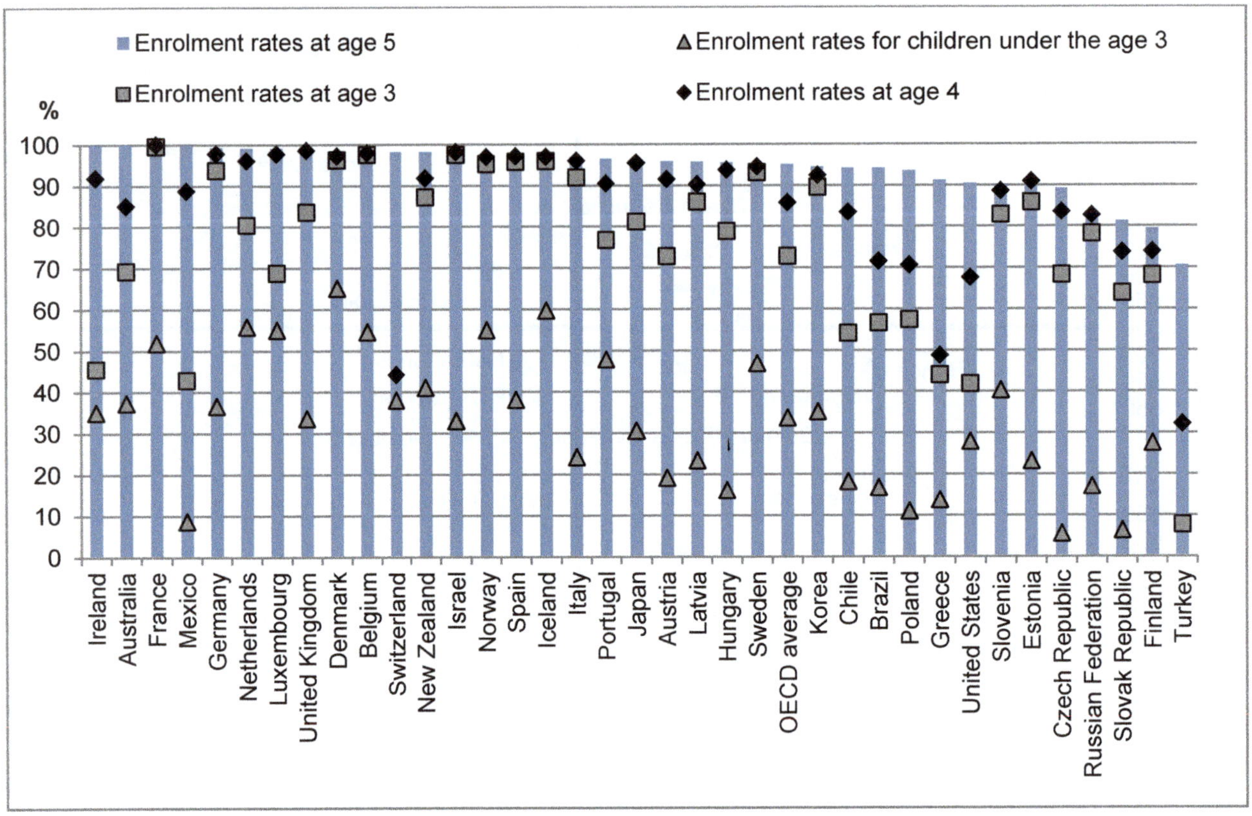

1. Children under the age of 3 are enrolled in formal childcare (ISCED 0 and other registered ECEC services); children at ages 4 and 5 can already be enrolled in primary education in a small gorup of countries.

Sources: OECD (2017c), OECD Family Database, OECD, Paris, http://www.oecd.org/els/family/database.htm and OECD (2016), Education at a Glance 2016: OECD Indicators, http://dx.doi.org/10.1787/eag-2016-en.

StatLink http://dx.doi.org/10.1787/888933487156

Enrolment in ECEC settings has continued to rise over the last decade, partly due to the extension of legal entitlements to a place in ECEC, as well as efforts to ensure free access, at least for some ages and selected population groups.

The increase in access has been made possible, in part, by the extension of legal entitlements of a place for younger children, and efforts to ensure free access for the older age group (e.g. 3-5). However, there are major differences across countries in the age groups covered by legal entitlements to a place in ECEC. For instance, some countries, such as Norway and Germany, cover ages 1 to 5 (or even 7 or 8 years in some cases in Germany), while others, such as the Czech Republic and Portugal, only guarantee children a place for the year before entering primary school.

Similarly, the time per week covered by the legal entitlements to a place in ECEC also differs greatly across countries and jurisdictions. For example, Norway grants universal access to 41 hours of ECEC, French pre-primary schools provide 24 hours, Austria provides between 16 and 20 hours for the year before entering primary school, and Scotland (United Kingdom) provides only 16 hours for 3-4 year-olds (Table 2.2 and OECD, 2015).

The legal entitlement to a place in ECEC is not a guarantee of free access, especially for younger children. However, most countries with available data provide free access to all children for at least the last year before entering primary school (Figure 2.9).

The share of children under the age of 3 enrolled in ECEC settings is also on the rise in most countries.

On average across OECD countries, around one third of children under the age of 3 are enrolled in formal childcare (ISCED 0 and other registered ECEC settings outside ISCED 2011). However, enrolment rates at these ages vary significantly across countries, and range from less than 10% in the Czech Republic, Mexico and the Slovak Republic, to more than 45% in Nordic countries, except Finland, in "Benelux" OECD countries (Belgium, Luxembourg and the Netherlands), and in France and Portugal (Figure 4.2; OECD, 2017b; OECD, 2017c).

Despite significant differences across countries, a common pattern has emerged: the share of young children enrolled in ECEC settings is on the rise. On average across OECD countries, enrolment rates for children under the age of 3 increased by over eight percentage points between 2005 and 2014, from 26% to 34% (Figure 4.4). These trends are the result of policy initiatives across OECD countries that have aimed to expand ECEC services and simultaneously improve the quality of early childhood education (see more details at the end of Chapter 4).

This move is particularly marked in many European countries, and is the result of a further stimulus by the 2010 objectives set by the European Union (EU) at its Barcelona meeting in 2002 (e.g. supply subsidised full-day places for one-third of children under the age of 3). In 2014, fourteen EU countries – Belgium, Denmark, France, Germany, Iceland, Ireland, Luxembourg, the Netherlands, Norway, Portugal, Slovenia, Spain, Sweden and the United Kingdom – had reached the Barcelona targets, although at different levels of quality and at different level of intensity in participation (see Chapter 4).

However, significant differences are still persistent across OECD countries in the quality of ECEC programmes provided to young children and in the usual number of hours per week that each child is enrolled.

While participation rates by age provide a proxy of how long children are enrolled in ECEC over their childhood (e.g. in years), they do not provide any information about the intensity of participation in ECEC services (i.e. whether children participate only for a few hours per day or full-time), or globally about the quality ECEC services. Quality in ECEC settings is a complex endeavour, and countries are at differing stages in the development of a quality monitoring system (see OECD, 2015 for an overview of quality monitoring systems and challenges).

Figure 1.4. Access to early childhood services versus intensity of participation (2014)

Enrolment rates in formal childcare (ISCED 0 and other registered ECEC settings outside ISCED 2011) of children under the age of 3, and intensity of participation in these services during a usual week

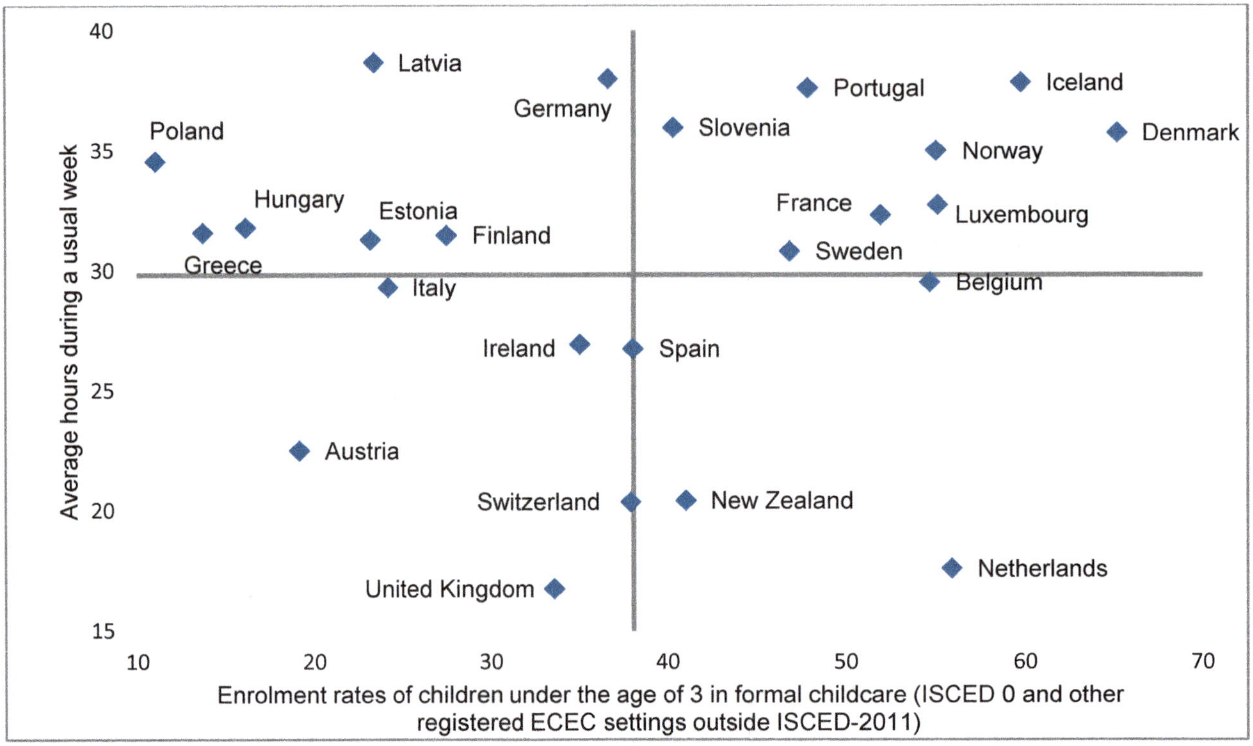

Sources: OECD (2017b), OECD Online education database, OECD, Paris, http://www.oecd.org/education/database.htm and OECD (2017c), OECD Family Database, OECD, Paris, www.oecd.org/els/family/database.htm.

StatLink http://dx.doi.org/10.1787/888933487161

The intensity of participation is easier to capture, and significant variations are observed across and within countries in what is provided to young children. Thus, when participation rates and average hours during a usual week are analysed together, different patterns emerge, reflecting policy choices made by countries. For example, ECEC settings in some countries, such as Estonia, Finland, Greece, Hungary, Latvia and Poland, provide long hours per week to a small proportion of the children under the age of 3. The opposite is observed in the Netherlands and New Zealand. In these two countries, fewer hours per week are provided to an above-average proportion of children under the age of 3 (Figure 1.4).

Curriculum frameworks

Access is not a guarantee of high-quality ECEC. Therefore, in many countries, the curriculum framework in pre-primary education has recently been extended to enhance ECEC quality and to ensure better transition between pre-primary and primary education.

Curriculum frameworks can play a pivotal role in ensuring the quality of ECEC services. In 2015, as in 2011, most OECD countries and jurisdictions with data for both reference years still placed a high importance on arts, literacy, music, numeracy, physical education and science in their curriculum frameworks designed for pre-primary education. In contrast, practical skills were slightly less common content areas of the frameworks/guidelines in 2015 than in 2011, while the importance in the curriculum frameworks given by countries to social sciences significantly decreased between 2011 and 2015. Data on play time were only collected in 2015. However, countries place importance on "unguided playtime" in their curriculum framework. In addition, as mentioned by several of them, this field now being embedded into other content areas to stimulate learning through play (Figure 1.5)

Figure 1.5. Content areas included in ECEC curriculum (2011 and 2015)

Proportion of countries and jurisdictions which declared in 2011 and 2015 that the following content areas are included in their ECEC curriculum framework

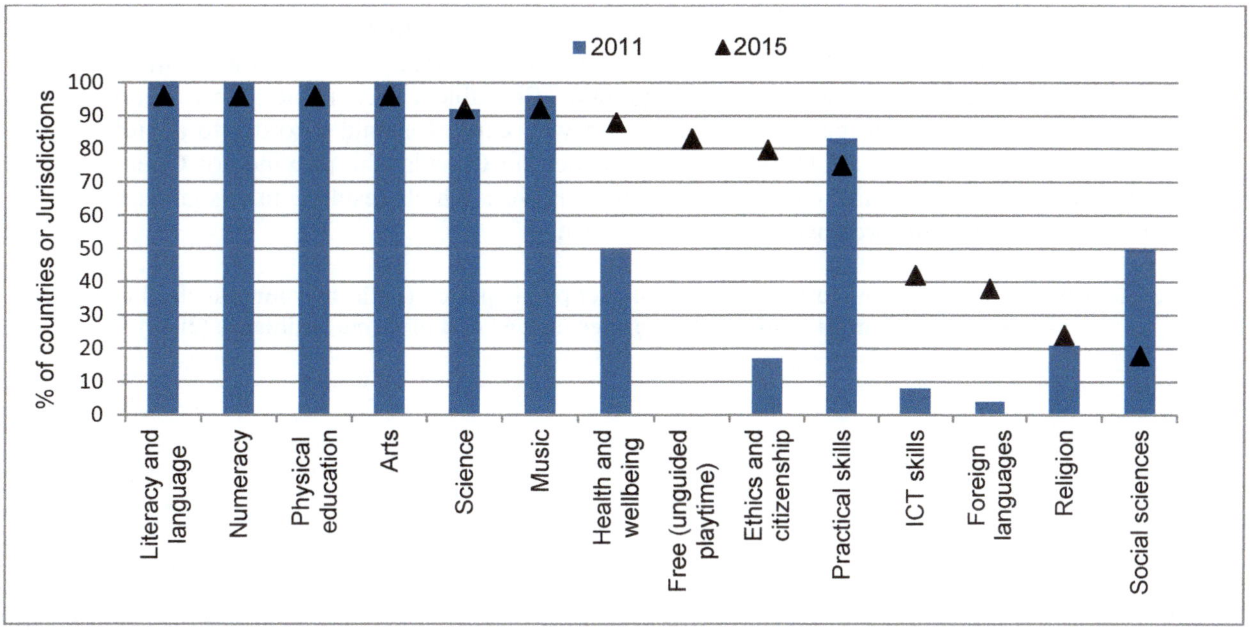

Notes: The figures are reported in percentage of total number of answers. The chart includes only the 24 countries and jurisdictions that participated in the survey in 2011 and 2015. Data on Free (unguided playtime) for 2011 are missing.

Countries are ranked in descending of order of the percentage of countries and jurisdictions declaring that the following content areas are included in their ECEC curriculum framework in 2015.

Sources: OECD (2017d), Starting Strong V, http://dx.doi.org/10.1787/9789264276253-en, OECD (2012), Starting Strong III: A quality toolbox for ECEC, http://dx.doi.org/10.1787/9789264123564-en.

StatLink http://dx.doi.org/10.1787/888933487179

A significantly higher proportion of respondent countries have included newly emerging subject matters in their pre-primary curriculum, which responds to changing needs in present-day society. By including these new fields, such as ICT skills, learning foreign languages, developing ethics and citizenship values, learning religion or ensuring health and well-being for children, pre-primary curriculum has been aligned with the content areas of primary education. The increase between 2011 and 2015 is particularly marked for ICT skills, with around 40% of respondent countries (Chile, Finland, Greece, Italy, Korea, Mexico, New Zealand, Norway, Portugal, Slovak Republic, Spain, Sweden, some provinces in Canada and some regions in Germany) citing ICT skills as a content area of their curriculum framework in 2015 (Figure 1.5).

Access to early childhood education and participation of women in the labour market

Affordable and high-quality ECEC with an adequate number of hours per week can contribute to an increase in the participation of women in the labour force.

In recent decades, policies implemented in most countries for children under the age of 3 emphasised the expansion of services as a necessary support for maternal employment in a strong economy, rather than as a public service that can benefit both children and parents. However, there are recent signs of convergence among OECD countries, and the concept of services for children under the age of 3 is progressively broadening from "childcare" to support working parents to include educational and pedagogical, gender equality, social integration, and family support objectives.

Working parents, mothers in particular, are more likely to drop out of the labour market or work fewer hours to take up childcare duties, especially when their children are young. Therefore, women need high-quality, affordable ECEC to be able to return to work with confidence that their children are well cared for, and in order to achieve a better work balance (OECD, 2011). For instance, in Canada, the province of Quebec introduced a low-fee child care policy in the mid-90s, which resulted in a significant increase in the labour force participation of women.

Figure 1.6. Relationship between mother's labour market participation (with the youngest child under the age of 3) and enrolment rates of children under the age of 3 in formal childcare (2014)

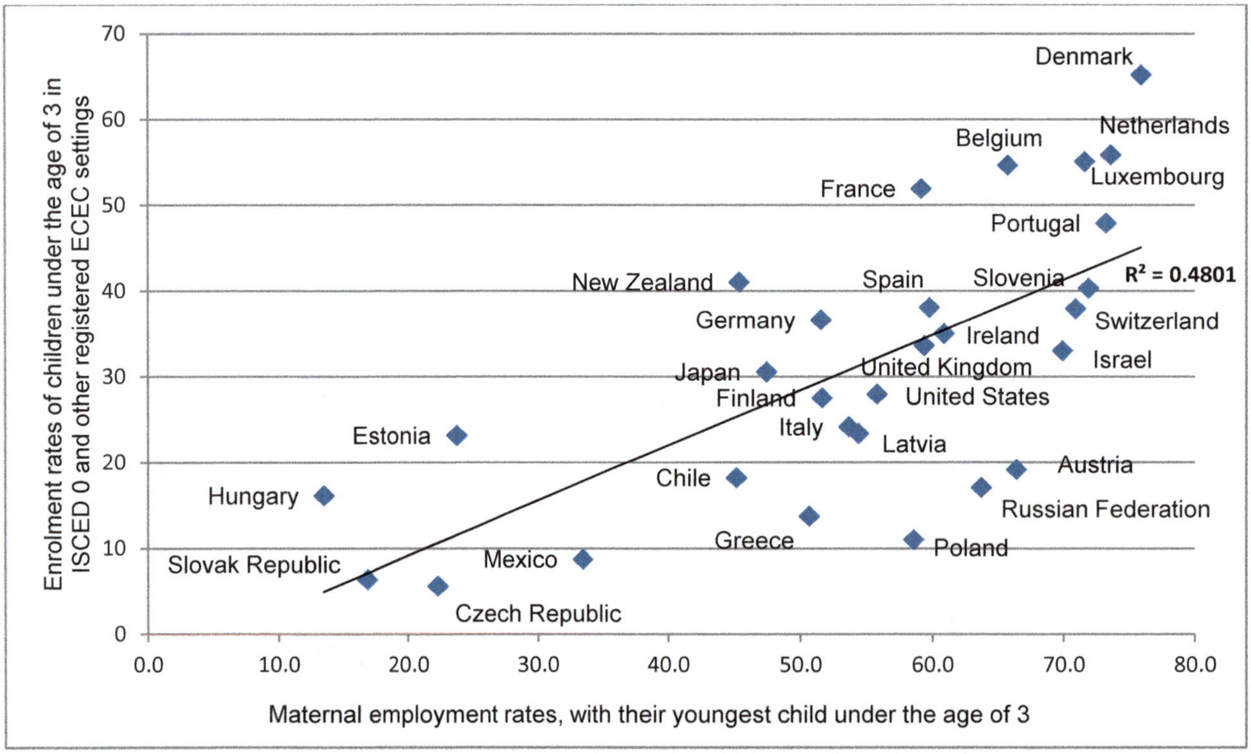

Sources: OECD (2017b), OECD Online education database, OECD, Paris, www.oecd.org/education/database.htm and OECD (2017c), OECD Family Database, OECD, Paris, www.oecd.org/els/family/database.htm.

StatLink http://dx.doi.org/10.1787/888933487187

The relationship between a mother's labour market participation and enrolment rates in formal childcare is strong, especially for mothers with their youngest child under the age of 3. Thus, in countries where mothers' labour market participation rates are the highest, such as Denmark, Luxembourg, the Netherlands, Portugal, Slovenia and Switzerland (above 70% employment among women aged 15 to 64 with their youngest child under the age of 3), the proportions of young children enrolled in formal childcare (ISCED 0 and other registered ECEC settings outside ISCED 2011) are also the highest. In contrast, the enrolment rates in formal childcare for children under the age of 3 is less than 10% in the Czech Republic, the Slovak Republic and Mexico, while employment among women aged 15 to 64 with their youngest child under the age of 3 is significantly below the OECD averages in all of these countries (Figure 1.6).

A relationship between enrolment rates at ages 3 to 5 and maternal employment among women aged 15 to 64 with their youngest child aged 3 to 5 is still strong, but the correlation is weaker compared to younger ages (Figure 5.10).

Child development research on the benefits of full-time as compared to part-time programmes is less conclusive than evidence regarding the benefits of a longer period of participation. However, from a labour market perspective, the availability of full-day ECEC services is a crucial factor allowing parents of young children, especially mothers, to take up near full-time employment and secure higher earnings. An adequate number of hours per week of these services can also contribute to increases in the full-time participation of women in the labour force. The usual number of hours per week that children under the age of 3 are enrolled in formal childcare is highly correlated with the part-time employment of women with at least one child aged 0 to 14.

In some countries (e.g. Latvia, Portugal and Slovenia), the average number of hours during a usual week is over 35, and part-time employment is below 10% among women aged 15 to 64 with at least one child aged 0 to 14. At the other extreme, in Austria, the Netherlands and the United Kingdom, children under the age of 3 spend on average 22 hours or less in formal childcare during a usual week, while more than 25% of women with at least one child aged 0-14 are employed part-time (Figure 5.11).

Number of years of ECEC and academic performance at age 15

High-quality ECEC can result in better outcomes in subsequent stages of life. The number of years spent in ECEC (ISCED 0) is a strong predictor of level of performance reached at later stages. However, the extent of its benefits heavily depends on the quality of the ECEC services.

A growing body of research recognises that ECEC can improve children's cognitive abilities and socio-emotional development, help create a foundation for lifelong learning, make children's learning outcomes more equitable, reduce poverty, and improve social mobility from generation to generation. PISA 2015 data relies on retrospective self-reporting from 15-year-olds (e.g. PISA students participating in ECEC 10-15 years ago, between 2000 and 2005), but these data show, as previous editions of PISA, that in practically all OECD countries, 15-year-old students in 2015 who had attended ECEC settings outperformed students who had not, at least before accounting for student and school-level socio-economic status.

For instance, the difference between students who had attended more than one year of ECEC (ISCED 0) and those who had attended one year or less of early childhood education averaged 41 score points in the PISA 2015 science assessment, with one year of formal schooling equivalent to around 30 score points. The performance gap reduces but remains significant when comparing students from similar backgrounds. After accounting for student and school-level socio-economic status, students who had attended early childhood education for one year or more scored an average of 25 points higher in the PISA science assessment compared to those who had not (Chapter 5).

Figure 1.7. Average score-point difference in science performance across OECD countries, by number of years spent by 15-year-old students in ECEC (ISCED 0) - before and after accounting for socio-economic status (PISA 2015)

Comparison made with all 15-year-olds in OECD countries having attended early childhood education for three years or more (e.g. >3)

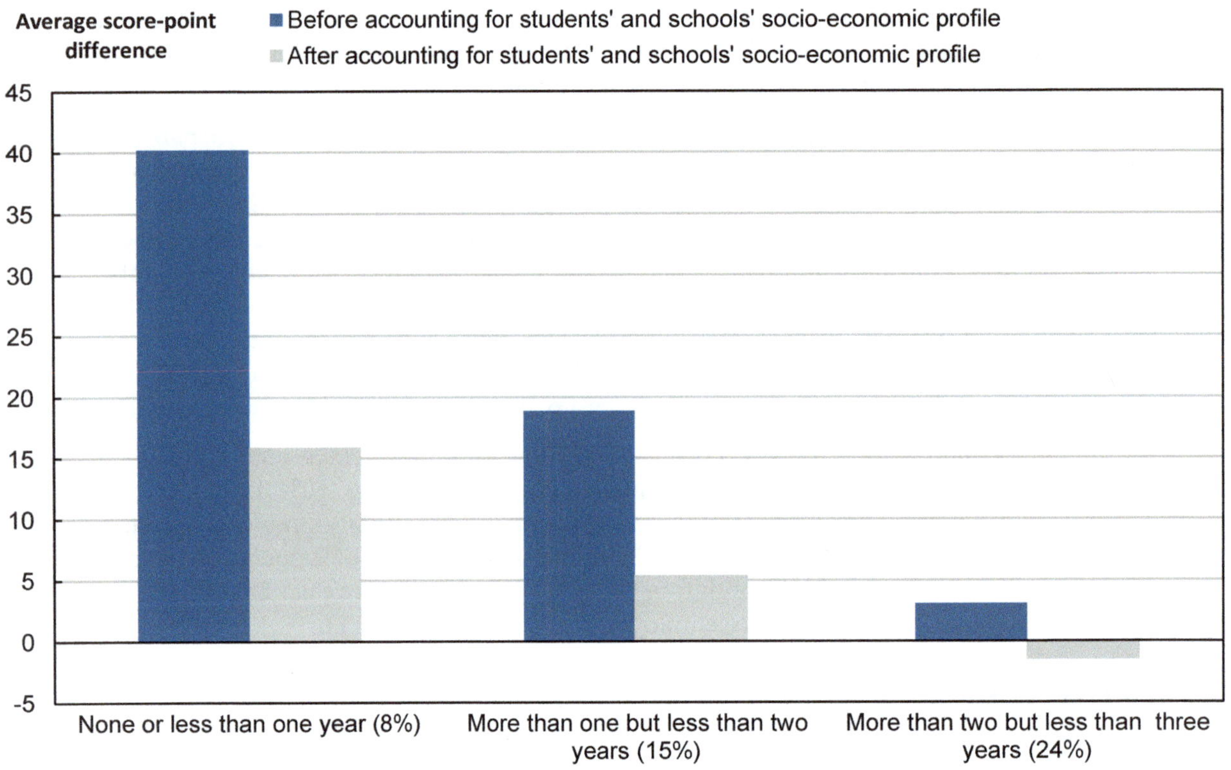

Notes: **How to read this chart?** For instance, before accounting for student and school-level socio-economic status, students who had attended early childhood education for three years or more scored an average of 40 points higher in the PISA science assessment compared to those who had attended ECEC for less than one year. The difference is still significant at 16 points after accounting for socio-economic background.

On average among 15-year-old students who remember about early childhood education (ISCED 0), 53% of them had attended early childhood education for at least three years. The percentages of 15-year-olds who attended early childhood education (ISCED 0) in each of the other categories are added into brackets next to each category.

Source: OECD (2017a), PISA online education database, OECD, Paris, http://www.oecd.org/pisa/data/.

StatLink http://dx.doi.org/10.1787/888933487196

The positive and statistically significant effect of ECEC attendance on PISA performance in science is not limited to this comparison. The number of years spent in ECEC (ISCED 0) is a strong predictor of level of performance in and out of schools reached at later stages. For instance, across the 35 OECD countries with available data, 15-year-old students who had attended more than two years and less than three years of ECEC (e.g. >=2 and <3) scored, on average, 16 points higher than those who attended more than one year and less than two years (e.g. >=1 and <2), and 7 points more after accounting for socio-economic background.

The same positive effect is not found when the comparison is made between 15-year-old students who had attended early childhood education for 3 years or more (e.g. >3) over those who had attended early childhood education for more than 2 years and less than 3 years (e.g. >=2 and <3). In this case, the difference is statistically non-significant in most countries after accounting for socio-economic status, suggesting that two years of early childhood education is the minimum duration needed to have a good chance to reach a good level of performance at age 15 (Figure 1.7).

The extent of the benefits of ECEC heavily depends on the quality of the services. PISA 2015 data reveal that the correlation between enrolment in pre-primary education and performance obtained at the age of 15 is generally stronger in education systems where participation in early childhood education (ISCED 0) lasts more than two years (Figure 5.3), and the link is stronger in settings where the child-to-teacher ratio is lower and public expenditure per child is higher. In other words: input policies, such as the child-to-teaching-staff ratio, affect learning outcomes. However, the duration of ECEC is, among all these variables, the strongest predictor of low performance at age 15 (Figure 5.5).

Over the past two decades, many countries have taken initiatives to increase access to ECEC services, especially for disadvantaged children. However, PISA data show that inequities persist in many countries.

On average among 15-year-old students who remember about early childhood education (ISCED 0), 92% of them declared in PISA 2015 that they had attended early childhood education for at "least one year" and, 77% for "at least two years". However, advantaged 15-year-old students were more likely than disadvantaged students to attend early childhood education when they were younger in most countries. For instance, an average of 72% of disadvantaged 15-year-old students in 2015 had attended ECEC for at least two years, while this figure was 82% for advantaged students.

The differences in enrolment between advantaged and disadvantaged students are the largest (between 15 and 30 percentage points) in Slovenia, the Slovak Republic, Turkey and the United States. This means that the students who could benefit the most from these programmes – those from disadvantaged backgrounds – are less likely to participate in ECEC (Figure 5.7).

What are the key challenges on early childhood education and care?

The chapters of this publication present the key indicators on ECEC and highlight some key challenges for countries regarding the different dimensions of ECEC included in the scoreboard: governance, financing, teaching workforce, access and intensity of participation, equity in access, and quality of ECEC settings (Table 1.1). Many of these challenges were already identified in previous versions of Starting Strong. For some, international efforts are necessary to identify and address the existing data gaps in the field and the immediate priorities for data collection and monitoring. The challenges highlighted by the indicators on ECEC are the following:

- **Financing**: Developing clear and consistent strategies for efficiently allocating public resources on ECEC priority areas.

Evidence suggests that significant public funding is necessary to support a sustainable and equitable early childhood system. Without this investment, there is likely to be a shortage of good quality programmes, unequal access, and the segregation of children according to income. The key is therefore to invest not only in expanding access, but also in improving the quality of ECEC services that is affordable for all children (e.g. under or above the age of 3).

In well-functioning systems, governments develop clear and consistent strategies for efficiently allocating resources, including investment in long-term planning and quality initiatives. Investment should be directed towards achieving high-quality pedagogical goals, rather than the simple creation of places. In setting out quality goals, countries face challenges such as: 1) building consensus on the goals; 2) aligning ECEC goals with the goals of other levels of education or other child-focused services; and 3) translating the goals into action.

- **Teaching workforce**: Improving the working conditions and professional education of ECEC staff.

Attention to the level of recruitment of early childhood workers, their professional development and their working conditions are important for ensuring quality. In several countries, such attention is also critical for teachers' development and the long-term sustainability of recruitment in early childhood services. Several weaknesses in staff policies emerged from the indicators, such as: low recruitment and pay levels, particularly in childcare services (based on national data because no international indicators exist); the feminisation of the workforce; and the failure of pedagogical teams to reflect the diversity of the neighbourhoods they serve.

Good working conditions can improve the quality of ECEC services. Research has indicated that staff job satisfaction and retention – and thereby the quality of ECEC environments – can be improved by: 1) low child-to-staff ratios and low group size; 2) competitive wages and other benefits; 3) reasonable schedule/workload; 4) low staff turnover; 5) good physical environment; and 6) a competent and supportive centre manager. Common challenges that countries face in encouraging a high-quality workforce include: 1) raising staff qualification levels; 2) recruiting, retaining and diversifying a qualified workforce; 3) continuously up-skilling the workforce; and 4) ensuring the quality of the workforce in the private sector. Chapter 3 covers some of these challenges.

- **Parents**: Engaging families and communities.

Parents and communities should be regarded as "partners" working towards the same goal. Home learning environments and neighbourhood are important for healthy child development and learning. Parental and community engagement is increasingly seen as an important policy lever to enhance healthy child development and learning. Parental partnership is critical in enhancing the knowledge of ECEC staff about the children. Parental engagement – especially in ensuring high-quality children's learning at home and communicating between ECEC staff and parents – is strongly associated with children's later academic success, high school completion, socio-emotional development and adaptation in society (OECD, 2015).

Countries face challenges such as: 1) lack of awareness and motivation from parents; 2) lack of communication and outreach of ECEC services with parents; 3) parents' time constraints to being engaged; and 4) increasing inequity and diversity among parents. There are also particular challenges associated with engaging ethnic minority parents.

Community engagement is increasingly seen as an important policy lever. There are also some unique challenges in community engagement, such as the challenges of managing dysfunctional communities and facilitating co-operation between ECEC services and other services, as well as between ECEC and other levels of education. International indicators should be further developed to capture this key quality dimension of ECEC, especially for ECEC settings that enrol children under the age of 3.

- **Curriculum**: Developing broad guidelines and curricular standards for all ECEC services.

Guiding frameworks help to promote a more even level of quality across age groups and provision, guide and support professional staff, and facilitate communication between staff and parents. Curriculum frameworks gain in effectiveness when co-constructed with the main stakeholders. Almost all OECD countries have a curriculum or learning standards from age 3 until compulsory schooling. In recent years, curricula or learning standards are often embedded within a lifecycle or lifelong learning approach, and a growing number of countries and regions have started to frame continuous child development from early childhood up to entry to primary education (Figure 1.5).

While the age groups covered may differ, curricula aligned with those of primary schooling or beyond also facilitate transition to the next level of education (Eurydice, 2009; Kagan and Kauerz, 2006). An aligned curriculum contributes to avoiding the fade-out effects of ECEC (Pianta et al., 2009).

Key challenges regarding curriculum or standards (OECD, 2012) include: 1) defining goals and content; 2) aligning them with the school-level framework; 3) communicating it to relevant staff when it is created or revised; 4) implementing it effectively; and 5) evaluating its contents and its implementation.

- **Access and governance**: Increasing public provision for children under 3 and facilitating the transition from childcare to early education are two key challenges, especially for countries with split systems.

In many countries, the concept of services for children under 3 is broadening from a labour market perspective to the inclusion of quality objectives, especially in integrated systems. However, significant differences are still persistent across OECD countries in the quality of ECEC programmes provided to young children, and in the usual number of hours per week that each child is enrolled in these programmes, especially in countries with split systems.

Similarly, transitions for young children are critical: they can be a stimulus to growth and development, but if too abrupt and handled without care, they carry – particularly for young children – the risk of regression and failure. Some children, for example, may transit daily between different types of services. Indicators show that such transitions are often linked to affordability, the absence of appropriate full-day services, or to the operation of "slot" systems, where parents who work part-time are encouraged to drop off their young child at a childminding service for a few hours daily or weekly (see Chapters 3 and 4). A full-time place may then be occupied by several children on a daily basis, making it difficult for staff to follow the progress of each child, and for the child to make relationships with other children. The risks are even greater in systems where staff are inexperienced and there is a high turnover.

In principle, the issue of disturbing the transition from childcare to early education does not arise in countries with an integrated administration of early childhood services, and where a common curriculum across the ages of 1-5 years is generally employed, which applies to more than half of the countries with available data. By contrast, fundamental differences in goals, means and quality can characterise the "childcare" and "early education" sectors in countries operating split or two-tiered early childhood systems. The result can be a lack of coherence for children and families, with a confusing variation in objectives, funding streams, operational procedures, regulatory frameworks, staff training and qualifications.

There seem to be few initiatives to provide continuity when children move from the childcare sector into early education, unless the ECEC sector has been integrated or a common pedagogical approach is used in both sectors. In addition, many childcare services are private (Figure 4.6), and may use a broad range of models and approaches to young children in their programmes, unlike the approach used in the public early education domain.

- **Equity in the access to ECEC**: Ensuring equitable access for all children to attend quality ECEC, with a focus on children under the age of 3.

Growing inequity in the economic, social and cultural backgrounds of children in ECEC centres is becoming a challenge in many OECD countries. It is often reported that despite the children of deprived families needing high-quality ECEC the most, these families often have lower interest, lack of knowledge and lack of time to be engaged in ECEC.

Increasing diversity can also be a challenge for getting parents engaged in ECEC services. Often reported barriers include different cultural needs, views or languages. Uneven parental engagement with different socio-economic backgrounds can result in greater inequity. It is therefore particularly important that real efforts are made to reach out to the most deprived families. Collaboration with parents is especially important in low-income, minority families, where differences in socio-economic background and cultural values about child rearing and education are likely to affect the home learning environment.

Many initiatives have been taken to tackle this challenge, some of which are included in the set of indicators covered by this publication ("prioritising participation of children with an immigrant or low-educational background"; "providing free ECEC services to families in need', "providing support in different languages"). Some others were included in a previous edition of Starting Strong ("providing training for parents", "assisting parents to provide qualitative home learning environments", "providing home visits"), however no robust indicator exists at the international level.

- **Quality monitoring**: Advancing data collection, research and monitoring.

Data, research and monitoring are powerful tools for improving children's outcomes and driving continuous improvement in-service delivery. Data and monitoring can help establish facts, trends and evidence about whether children have equitable access to high-quality ECEC and are benefiting from their participation. They are essential for accountability and/or programme improvement. They can also help parents make informed decisions about their choice of services.

Research and the European Quality Framework suggest that better data systems and monitoring can improve child outcomes if they are developed and aligned with quality goals (OECD, 2015), and if there are links between child-level data, practitioner-level data and programme-level data. Country experiences have shown seven targets or purposes of monitoring: 1) child development; 2) staff performance; 3) service quality; 4) regulation compliance; 5) curriculum implementation; 6) parent satisfaction; and 7) workforce supply and working conditions. Despite improvement, more can be done, especially to assess services for children under the age of 3.

An increasing number of countries and regions are making efforts to develop effective data systems – not simply for the sake of data collection or monitoring, but by first defining a purpose. The purpose of data collection and quality monitoring should be aligned with the purposes of system improvement. There is a growing trend to use quantitative research methods, such as comparing the effectiveness of different programme types or different pedagogical strategies.

However, there is also a growing recognition that qualitative research plays an essential role in informing practices with local values and democracy. Both quantitative and qualitative studies are needed to advance research in ECEC. Countries reported challenges in Starting Strong IV (OECD, 2015) regarding advancing research, such as: 1) a need for more analysis on the effects of ECEC and a cost-benefit analysis; 2) under-researched areas or areas with newly growing interest; and 3) dissemination. In recent years, countries have focused their efforts on linking research to policy and practice, improving the quality and quantity of ECEC research, and disseminating findings internationally.

A challenge for OECD: identify and address the existing data gaps in the field and the immediate priorities for data collection and monitoring.

While much progress has been accomplished in recent years, additional efforts are needed to fill in remaining gaps in system-level indicators and to develop the scope of available data on ECEC.

Despite recent progress, member countries and the OECD continue to strive to strengthen the link between policy needs and the best available internationally comparable data. However, additional efforts are needed to fill remaining gaps in system-level indicators, for instance: by collecting more robust and comparable indicators on ECEC settings that enrol children under the age of 3; by improving the definitions of public and private funding; and by improving the country coverage, time series and quality of the key ECEC indicators related to actual child-to-staff ratios, content areas of the curriculum, public support to families, and average time children spend on intentional pedagogical or educational activities.

Systematic attention to monitoring and data collection also requires coherent procedures to collect and analyse data on the status of young children, ECEC provision, and the early childhood workforce. The OECD will continue to address these challenges vigorously and develop ECEC indicators where it is feasible and promising to develop data; it will also advance in areas where considerable investment still needs to be made in conceptual work. International efforts are also necessary to develop new indicators, especially on child outcomes and process quality (e.g. on the quality of pedagogical interactions between ECEC staff and children, the quality of communications between staff and parents, and, most importantly, the quality of interactions among children, as well as the quality of interaction of children with space and materials). Therefore, the OECD programme of work over the period 2017-2020 includes a series of projects to develop the scope of available data on ECEC. These include:

- The **Teaching and Learning International Survey (TALIS), Starting Strong,** is the first international survey of ECEC staff and the quality of the learning and well-being environment in different ECEC settings across OECD member and non-member economies. The objective is to collect data on staff characteristics, pre-service and in-service education, pedagogical practices and beliefs, organisation and management, and working conditions to give countries an internationally framed assessment of what actually happens in their ECEC settings from the perspective of those that experience it first hand: ECEC staff and centre leaders. This will contribute to a better understanding of the quality of the learning and well-being environment that children experience (instrument development and pilot study in 2015/16, main study in 2018 and reporting in 2019).
- The **Policy Review on Quality in ECEC** is a project that aims to influence how to interpret quality dimensions, in particular, quality beyond regulations, for which a common understanding is yet to be established at the international level. The project will enable countries to draw on the most recent available international evidence on the effectiveness of both structural and process quality standards, and to learn from other countries' experiences and challenges in this regard. The project will explore the scope of quality dimensions and analyse how they are interrelated, as well as their relationship with the child's outcome, where research is available. It will also enlarge the scope of quality dimensions, recognising different institutional ECEC arrangements and ECEC cultures. The project started in 2017 and will undertake different steps until 2020.
- The **International Early Learning and Child Well-being Study** is an international study to measure the non-cognitive and cognitive learning outcomes of children. The results of this pilot study will show what is possible in children's early learning in various socio-emotional and cognitive domains, and will help countries monitor progress at a system level. The conceptual framework for the assessment of children's learning was developed in 2015, with a scoping exercise conducted in 2016 and reporting scheduled for 2020.

The next versions of this publication will include some of these new materials and will contribute to the trend to move the debate from the structural to the process quality of ECEC settings.

References

Bennett, J. (2008), "Early Childhood Education and Care Systems in the OECD Countries: the Issue of Tradition and Governance", *Encyclopedia on Early Childhood Development*, Centre of Excellence for Early Childhood Development and Strategic Knowledge Cluster on Early Child Development, Montreal, www.child-encyclopedia.com/pages/PDF/BennettANGxp.pdf.

Eurydice (2009), *Early Childhood Education and Care in Europe: Tackling Social and Cultural Inequalities*, Eurydice, Brussels.

Huntsman, L. (2008), *Determinants of quality in child care: A review of the research evidence*, Centre for Parenting and Research, NSW Department of Community Services.

Kaga, Y., J. Bennett and P. Moss (2010), *Caring and Learning Together: A cross-national study on the integration of early childhood care and education within education*, UNESCO, Paris.

Kagan, S. and K. Kauerz (2006), "Preschool Programs: Effective Curricula", *Encyclopedia on Early Childhood Development, Centre of Excellence for Early Childhood Development and Strategic Knowledge Cluster on Early Child Development*, Montreal, www.child-encyclopedia.com/documents/Kagan-KauerzANGxp.pdf.

Mahon, R. (2011), "Child Care Policy: A Comparative Perspective", *Encyclopedia on Early Childhood Development*, Centre of Excellence for Early Childhood Development and Strategic Knowledge Cluster on Early Child Development, Montreal, www.child-encyclopedia.com/pages/PDF/MahonANGxp2.pdf.

NIEER (2004a), "Better Practitioners, Better Preschools: Student Achievement Linked to Teacher Qualifications", *Policy Brief*, National Institute for Early Education Research, New Jersey.

OECD (2017a), *PISA online education database*, OECD, Paris, www.oecd.org/pisa/data/.

OECD (2017b), *OECD Online education database*, OECD, Paris, www.oecd.org/education/database.htm.

OECD (2017c), *OECD Family Database*, OECD, Paris, www.oecd.org/els/family/database.htm.

OECD (2017d), *Starting Strong V: Transitions from Early Childhood to Primary Education*, http://dx.doi.org/10.1787/9789264276253-en

OECD (2016), *Education at a Glance 2016: OECD Indicators,* OECD Publishing, Paris, http://dx.doi.org/10.1787/eag-2016-en.

OECD (2015), *Starting Strong IV: Monitoring Quality in Early Childhood Education and Care (ECEC)*, OECD Publishing, Paris, http://dx.doi.org/10.1787/9789264233515-en.

OECD (2014), *Education at a Glance 2014: OECD Indicators*, OECD Publishing, Paris, http://dx.doi.org/10.1787/eag-2014-en.

OECD (2012), *Starting Strong III: A Quality Toolbox for Early Childhood Education and Care*, OECD Publishing, Paris, http://dx.doi.org/10.1787/9789264123564-en.

OECD (2011), *Doing Better for Families,* OECD Publishing, Paris, www.oecd.org/els/family/doingbetterforfamilies.htm.

OECD/Eurostat/UNESCO Institute for Statistics (2015), *ISCED 2011 Operational Manual: Guidelines for Classifying National Education Programmes and Related Qualifications*, OECD Publishing, Paris, http://dx.doi.org/10.1787/9789264228368-en.

Pianta, R.C. et al. (2009), "The Effects of Preschool Education: What We Know, How Public Policy Is or Is Not Aligned With the Evidence Base, and What We Need to Know", *Psychological Science in the Public Interest*, Vol.10/2, pp.49-8.

Tables of Chapter 1

StatLink http://dx.doi.org/10.1787/888933487206

Table 1.1. Scoreboard: Key OECD indicators on early childhood education and care (2013, 2014 and 2015)

	Access and intensity of participation (2014)						Financing (2013)			
Indicator name:	Enrolment rates of children under the age of 3 in formal childcare, split between ISCED 0 programmes and other registered ECEC settings outside ISCED 2011			Usual average weekly hours received by children under the age of 3	Enrolment rates of 3-5 year-olds	Annual number of teaching hours received by children the last year of ECEC	Annual expenditure on ECEC settings per child		Public funding in percentage of total expenditure on ECEC settings	
ISCED 2011 coverage:	ISCED 0	Outside ISCED-2011	Total	Total	ISCED 0 and ISCED 1	ISCED 02	ISCED 01	ISCED 02	ISCED 01	ISCED 02
Table/Figure:	Figure 4.2	Figure 4.2	Figure 4.2	Figure 4.3	Figure 5.10	Figure 3.3	Figure 3.1	Figure 3.1	Figure 3.4	Figure 3.4
Column:	(1)	(2)	(3)	(4)	(5)	(6)	(7)	(8)	(9)	(10)
OECD average	**20**	**15**	**34**	**30**	**85**	**911**	**12 555**	**7 927**	**69**	**83**
Australia	37	0	37	-	85	584	-	-	4	42
Austria	16	3	19	22	87	720	10 307	8 737	73	88
Belgium	18	37	55	30	98	-	-	7 576	-	96
Canada	-	-	-	-	-	-	-	-	-	-
Chile	21	0	21	-	84	1 417	7 032	6 408	86	85
Czech Republic	4	2	6	-	80	-	-	4 655	-	92
Denmark	61	5	65	36	98	-	X(8)	16 341	-	-
Estonia	23	0	23	31	90	-	X(8)	1 987	-	-
Finland	28	0	28	31	74	700	18 668	10 477	91	89
France	4	48	52	32	100	864	-	7 507	-	93
Germany	37	0	37	38	97	-	14 886	9 167	71	79
Greece	14	0	14	32	71	1 480	-	-	-	-
Hungary	X(3)	X(3)	16	32	90	720	-	5 074	-	91
Iceland	45	14	60	38	93	-	14 167	10 956	89	84
Ireland	0	35	35	27	79	570	-	-	-	100
Israel	33	0	33	-	98	-	4 219	4 302	25	90
Italy	5	19	24	29	95	1 400	-	6 233	-	92
Japan	0	30	31	-	91	780	-	6 247	-	44
Korea[1]	35	0	35	-	92	-	-	6 227	-	78
Latvia	X(3)	X(3)	23	39	91	-	-	4 854	-	98
Luxembourg	2	53	55	33	88	936	-	19 233	-	98
Mexico	3	6	9	-	82	800	X(8)	2 575	-	-
Netherlands	0	56	56	18	92	880	-	8 305	-	88
New Zealand	41	0	41	20	92	924	13 579	10 252	72	86
Norway	55	0	55	35	97	1 680	24 329	14 704	93	93
Poland	2	9	11	35	74	905	-	5 552	-	77
Portugal	0	48	48	38	88	950	-	6 604	-	65
Slovak Republic	4	2	6	-	73	-	-	4 996	-	85
Slovenia	37	4	40	36	87	-	11 857	8 101	75	76
Spain	33	5	38	27	97	875	8 160	6 021	58	82
Sweden	46	1	47	31	94	630	14 787	12 833	94	94
Switzerland	0	38	38	20	48	608	-	-	-	-
Turkey	-	-	-	-	37	1 080	-	3 172	-	73
United Kingdom	7	27	34	17	94	-	8 668	8 727	60	66
United States	X(3)	X(3)	28	-	67	-	-	9 986		74
Brazil	17	0	17	-	-	-	-	-		
Russian Federation	17	0	17	-	81	-	-	-	69	83
Data Source[2]	**ECEC**	**ECEC**	**ECEC**	**FD**	**EAG**	**ECEC**	**EAG**	**EAG**	**EAG**	**EAG**

	Governance				Legal access entitlement (2015)		
Indicator name:	Integrated or split ECEC system, i.e. with regards to curricula and governing authority (2015)	% of final funds from central level of government (after transfers) (2013)	Percentage of private ECEC settings (2014)		Age group covered by the free access entitlement for all children	Entitlement to free access: Conditional is based on certain conditions; Unconditional is for all children	Number of hours per week the child has free access to ECEC
ISCED 2011 coverage:	ISCED 02	ISCED 02	ISCED 01	ISCED 02	ISCED 02		
Table/Figure:	Tables: 2.1, 2.3	Figure 3.5	Figure 4.6	Figure 4.6	Figure 2.9 and Table 2.2		
Column:	(11)	(12)	(13)	(14)	(15)	(16)	(17)
OECD average	**I:60%,S:40%**	**32**	**56**	**32**	-	-	-
Australia	Integrated	83	-	77	-	-	-
Austria	Integrated	0	67	28	6	Unconditional	16-20
Belgium	Split	23	-	53	2.5-5	Unconditional	23-28
Canada	-	-	-	-	-	-	-
Chile	Integrated	76	31	56	4-5	Unconditional	22
Czech Republic	Split	8	-	3	5	Unconditional	>=40
Denmark	Integrated	-	53	17	-	-	-
Estonia	Integrated	0	-	-	-	-	-
Finland	Integrated	2	12	9	6	Unconditional	20
France	Split	49	-	13	2.5-5	Unconditional	24
Germany	Integrated	0	73	65	3-5	Differ across landers	
Greece	m	-	-	-	-	-	-
Hungary	Integrated	-	-	9	-	-	-
Iceland	Integrated	0	19	13	-	-	-
Ireland	Split	100	-	-	3-5	Unconditional	15
Israel	Split	62	100	38	-	-	-
Italy	Split	71	-	29	3-5	Unconditional	40
Japan	Split	5	-	73	3-5	Conditional	20-50
Korea[1]	Split	-	92	81	3-5	Unconditional	20-25
Latvia	Integrated	0	-	6	-	-	-
Luxembourg	Integrated	72	-	-	3-5	Unconditional	<=26
Mexico	Integrated	-	63	14	3-5	Unconditional	15-20
Netherlands	Split	80	-	29	-	-	-
New Zealand	Integrated	100	98	98	3-5	Unconditional	20
Norway	Integrated	0	51	46	3-5	Conditional	20
Poland	Split	0	-	20	-	-	-
Portugal	Split	75	-	46	3-5	Unconditional	25
Slovak Republic	Split	8	-	5	3-6	Unconditional	m
Slovenia	Integrated	7	5	3	11 months to 5	Conditional	45
Spain	Integrated	10	48	31	-	-	-
Sweden	Integrated	-	20	17	3-6	Unconditional	15
Switzerland	Split	0	-	5	-	-	-
Turkey	Split	-	100	13	-	-	-
United Kingdom	m	8	59	30	3-4	Unconditional	12.5-15
United States	m	-	-	41	-	-	-
Brazil	Integrated	1	-	25	-	-	-
Russian Federation	Integrated	-	-	-	-	-	-
Data Source[2]	**ECEC**	**EAG**	**EAG**	**EAG**	**ECEC**	**ECEC**	**ECEC**

	Teaching workforce (2014)						Equity				
Indicator name:	Teacher's qualification (upper secondary: ISCED 3; Short tertiary: ISCED 5; Bachelor's: ISCED 6, Master's: ISCED 7)	Teacher's statutory salary after 15 years of exercise	Teacher's annual statutory contact time time in hours , public settings	Teacher's annual statutory working time at school in hours, public settings	Child-to-staff ratios	Child-to-teacher ratios	Maternal employment rates, with at least one child under the age of 3	Maternal employment rates, with at least one child aged 3 to 5 year-olds	% of ECEC teachers who are women (2014)	Percentage of 15-year-old pupils who attended early childhood education (ISCED 0) for "two years and more", by socio-economic backgrounds (2015)	
coverage:	ISCED 02						Women aged 15 to 64 year-olds (2014)		ISCED 02	Disadvantaged (bottom quarter)	Advantaged (top quarter)
Table/Figure:	EAG 2014	Figure 3.7	Figure 3.9	EAG 2016	Figure 3.10	Figure 3.10	Figure 5.10	Figure 5.10	Figure 3.6	Figure 5.7	Figure 5.7
Column:	(18)	(19)	(20)	(21)	(22)	(23)	(24)	(25)	(26)	(27)	(28)
OECD average	**B:75%**	**35 664**	**1 047**	**1 417**	**11**	**14**	**53**	**66**	**97**	**72**	**82**
Australia	Bachelor	57 445	885	1226	4	5	-	-	-	43	57
Austria	ISCED 5	-	-	-	9	14	66	75	99	84	94
Belgium	Bachelor	-	-	-	15	15	66	70	97	94	98
Canada	Bachelor	-	-	-	-	-	66	72	-	40	55
Chile	Bachelor	23 199	1 146	2 006	12	26	45	55	99	51	63
Czech Republic	Bachelor	16 790	1 159	1 664	13	14	22	72	100	90	95
Denmark	Bachelor	45 898	1 417	1 680	6	10	76	80	-	91	95
Estonia	Bachelor	-	1 320	1 610	-	-	24	81	99	86	95
Finland	Bachelor	-	-	-	-	10	52	78	97	62	79
France	Master	31 865	924	972	15	22	59	76	92	89	97
Germany	Post-sec.	-	1 482	1 757	9	10	52	70	97	87	94
Greece	Bachelor	21071	684	1140	12	12	51	50	99	76	82
Hungary	Bachelor	17 858	1 152	1 152	13	13	13	68	100	95	99
Iceland	Master	-	-	-	-	-	-	-	-	94	97
Ireland	Post-sec.	-	-	-	-	-	61	58	-	44	54
Israel	Bachelor	27 588	1 025	1 051	-	-	70	75	-	87	94
Italy	Master	30 048	930	-	13	13	54	55	-	91	92
Japan	Bachelor	-	-	1 891	14	15	47	61	97	92	94
Korea[1]	ISCED 5 and 6	40 548	585	1 520	14	14	-	-	99	81	83
Latvia	Bachelor	-	-	-	-	11	54	70	100	88	91
Luxembourg	Bachelor	90 208	880	1 060	11	11	72	80	96	81	91
Mexico	Bachelor	22 148	532	772	25	25	33	43	-	76	89
Netherlands	Bachelor	44 847	930	1 659	14	16	74	73	-	-	-
New Zealand	Bachelor	-	-	-	-	7	45	63	98	76	81
Norway	Bachelor	40 520	1 508	1 508	5	11	-	-	91	81	94
Poland	Master	20 325	1 137	1 800	-	16	59	65	98	41	78
Portugal	Master	35 270	945	1 095	-	17	73	76	99	23	32
Slovak Republic	ISCED 3, 6 and 7	11 648	1 109	1 568	12	13	17	59	100	73	92
Slovenia	Bachelor	29 594	1 314	-	9	9	72	79	98	66	85
Spain	Bachelor	39 371	880	1 140	-	15	60	59	93	88	96
Sweden	Bachelor	35 086	-	1 792	6	6	-	-	-	83	93
Switzerland	Bachelor	59122	-	-	-	16	71	76	99	79	82
Turkey	Bachelor	27 746	1 080	1 160	-	17	22	30	95	10	33
United Kingdom	Master	-	-	-	10	18	59	62	96	63	70
United States	Bachelor	52 076	-	1 365	10	12	56	63	94	51	77

	Teaching workforce (2014)						Equity				
Indicator name:	Teacher's qualification (upper secondary: ISCED 3; Short tertiary: ISCED 5; Bachelor's: ISCED 6, Master's: ISCED 7)	Teacher's statutory salary after 15 years of exercise	Teacher's annual statutory contact time time in hours , public settings	Teacher's annual statutory working time at school in hours, public settings	Child-to-staff ratios	Child-to-teacher ratios	Maternal employment rates, with at least one child under the age of 3	Maternal employment rates, with at least one child aged 3 to 5 year-olds	% of ECEC teachers who are women (2014)	Percentage of 15-year-old pupils who attended early childhood education (ISCED 0) for "two years and more", by socio-economic backgrounds (2015)	
coverage:	ISCED 02						Women aged 15 to 64 year-olds (2014)		ISCED 02	Disadvantaged (bottom quarter)	Advantaged (top quarter)
Table/Figure:	EAG 2014	Figure 3.7	Figure 3.9	EAG 2016	Figure 3.10	Figure 3.10	Figure 5.10	Figure 5.10	Figure 3.6	Figure 5.7	Figure 5.7
Column:	(18)	(19)	(20)	(21)	(22)	(23)	(24)	(25)	(26)	(27)	(28)
OECD average	**B:75%**	**35 664**	**1 047**	**1 417**	**11**	**14**	**53**	**66**	**97**	**72**	**82**
Brazil	Bachelor	-	-	-	15	17	-	-	-	69	80
Russian Federation	Bachelor	-	-	-	-	-	64	86	-	72	90
Data Source²	**EAG**	**EAG**	**EAG**	**EAG**	**EAG**	**EAG**	**FD**	**FD**	**EAG**	**PISA**	**PISA**

Notes: The scoreboard highlights countries in the bottom 25% (light blue), countries in the top 25% (dark blue) and those around the OECD average (in white).A sharp threshold has been applied, which means that some countries can be classified in one group (e.g. the bottom 25%) but be close to the other group (e.g. average).

1. Data from Education at a Glance cover only Kindergarten.

2. Education at a Glance online database (EAG), OECD Family Database (FD), PISA 2015 database (PISA) and OECD ECEC Network data collections (ECEC).

Sources: OECD (2017a), PISA online education database, OECD, Paris, http://www.oecd.org/pisa/data/, OECD (2017b), OECD Online education database, OECD, Paris, www.oecd.org/education/database.htm and OECD (2017c), OECD Family Database, OECD, Paris, www.oecd.org/els/family/database.htm and OECD (2016), Education at a Glance 2016: OECD Indicators, http://dx.doi.org/10.1787/eag-2016-en.

StatLink http://dx.doi.org/10.1787/888933487206

Chapter 2.

Contextual factors influencing policies on early childhood education and care

Ageing populations, declining fertility rates and a greater proportion of children living in lone parent families have been part of the changing demographic landscape in recent decades. Societies are also becoming more ethnically, culturally, and linguistically diverse. At the same time, women's labour force participation rates have increased substantially in most countries. Current demographic and labour market patterns are a further motivation for governments to take early childhood education and care (ECEC) provision seriously. Enrolment in ECEC settings has continued to rise over the last decade, partly because of the extension of the legal entitlement to a place in ECEC, and efforts to ensure free access, at least for some ages and selected population groups. This chapter is a general review of a range of socio-economic and other factors that may determine the need for ECEC, policy on ECEC, the kinds of ECEC provided and uptake of what is on offer. This chapter also includes a summary table with a full overview of the ECEC systems and provision across OECD countries.

The statistical data for Israel are supplied by and are under the responsibility of the relevant Israeli authorities. The use of such data by the OECD is without prejudice to the status of the Golan Heights, East Jerusalem and Israeli settlements in the West Bank under the terms of international law.

Key messages

The demographic landscape and family structure have been dramatically changing in recent decades.

- Fertility rates have declined in most OECD countries to levels that are well below those needed to secure generation replacement. Among OECD countries, Israel has the highest fertility rate, with 3 children per woman in 2014, while total fertility rates are lower than 1.3 in Greece, Korea, Poland, Portugal and Spain.
- The average age at which mothers have their first child has risen across all OECD countries with available data over the past 40 years. By 2000, the age had risen to over 26 on average across OECD countries, and by 2013 it had risen again to 29.
- An increasing proportion of children lived with only one parent or with cohabiting parents in 2014. On average, the proportion of children living with two married parents decreased between 2005 and 2014 – from 72% to 67%.
- Trend data and projections show that, on average across OECD countries, the child population under the age of 6 fell between 1970 and 2000, was relatively stable between 2000 and 2014, and is expected to slightly decrease until 2030. On average across OECD countries, children under the age of 6 represented 7% of the total population in 2014.
- The populations of OECD countries are becoming increasingly heterogeneous as a result of migration. On average across the OECD, the share of the foreign-born population increased from 6% to over 9% over the last two decades. Increased mobility leading to greater diversity requires particular efforts towards integration, especially in the early stages of education.
- Integrating young immigrant children into their new communities is of key importance in the long run. Education systems can help by encouraging their enrolment in early childhood education and care (ECEC) programmes.

Labour market participation.

- Joblessness is generally much higher for sole-parent families than for couples with children, and the growth in the incidence of sole-parent families has been a significant contributor to trends in family joblessness. Almost one in three children with a single parent lived in a jobless household.
- Lone parents, mostly mothers, must carry the dual responsibility of being the main breadwinner and the main carer. In 2011, sole-parent employment rates went up with the age of the youngest child. Thus, the proportion of sole parents with youngest child aged 6-14 in employment was almost twice as high as for sole parents with children under 3 years of age.
- Women labour force participation rates have increased substantially in most countries since 1980, except for those in the youngest age group (20 to 24 years), when many are still in education. On average across OECD countries, female employment rates increased between 1980 and 2014 from 53% to 73% among 25-54 year-olds.

Current demographic and labour market patterns are a further motivation for governments to take ECEC provision seriously.

- The growing need for ECEC is a consensus among OECD countries. However, the types of ECEC services available to children and parents in OECD countries and jurisdictions differ greatly.
- Variations exist in the targeted age groups, the ownership of centres, the funding of services, the intensity of participation (i.e. usual number of hours per week), the type of delivery (full-day versus part-day attendance), the care or education orientation of provision, and the locus of provision (either in centres/schools or at home).
- The definition of ECEC in the OECD's Starting Strong series is broader than the ISCED 2011 definition. It includes all arrangements providing care only or care and education for children under compulsory school age, regardless of setting, funding, opening hours or programme content.

ECEC provision differs across countries regarding governance and legal entitlement, however, some trends have emerged.

Research tells us that:

- The literature shows that having integrated ECEC systems administered under the responsibility of one ministry (or agency) is associated with better ECEC quality and helps enhance universal entitlement, more affordable access, better qualified staff and smoother transitions.
- By contrast, split systems have negative effects, in particular for childcare services, as they are less developed and less affordable, staff are less qualified and there are worse working conditions.

International comparisons reveal some clear trends:

- A move towards integrated ECEC settings regarding curricula and governing authority is observed in several OECD countries. In 2014, more than half of OECD countries had an integrated ECEC system. In the others, ECEC settings were officially registered, but provided in distinct settings and under the responsibility of different ministries (split model).
- In split systems, the settings enrolling most children under the age of 3 are often under the authority of the Ministry of Social Affairs, while the settings providing ECEC for older children are under the authority of the Ministry of Education. In these countries, different standards are often set for different ECEC settings. In contrast, in all countries with an integrated system, the same standards are applied to any ECEC setting.
- Enrolment in ECEC settings have continued to rise over the last decade, partly because of the extension of the legal entitlement to a place in ECEC, and efforts to ensure free access, at least for some ages and selected population groups. However, there are major differences across countries in the age groups covered by legal entitlements to a place in ECEC.
- The legal entitlement to a place in ECEC is not a guarantee of free access, especially for younger children. However, most countries provide free access to all children for at least the last year before entering primary school.

Changes in demographic landscape over the last decades

Fertility rates have declined in most OECD countries to levels that are well below those needed to secure generation replacement.

The demographic landscape for families has changed dramatically since 1970. Declining fertility rates, combined with longer life expectancies at birth and declining mortality rates, have contributed to the shift in the age structure of the population in OECD countries (OECD, 2011 and OECD, 2017a). Due to this declining total fertility rate (TFR), an increasing number of countries are now facing the challenge of securing generation replacement. In 1970, most OECD and partner countries had total fertility rates around or above the replacement rate of 2.1 children per women. Only the Czech Republic, Denmark, Finland, Germany, Hungary, Latvia, Luxembourg, the Russian Federation and Sweden already had below replacement fertility rates. By contrast, TFRs were above five children per women in Korea, Mexico and Turkey in 1970 (Figure 2.1).

Figure 2.1. Total fertility rates in 1970, 2000 and 2014

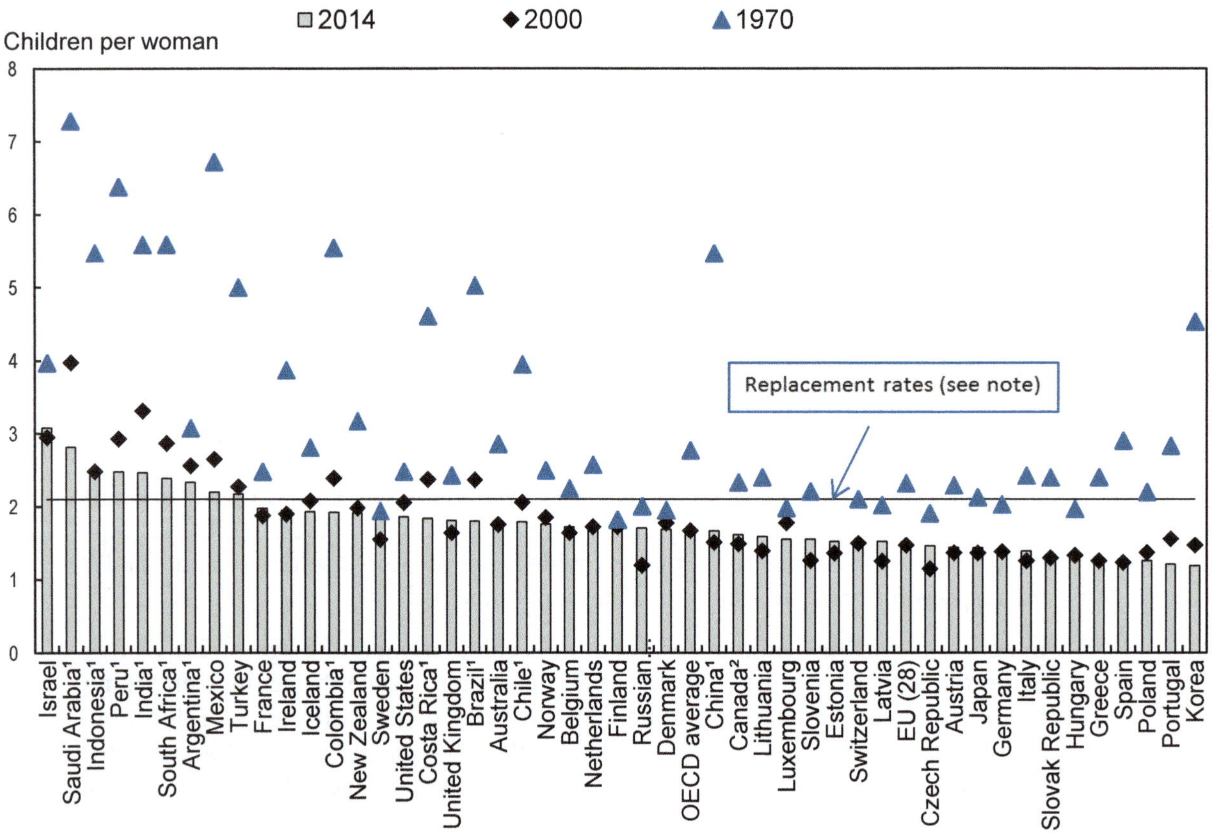

Notes: The dot line represents the average replacement rates. Assuming no migration and that mortality rates remain unchanged, a total fertility rate of 2.1 children per woman is generally sufficient to generate a stable population within a given country.

Countries are ranked in descending order of total fertility rates in 2014.

1. Year of reference 2013 instead of 2014.

2. Year of reference 2012 instead of 2014.

Source: OECD (2017a), OECD Family Database, OECD, Paris, www.oecd.org/social/family/database.htm.

StatLink http://dx.doi.org/10.1787/888933487214

This situation has dramatically evolved during the four last decades. In 2000, most countries had rates well below the replacement level. The situation became worse by 2014, when only three OECD countries (Israel, Mexico and Turkey) and six partner countries (Argentina, India, Indonesia, Peru, Saudi Arabia and South Africa) had total fertility rates at the level or higher than two children per women. In these countries, the need for the expansion of ECEC settings will be stronger compared to the countries where fertility rates are stable or have declined between 2000 and 2014.

Among OECD countries, Israel has the highest fertility rate, with three children per woman in 2014. Total fertility rates are lower than 1.3 in Greece, Korea, Poland, Portugal and Spain. Population issues are different in developing countries, where fertility rates are often much higher than in OECD countries. For example, China, India and Indonesia have developed active policies to control fertility, which have contributed to a decline in TFRs from above five children per woman at the beginning of the 1970s, to 2.5 children per woman in India and Indonesia and 1.7 in China in 2014 (OECD, 2017a).

The decreasing fertility rates observed in many OECD countries is strongly linked to the fact that more women and men are waiting until later in life to begin their families.

As family structures change, so do the relative ages of parents. The decreasing fertility rates observed in many OECD countries is strongly linked to the fact that more women and men are waiting until later in life to begin their families (OECD, 2017a). They do so for several reasons, including planning for greater financial security, taking more time to find a stable relationship, and committing to their careers before turning their attention to having children. Another important reason for the postponement of childbearing is an increase in the number of women in OECD countries entering tertiary education and undertaking longer studies than in the past (see effect on employment rates in Figure 2.4). Women who are university students are far less prone to have children.

Consequently, the number of countries with a current mean age at childbirth of 30 or above is considerably higher than in previous years. The average age at which mothers have their first child has also risen across all OECD countries with available data over the past 40 years. In 1970, Iceland had the lowest average age of mothers giving birth to their first child among OECD countries, at just over 21 years. Out of the 23 countries for which 1970 data are available, five other countries had an average age at first birth of under the age of 23, and the average age across all countries was just over 24. By 2000, the age had risen to over 27 on average across OECD countries, and by 2014 it had risen again to 29 (Figure 2.2).

Despite this trend, there is still a wide variation among countries. In 2014, Italy, Japan, Korea, Spain and Switzerland had the highest average age at first birth – older than 30. By contrast, the United States had the lowest average age – at just 26.

Figure 2.2. Trends in the age of first-time mothers (1970, 2000 and 2014)

Average age when mothers have their first child

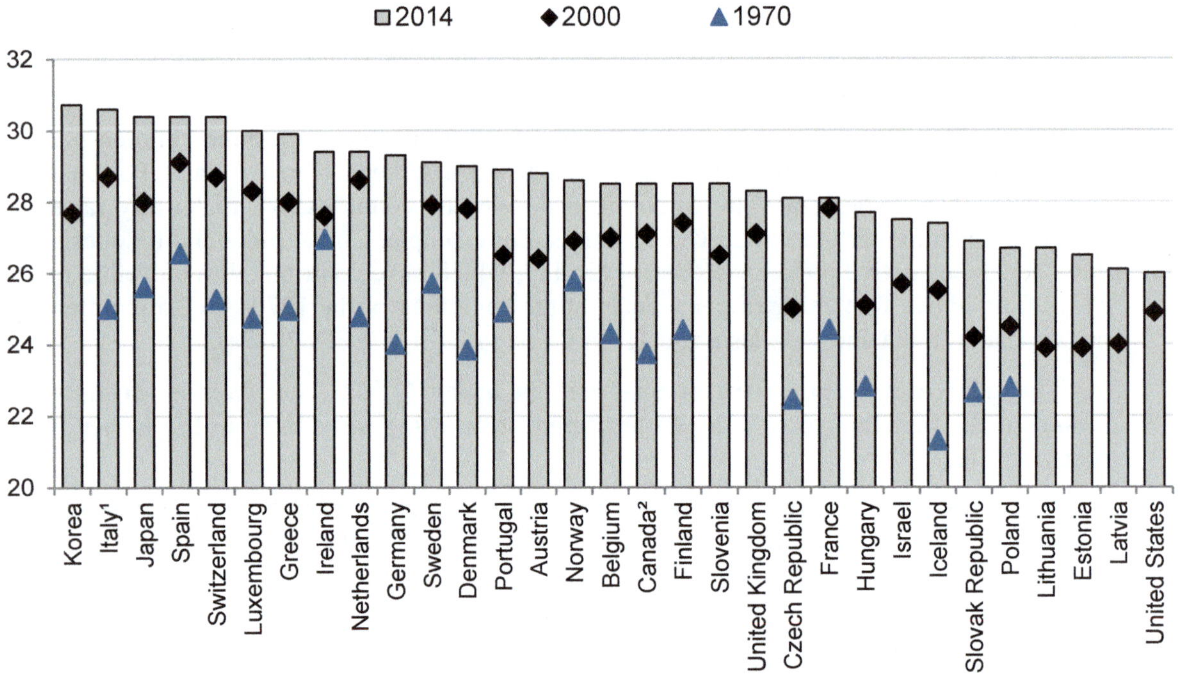

Notes: Countries are ranked in descending order of the average age when mothers have their first child in 2014.

1. Year of reference 1997 instead of 2000.
2. Year of reference 2011 instead of 2014.

Source: OECD (2017a), OECD Family Database, OECD, Paris, www.oecd.org/social/family/database.htm.

StatLink http://dx.doi.org/10.1787/888933487221

The structure of families is also changing: An increasing proportion of children live with only one parent or with cohabiting parents.

Today, living with two cohabiting parents (e.g. with two parents who are not married to each other) or with lone parents is increasingly common. For European countries, "married parents" in principle includes parents in registered partnerships, although actual practice may vary from country to country. These trends are mainly linked to the increase in divorce and separation observed in many OECD countries, and to a lesser extent a rise in births outside of partnership or marriage. On average across countries where detailed data are available, the proportion of children living with two married parents decreased slightly between 2005 and 2014 – from 72% to 67% – while the share of children living in households with a sole parent remained stable (from 17% to 18%). In the mid-1980s, only 6% of children grew up in this situation (OECD, 2017a).

The proportion of children living with cohabiting parents increased from 10% in 2005 to 15% in 2014, an increase of almost 50%. However, some exceptions exist across OECD countries. For instance, in Sweden, the share of children living with both parents has been stable since the beginning of the 2000s (so the share living with lone parents has not increased). Among children with separated parents in Norway and Sweden, many have shared residence, and the share is increasing. This means that fathers are now more involved than before in taking care of children (OECD, 2017a).

The rates of lone parenthood varied widely among countries in 2014. In Latvia and the United States, more than 25% of children aged 0 to 17 grow up in single-parent families, compared to fewer than 10% in Greece, Croatia, Poland, Romania and Turkey. On average, 85% of all single-parent families are female headed. In Estonia, Iceland and Lithuania, more than 90% of single parents are mothers (OECD, 2017a). The overall trend is expected to continue, and by 2030, the share of single-parent families among all households with children will rise across all OECD countries. In countries such as Austria, Japan and New Zealand, the share of single-parent families is expected to reach between 30% and 40% by 2030 (OECD, 2014 and OECD, 2017a).

Children living in households with a sole parent are more likely to be living in a jobless household than children in families with two parents living together.

The economic vulnerability of families is linked to parents' incapacity to reconcile employment and parenthood (OECD, 2011). The most disadvantaged families with children are those where no adults are in paid employment. On average, almost 9% of children aged 0 to 14 live in households where no adult is in paid work. However, there is a wide variation across OECD and European Union (EU) countries. In 2011, in Austria, Finland, Japan, Luxembourg, Slovenia and Sweden, fewer than 5% of children lived in jobless households, while this percentage was around 14% or more in Australia, Hungary, New Zealand Turkey and the United Kingdom (Figure 2.3).

Children living in jobless families are children living in households where no adult is in paid work, regardless of the number of adults (and their relationship) in the household. Joblessness is generally much higher for sole-parent families than for couples with children, and the growth in the incidence of sole-parent families has been a significant contributor to trends in family joblessness. Thus, almost one in three children with a single parent lived in a jobless household. The proportion of children with a jobless parent in sole-parent families was around 50% in Australia, New Zealand and the United Kingdom, and over 70% in Turkey.

Couple households, that is, households with two partnered adults either married or in a civil or registered partnership, or cohabiting. The "risk" of living with parents not in the labour force is much lower in other types of households: only 5% of children in couple households and around 9% of children in "complex" households (e.g. households with either several non-related cohabiting members or with members of two or more families sharing the same dwelling) live in a jobless household (Figure 2.3).

Figure 2.3. Proportion of children living in jobless families (2011)

Proportion (%) of children under age 15 for each type of household

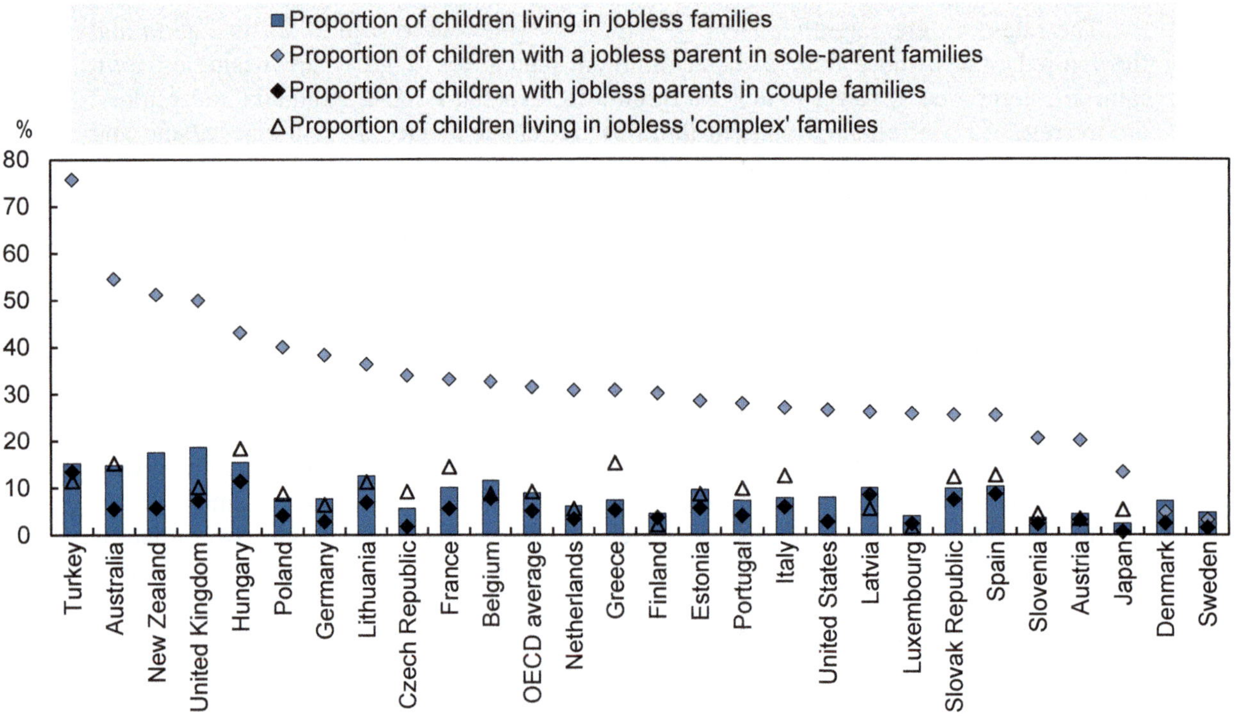

Note: Countries are ranked in descending order of the proportion of children with a jobless parent in sole-parent families.

Source: OECD (2017a), OECD Family Database, OECD, Paris, http://www.oecd.org/social/family/database.htm.

StatLink http://dx.doi.org/10.1787/888933487235

Lone parents face many challenges, and there are many consequences for ECEC policy.

Lone parents, mostly mothers, must carry the dual responsibility of being the main breadwinner and the main carer. They may wish to enter the labour market where caring responsibilities may not be recognised, and in the face of social arrangements that often continue to take for granted the flexibility of a mother's time (e.g. the time schedule of schools, the offer of childcare services, the opening hours of shops, public offices). In 2011, sole-parent employment rates increased with the age of the youngest child: the proportion of sole parents with a youngest child aged 6-14 in employment was almost twice as high as for sole parents with children under 3 years of age. Most sole parents with a child aged 6 to 14 are in full-time work, except in Germany and the Netherlands, where part-time work is most prevalent (OECD, 2017a and Figure 5.11).

There are many consequences of this trend for ECEC policy. For lone mothers to enter and remain in the labour market, there is a need for greater access to affordable ECEC. ECEC services need to be sensitive to the time and financial constraints faced by lone mothers when they conceive of opening hours, fees, and parental engagement objectives. The labour market also needs to respond with more flexibility so that lone parents – like other parents – can balance their work and family responsibilities (see Chapter 5 and OECD, 2011).

Changes in women labour force participation rates

The demographic landscape for families has changed dramatically since 1970. At the same time, women labour force participation rates have increased substantially in most countries.

Labour market developments appear to strongly influence family formation. Young people are waiting until they have completed more education and until one or both parents are more securely established in their careers before getting married and having children. This process is taking longer than in the past, as seen, for example, in the increasing age at first marriage and at first childbirth (Figure 2.2).

The most dramatic development over the past twenty years in many countries has been the increase in women labour force participation. Most women are obliged to juggle household and family demands with involvement in paid work structures. The availability and affordability of ECEC and other work-family provisions – such as temporary withdrawal from the labour market through parental leave – have a great influence on whether mothers are required to make a choice between labour market participation and childrearing (refer to Chapter 5 for further analyses).

The difficulties in managing paid work and childbearing are also seen in high levels of childlessness (especially among women with a high level of education). Therefore, in recent years, more government attention and expenditure have been given to increasing ECEC opportunities (see more details in Chapter 3).

Figure 2.4. More women are in paid work during childbearing years than in the past (2014)

Age-employment profiles of women, 1960-2014

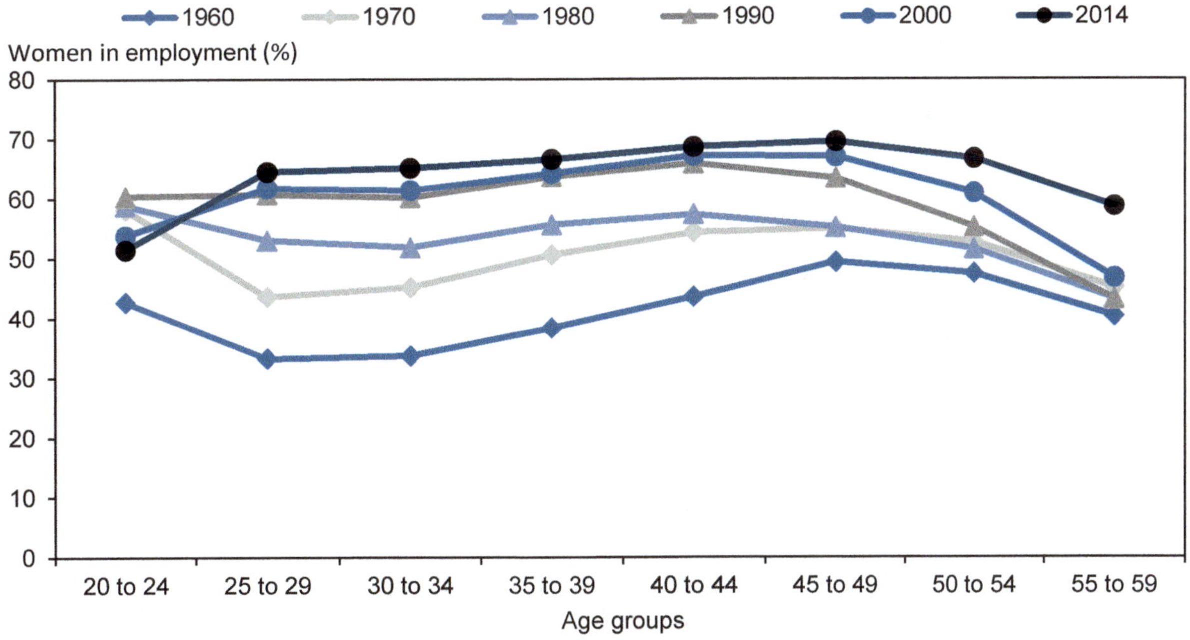

Source: OECD (2017b), OECD Employment Database, OECD, Paris, www.oecd.org/employment/emp/onlineoecdemploymentdatabase.htm.

StatLink http://dx.doi.org/10.1787/888933487246

As shown in Figure 2.4, women's transitions in and out of employment have noticeably changed in recent decades. Before 1990, on average in the OECD, women's age-employment profiles showed a marked trough during the childbearing years (between ages 25 and 34). This trough has gradually smoothed as more women remain in the labour market after childbirth. Employment rates in OECD countries have increased for women of all ages, except for those in the youngest age group (20 to 24 years), when many are still in education. This was not necessarily the case 30 years ago.

Some differences in age-employment profiles exist across countries. For example, in Nordic countries, women's age-employment participation profiles often closely resemble those of men, while in countries such as the Czech Republic, Hungary, Japan, Korea and the Slovak Republic, a more traditional profile is observed, as mothers find it more difficult to combine work with family commitments (OECD, 2012a and OECD, 2003a).

High female labour force participation is not incompatible with high fertility rates, especially in countries that provide well-developed ECEC services for young children, or good opportunities to temporarily withdraw from the labour market through parental leave.

Figure 2.5. Cross-country relationship between female employment rates and total fertility rates (1980 and 2014)

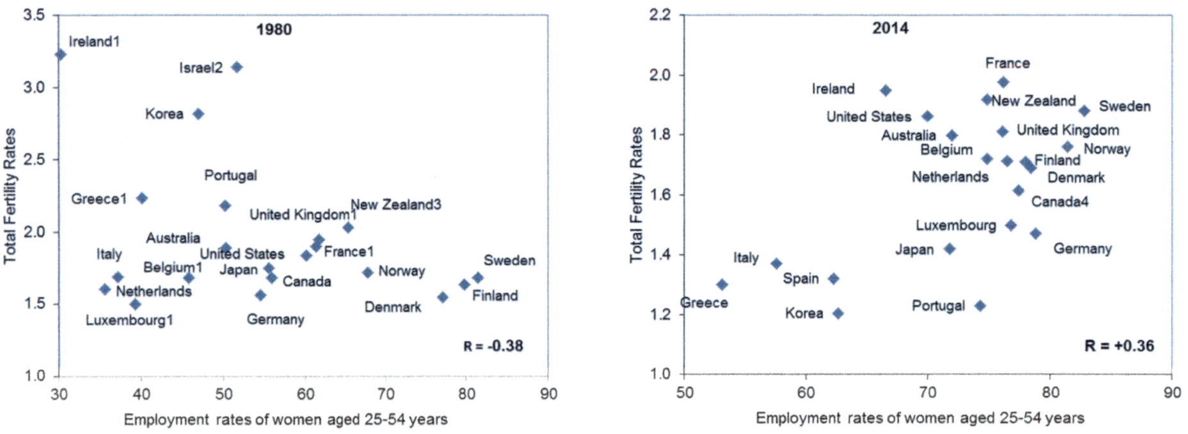

1. Year of reference 1983 instead of 1980.
2. Year of reference 1985 instead of 1980.
3. Year of reference 1986 instead of 1980.
4. Year of reference 2013 instead of 2014.

Sources: OECD (2017a), OECD Family Database, OECD, Paris, www.oecd.org/social/family/database.htm and OECD (2017b), OECD Employment Database, OECD, Paris, www.oecd.org/employment/emp/onlineoecdemploymentdatabase.htm.

StatLink http://dx.doi.org/10.1787/888933487252

Figure 2.5 shows that across OECD countries, the relationship between female employment and fertility has changed over the four last decades. Apart from the general increase in female employment observed between 1980 and 2014 (from 53% to 73% for 25–54 year-olds across OECD countries with available data for both years), there was a slight negative correlation (R= -0.38) between female employment and fertility rates in 1980, while the correlation was positive in 2014 (R= + 0.36).

In other words, in 1980, most countries with higher female employment rates had low fertility levels. By contrast, in 2014, the countries with low female employment rates tended to also have lower total fertility rates. The degree of incompatibility between paid work and having children still exists in some countries, but it has diminished. However, there are substantial cross-country differences: combining childrearing and employment is most difficult in some Mediterranean countries (Greece, Italy, Portugal and Spain), as well as in Korea. Whereas is seems most compatible in Nordic countries (OECD, 2006 and OECD, 2012a).

This reverse trend between 1980 and 2014 is not surprising, as during this period most countries expanded their ECEC provision, while more opportunities were offered to parents to temporarily withdraw from the labour market through parental leave. Thus, the Nordic case shows that an increase in female labour force participation followed by an expansion of ECEC facilities has led to an increase in fertility rates over the last four decades. Moreover, the relationship between mother's employability and enrolment rates in formal childcare was strong in 2014, especially for mothers with their youngest child under the age of 3 (refer to Chapter 5 for further analyses on policy outcomes).

Societies are becoming more ethnically, culturally, and linguistically diverse

The populations of OECD countries are becoming increasingly heterogeneous because of migration. On average across the OECD, the share of the foreign-born population has increased from 6% to over 9% in the last two decades. Increased mobility leading to greater diversity requires particular efforts towards integration, especially in the early stages of education.

The total foreign-born population living in OECD countries rose to 120 million people in 2014. On average, this represents approximately an additional three million per year since 2000. However, the growth pace decreased over the period 2010-14. Between 2000 and 2010, the foreign-born population gained a little over three million people every year, but since then it grew by only two million per year. Of these 120 million foreign-born, 46% live in an EU/EFTA country, and 35% in the United States. The average proportion of foreign-born persons in OECD countries rose from 10% in 2000 to 13% in 2014 (Figure 2.6). With the exception of Estonia, Israel and Poland, all countries contributed to this growth, and half saw the share of their foreign-born population rise by more than five percentage points over this period (OECD, 2016a).

Integrating young immigrant children into their new communities is of key importance in the long run. One of the ways in which education systems can help is by encouraging their enrolment in ECEC programmes. However, in most countries, the participation of immigrant children in these programmes is considerably lower than for those without an immigrant background. However, participation in at least one year of early childhood education is particularly beneficial for children with an immigrant background, and for children where mothers have not attained upper secondary education (Figure 5.8; Magnuson, Lahaie, and Waldfogel, 2006).

Figure 2.6. The foreign-born as a percentage of the total population in OECD countries, 2000 and 2014

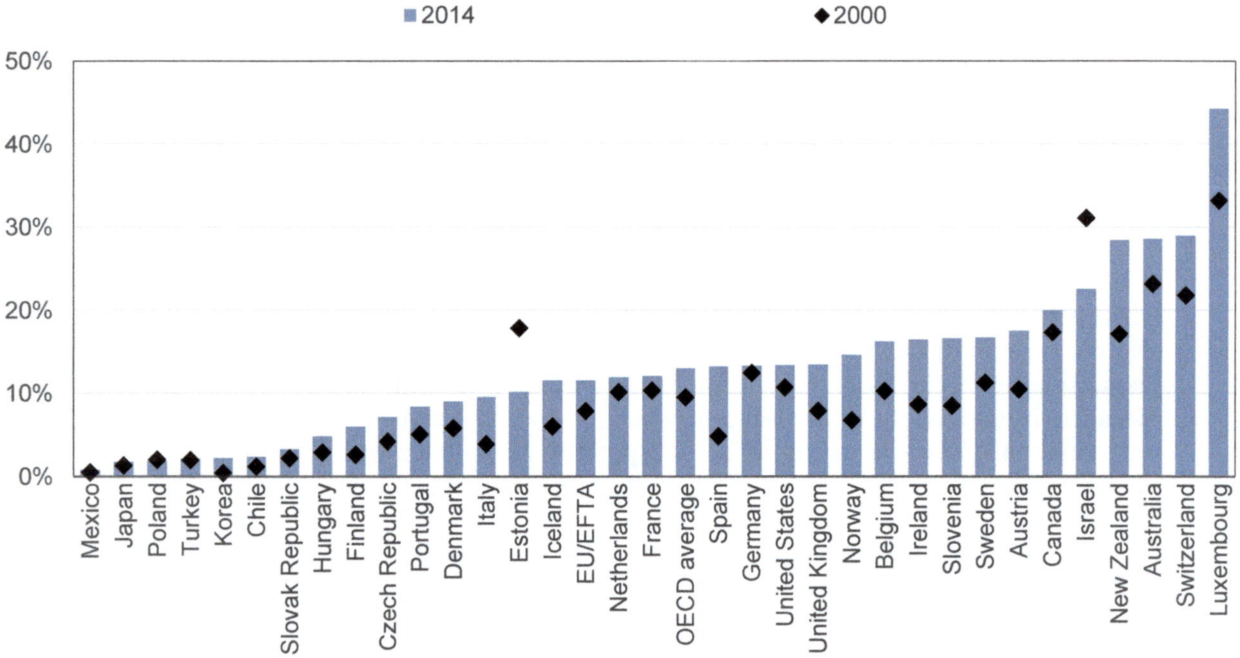

Notes: Data refer to 2000 or to the closest year with available data, and to 2014 or most recent available year. OECD average refers to the average of countries presented. The value for EU/EFTA is the percentage of the foreign-born population living in all EU/EFTA countries presented among the total population of these countries. Data refers to foreign instead of foreign-born population for Japan and Korea.

Source: OECD (2017c), "International migration database", OECD International Migration Statistics (database), http://dx.doi.org/10.1787/data-00342-en (accessed 24 April 2017).

StatLink http://dx.doi.org/10.1787/888933487269

Impact of demographic and societal changes on the evolution of the population of young children

On average across OECD countries, children under the age of 6 represented 7% of the total population in 2005 and in 2014. In most OECD countries, the variation in the proportion of children under the age of 6 was not significant over this period, and exceeded one percentage point only in Chile, the Czech Republic, Estonia, Japan, Korea, Mexico, the Netherlands, Slovenia and Turkey. In 2014, the proportion of children under 6 reached at least 6% and did not exceed 10% of the total population in 32 of the 48 OECD and partner countries with available data.

At 13%, Saudi Arabia is the country with the largest proportion of children under 6 years of age. Among OECD countries, Ireland, Israel, Mexico and Turkey have the highest proportion of young children as a percentage of the population, at more than 9.5% (Figure 2.7). In contrast, in Austria, Greece, Germany, Hungary, Italy, Japan, Korea and Portugal, the percentages are the smallest. Children under the age of 6 represent fewer than 6% per cent of the total population in these eight countries (OECD, 2017a and European Commission/EACEA/Eurydice/Eurostat, 2014).

Figure 2.7. Number of children under the age of 6 as a proportion of the total population (2005 and 2014)

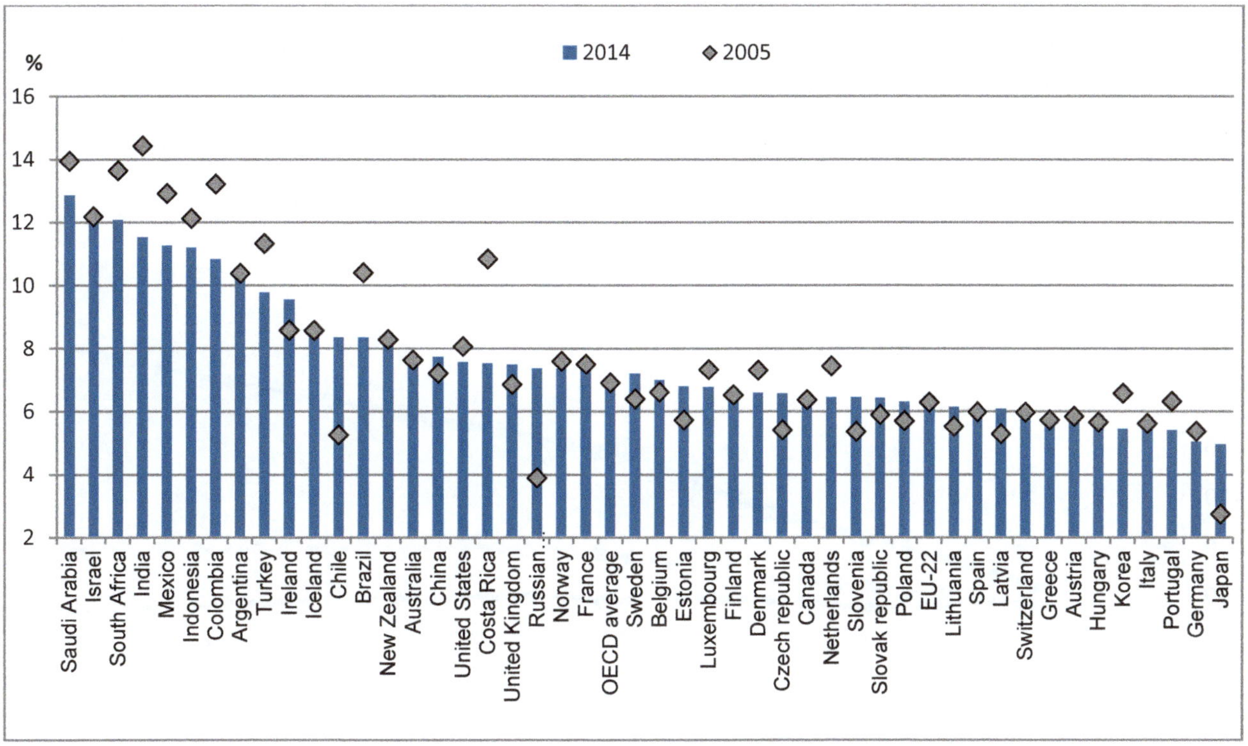

Note: Countries are ranked in descending order of the proportion of children under the age of 6 in 2014.

Source: OECD (2017d), OECD online education database, OECD, Paris, http://www.oecd.org/education/database.htm.

StatLink http://dx.doi.org/10.1787/888933487271

In most OECD and partner countries, trends and fluctuations in the child population size are partly explained by changes in the fertility rates and changes in the age of the first birth over the past few decades (Figures 2.1 and 2.2). However, the broad trend of young children cohorts being smaller among OECD countries is more apparent when comparing the evolution of the number of children under the age of 6 over four decades than over the last decade, as in Figure 2.7.

Trend data and projections shows that, on average across OECD countries, the population of children under the age of 6 fell between 1970 and 2000, was relatively stable between 2000 and 2014, and is expected to slightly decrease until 2030 (Figure 2.8 and OECD, 2016b: historical population data). In absolute numbers, in 2000 and 2014 there were around 91 million young children under the age of 6 across OECD countries; this means around 10 million fewer children in the OECD area compared to 1970. Population projections suggest that by 2030, the number of children under 6 will continue to decline and will fall to 89 million in 2030 in the OECD area (Figure 2.8).

As children under the age of 6 are those who benefit from ECEC provision, these findings are relevant for policy makers in their decision-making process as they will need to allocate resources to ECEC settings and target their investments according to needs over time. Policy makers will also need to handle local changes in demography, for example, if urbanisation leads to an increased number of children under 6 in one region and a decreased number in another. If there is an increase in the number of young children, ECEC provision needs to be expanded, if there is a decrease, policy makers can target their ECEC investment at improving the structural and process quality of ECEC provision (e.g. decrease child-to-staff ratio, increase teacher's salary, increase the intensity of participation during a usual week in ECEC).

Figure 2.8. Trend in child population and projections in selected OECD countries (2016)

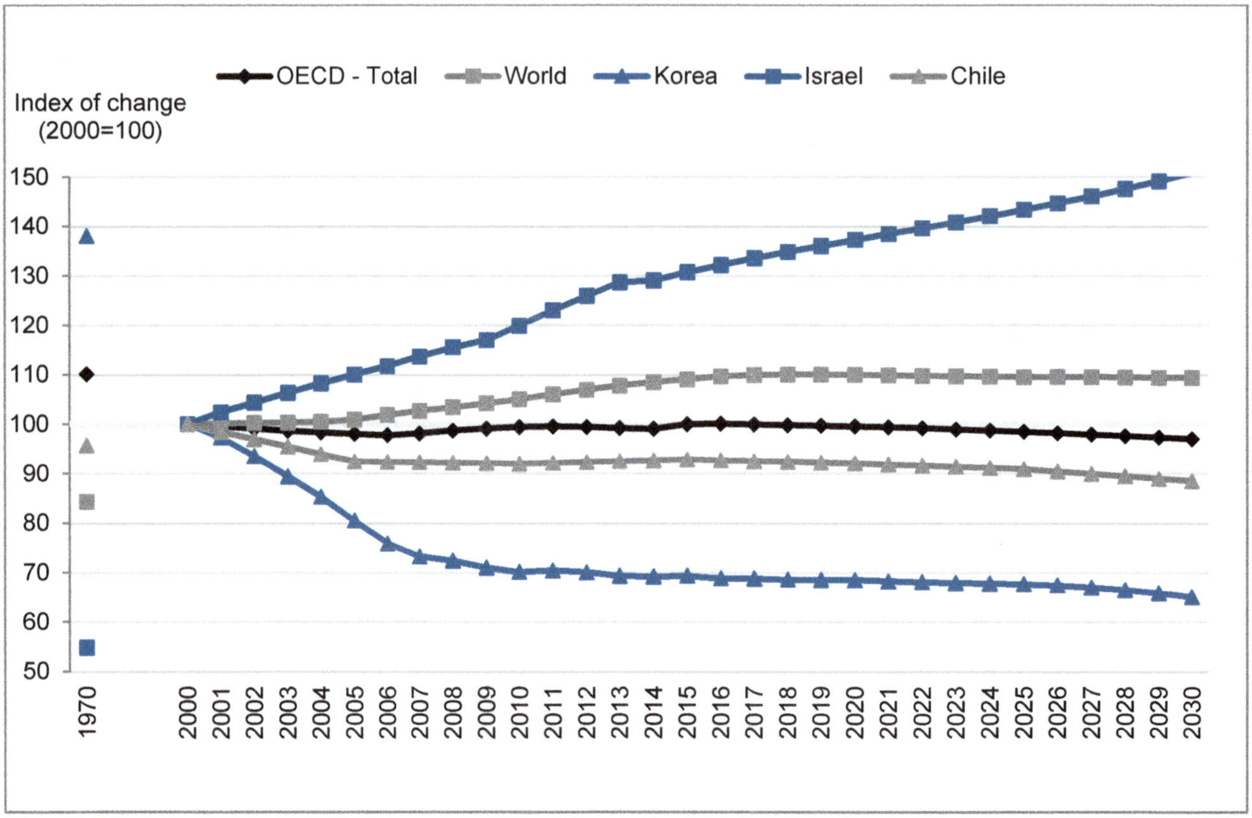

Source: OECD (2016b), OECD historical data and projections (1950-2050), OECD, Paris, https://stats.oecd.org/Index.aspx?DataSetCode=POP_PROJ.

StatLink http://dx.doi.org/10.1787/888933487284

The challenges across OECD countries are not the same, partly because trends in the child population are diverse. Thus, more than half of OECD countries (19 out 34 countries with available data) show small variations over the period 2000-2014, with the increases/decreases in the number of children under the age of 6 not exceeding eight percentage points in these countries (see Chile for example in Figure 2.8). By contrast, in 11 of the remaining OECD countries, the number of children under the age of 6 has significantly increased since 2000. For instance, increases exceed 20% between 2000 and 2014 in Ireland, Israel and Spain (see Israel in Figure 2.8).

In the five remaining OECD countries (Germany, Hungary, Korea, Japan and Portugal), the pattern is different, and the number of children under the age of 6 significantly fell between 2000 and 2014, with the decline in Korea (31%) particularly sharp. In these countries, the challenge to renew the generation is a priority, especially because demographic projections predict another fall of the child population between 2014 and 2030 (OECD, 2016b and Korea in Figure 2.8).

Overview of early childhood education and care system and provision

Current demographic patterns are a further motivation for all governments to take ECEC provision seriously. Additionally, as parents are more likely to be in the workforce today, there is a growing need for ECEC.

The likely long-term shrinkage of the working-age population means that the skills of women will be increasingly needed in paid employment to ensure the continued competitiveness of OECD economies. While the number of children in the ECEC age group is likely to decrease in many countries, the demand for ECEC and for ECEC staff generally will continue to increase, given that the provision of services for the youngest children have not been giving full coverage according to demand in many countries, and that more women will enter the labour market. Moreover, smaller family sizes mean that many children are growing up in families with few or no siblings. Informal opportunities for socialisation – in both rural and urban areas – are becoming rarer, leading to a greater need for ECEC settings where young children can interact with other children and adults (OECD, 2015 and OECD, 2012).

In addition, there is increasing awareness of the key role that early childhood education plays in children's well-being and cognitive and social-emotional development. As a result, ensuring the quality of ECEC has become a policy priority in most OECD countries. Enrolling children in ECEC can also mitigate social inequalities and promote better student outcomes overall (see Chapter 5). Many of the inequalities found in education systems are already evident when children enter formal schooling, and persist (or increase) as they progress through the school system.

Today, the type of ECEC services available to children and parents varies significantly across OECD countries.

There is a consensus among OECD countries about the growing need for ECEC. However, the types of ECEC services available to children and parents in OECD countries and jurisdictions differ greatly. Variations exist in the targeted age groups, the ownership of the centres, the funding of services, the intensity of participation (e.g. usual number of hours per week) and the type of delivery (full-day versus part-day attendance), the care or education-orientation of provision, as well as the locus of provision, either in centres/schools or at home (see Starting Strong series). Despite those differences, most ECEC settings typically fall into one of the five following categories:

- **Regular centre-based ECEC:** more formalised ECEC centres typically belong to one of these three sub-categories:
  - *Centre-based ECEC for children under the age of 3*: often called "crèches", these settings may have an educational function, but are typically attached to the social or welfare sector and associated with an emphasis on care. Many of them are part-time and provided in schools, but they can also be provided in designated ECEC centres.
  - *Centre-based ECEC for children from the age of 3:* often called kindergarten or pre-school, these settings tend to be more formalised and are often linked to the education system.
  - *Age-integrated centre-based ECEC for children from birth or one year-old, up to the beginning of primary school*: can be called kindergarten, pre-school,

or pre-primary, and offers a holistic pedagogical provision of education and care (often full-day). To an increasing degree, these settings are linked to the educational system.

- **Family day care ECEC:** licensed home-based ECEC, which is most prevalent for children under the age of 3. These settings may have an educational function and be part of the regular ECEC system, or not. The minimum requirements defined for licensed family day care services vary widely across countries. Requirements range from registration with an initial (one off) health and safety check, to registration with annual safety and health checks (the most usual form of licensing imposed on providers), to – in the most advanced cases – registration with requirements for staff and curriculum standards, annual pedagogical inspection, in-training requirements, and pedagogical supervision regularly ensured by an accredited supervisory body. Registered family day care refers to providers who are recruited, supported, and, in some cases, employed, by a public authority or publicly-funded private organisation.
- **Licenced or formalised drop-in ECEC centres:** often receiving children across the entire ECEC age bracket and even beyond, these drop-in centres often complement home-based care or services of other centre-based settings, and allow parents to complement home-based care by family members or family day care with more institutionalised services. They may also cater for children outside the opening hours of other centre-based ECEC settings, such as nursery schools. This type of ECEC setting allows children and children accompanied by caretakers (parent, guardian, relative or childminder) to attend a playgroup led by ECEC professionals on a drop-in basis (without having to apply for a place).

In practice, the boundaries between these categories are blurred in many countries and jurisdictions. For example, licenced family day care may operate for a larger age bracket, or in combination with centre-based care with more limited opening hours. Family day carers may equally establish networks in some countries and jurisdictions, or co-operate with ECEC centres in their work.

Despite the expansion of formalised and licensed ECEC services, informal care services continue to play an important role in many participating countries and jurisdictions. While this may be a full-time arrangement for children under the age of 3 in several countries, it often becomes part-time for older children until the age of school entry. These services can be undertaken by relatives, friends, neighbours, babysitters or nannies, or by unlicensed or unregulated centres. This informal service provision can be home-based (e.g. unlicensed family day care) or can take place outside the parental home (e.g. unregulated drop-in services and non-registered childminders). In the case of unlicensed family day care, for instance, providers are self-employed and make private arrangements directly with parents. Generally speaking, such services are used less if coverage with formal ECEC is higher. For example, in Finland, Sweden and Norway, fewer than 10% of children under compulsory school age receive informal care (OECD, 2017a and EU, 2013).

In the OECD indicators on ECEC, "formal" ECEC settings can be split into two categories: those in adherence to ISCED 2011 criteria, and other registered ECEC services outside the scope of ISCED 2011.

The type of ECEC services varies greatly from country to country in terms of provision, but also regarding the age of children attending different types of settings, the intensity of participation (number of hours and number of days), staff qualification and curriculum framework. There are also a range of different approaches to identifying the boundary between early childhood education and childcare. Globally, formal ECEC settings can be classified in two categories: those in adherence with the criteria defined in the ISCED 2011 classification, and other ECEC arrangements providing care and education for children under compulsory school age. Informal care services (generally unregulated care arranged by the child's parent either in the child's home or elsewhere, provided by relatives, friends, neighbours, babysitters or nannies) do not enter in this nomenclature.

- ECEC services in adherence to ISCED 2011 criteria

In ISCED 2011, ISCED 0 covers ECEC for all ages, including very young children. As the educational properties of ISCED 0 programmes can be difficult to assess directly, several criteria are used to develop a technical definition. For a programme of an ECEC setting to be reported as ISCED level 0 it must have: adequate intentional educational or pedagogical properties; be delivered by qualified staff members; take place in an institutionalised setting; meet a minimum intensity/duration (an intensity of at least 2 hours per day; and a duration of at least 100 days a year) and be targeted at children from age 0 until entry into ISCED level 1.

In ISCED 2011, programmes are sub-classified into two categories depending on age and the level of complexity of the educational content: early childhood educational development (ISCED 01) and pre-primary education (ISCED 02). ISCED 01 programmes are generally designed for children younger than 3. This is a new category not covered by ISCED 1997. ISCED 02 is designed for children from the age of 3 to the start of primary education. It corresponds exactly to level 0 in ISCED 1997 (see ISCED operational manual). Age-integrated ECEC services are reported according to the age of the children (OECD/Eurostat/UNESCO Institute for Statistics, ISCED 2011 operational manual, 2015).

- Other registered ECEC services

The definition of ECEC in the OECD's Starting Strong series is broader than the ISCED 2011 definition. The term ECEC includes all arrangements providing care only or care and education for children under compulsory school age, regardless of setting, funding, opening hours or programme content. This means that settings considered an integral part of countries' ECEC provision, but not covered by the ISCED classification, still fall under the terminology of ECEC.

For example, Ireland offers integrated programmes that include education and childcare services. However, early childhood educational development programmes (ISCED 01), as defined in ISCED 2011, are not formally structured in Ireland, although some ECEC services for children under 3 have an intentional educational aim. These programmes are outside the definition of ISCED 2011, but enter in this category. Belgium (except in the Flemish Community), the Czech Republic, France, Italy, Japan, Luxembourg, the Netherlands, Poland, Portugal, the Slovak Republic and Switzerland are in the same situation as Ireland (Table 2.1).

As the ISCED 2011 classification has been newly introduced in international educational statistics (e.g. in 2015), the decision to allocate some ECEC programmes into the ISCED 01 category is still subject to discussions in some of the countries listed in the above paragraph, especially in those where younger children are typically under the authority of welfare and health authorities. However, all the indicators presented in this publication specify which ECEC settings are covered in the reporting. In some indicators, only ISCED 0 programmes (in the ISCED 2011 nomenclature) will be taken into account. In the remaining indicators, other registered ECEC services (outside the scope of ISCED 2011) will also be considered (see for instance Figure 4.2 showing enrolment rates in formal childcare for children under the age of 3). Table 2.1 provides a full overview of the ECEC settings available in OECD countries, and specifies if they have been reported to be in adherence or not with the ISCED 2011 classification.

Legal entitlements to a place to early childhood education and care and to free access

Enrolment in ECEC settings have continued to rise between 2005 and 2014, partly because of the increased public spending to extend the legal entitlements to a place in ECEC, as well as efforts to ensure free access, at least for some ages and selected population groups.

Across OECD member economies and beyond, the share of children enrolled in ECEC services is on the rise, increasingly for children under the age of 3 (see Chapter 4). This has been made possible, in part, by the extension of legal entitlements to a place, and by efforts to ensure free access for the older age group (e.g. 3-5) and selected population groups, such as the younger age group (e.g. 0-2) or those who are disadvantaged. Eighteen jurisdictions participating in the previous edition of Starting Strong (OECD, 2015) responded that they encourage access through a legal right to ECEC provision for all or certain groups of children.

However, there are major differences in legal entitlements to a place in ECEC across jurisdictions, which reflects the diversity of ECEC systems. Some countries, such as Norway and Germany, cover ages 1 to 5 (or even 7 or 8 years in some cases in Germany), while others, such as the Czech Republic, only guarantee children a place for the year before entering primary school. A legal access entitlement around the age of 1 (rather than after birth) in some countries is mainly explained by the fact that in several cases, including Germany, Norway, Slovenia and Sweden, the duration of well-paid parental leave is around one year, in line with the legal entitlement (OECD, 2015 and Table 1.1).

The time per week covered by the legal entitlements to a place in ECEC differs greatly across countries and jurisdictions. For example, Norway grants universal access to 41 hours of ECEC, 24 hours is provided in French pre-primary schools, 20 hours in Finland, between 16 and 20 hours in Austria for the year before entering primary school, and only 16 hours for 3-4 year-olds in Scotland (United Kingdom). In Chile and Japan, the legal entitlement to a place for the youngest children is targeted based on certain conditions, such as low income and benefit entitlements (Table 2.2). Throughout Table 2.2, the upper boundary of the age bracket should be taken as included in the definition of the respective setting or regulation (i.e. 3-5-year-olds includes all children between their third and sixth birthday).

Figure 2.9. Number of hours per week and ages at which children have free access entitlement to pre-primary education (ISCED 02), 2015

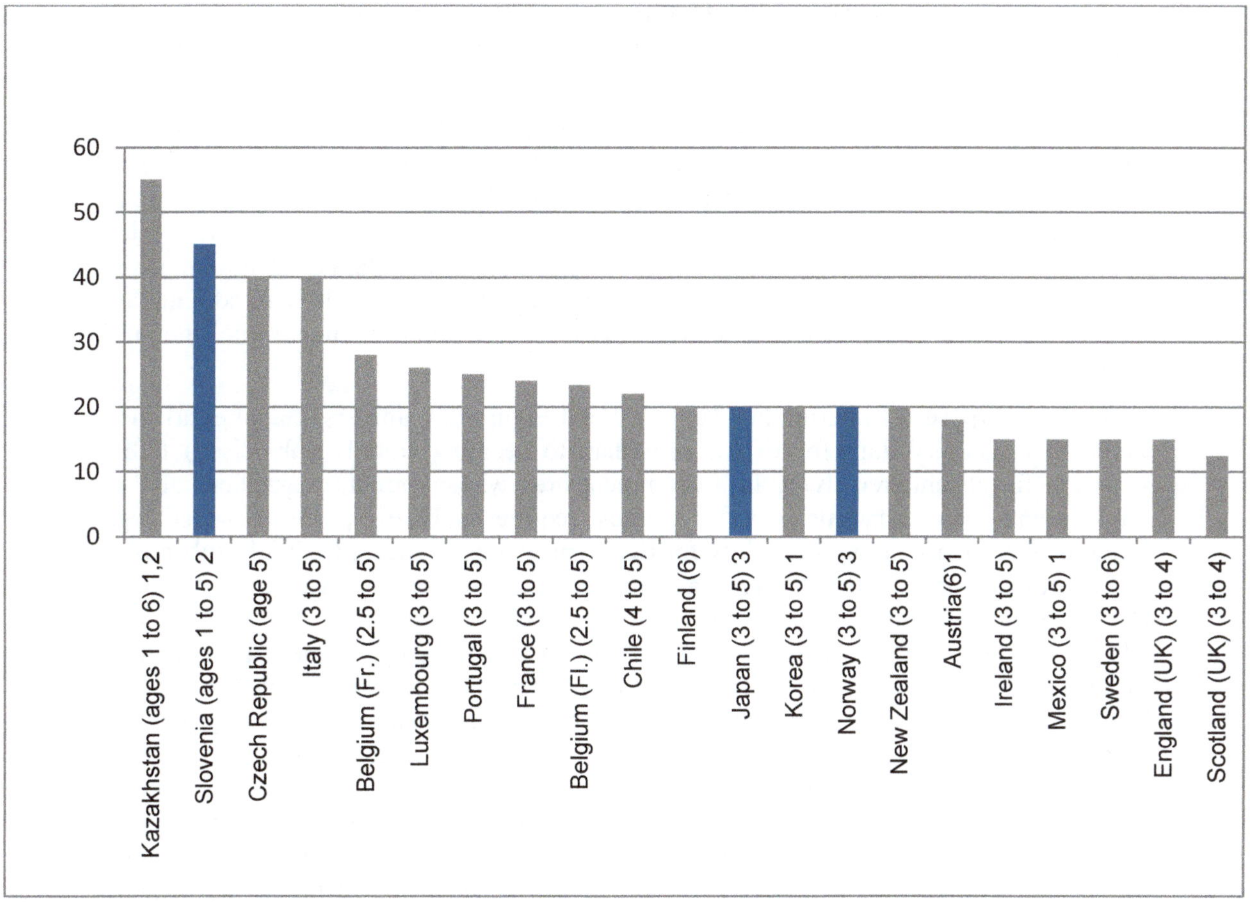

Notes: The age groups covered by the free access are added into brackets next to the country names.

1. Austria 16-20 hours, Mexico : 15-20 hours, Korea 15-25 hours, Kazakhstan 50-60 hours.
2. Integrated ECEC services, including early childhood development programmes (ISCED 01).
3. Low-income families have free access to 20 hours a week in kindergartens.

Source: OECD. Starting Strong 2017: Key OECD indicators on early childhood education and care, Table 2.2.

StatLink http://dx.doi.org/10.1787/888933487291

The legal entitlement to a place in ECEC is not a guarantee of free access, especially for younger children. Both variables are independent. In pre-primary education (ISCED 02), most countries provide free access to ECEC to all children for at least the year before entering primary school. However, exceptions include Japan, Norway and Slovenia, where free access to the last year of ECEC is provided, but only on a needs basis. In Slovenia, around 3% of all children aged from 11 months to 5 years have free access to ECEC. In other countries, free access to ECEC is common, but the number of years and the number of hours covered varies significantly.

The Czech Republic (only for the year before entering primary school), Italy and Kazakhstan (for all children aged 3 to 5) offer 40 hours or more of free ECEC for all children enrolled in pre-primary education. In Finland, all children have legal access to ECEC from the end of the parental leave period (e.g. 9 months) until the start of school. The subjective right is 20 hours per week, but it can also be full-time, depending on the child and family's circumstances (Figure 2.9). The fees depend on the number of children and income in the family. Families with low income do not pay fees at all. Universal free access (i.e. no fees) is only offered to all children in the year preceding the start of school (age 6).

By contrast, in Mexico and Sweden, all 3-5 year-old children may use 15 hours of free ECEC per week. England (United Kingdom) offers 15 hours per week for all children aged 3 to 4, and Scotland (United Kingdom) 12.5 hours for the same age group, albeit with some variations within Scotland. Unconditional free access to ECEC is less common for younger age groups than for older ones. For instance, Belgium, Chile, Finland, France, Japan, Luxembourg, the Netherlands, Slovenia and the United Kingdom provide free access, but only on a needs basis for all children under the age of 3 (Table 2.2 and Figure 2.9).

For the purposes of interpreting Table 2.2 and Figure 2.9, universal legal entitlement refers to a statutory duty for ECEC providers to secure (publicly subsidised) ECEC provision for all children living in a catchment area whose parents, regardless of their employment, socio-economic or family status, require an ECEC place. Targeted legal entitlement refers to the statutory duty for ECEC providers to secure (publicly subsidised) ECEC provision for children living in a catchment area who fall under certain categories. These categories can be based on various attributes, including the employment, socio-economic or family status of their parents. In this category, "none" means that for the respective age group, children or parents do not possess a legal entitlement to a place. This does not necessarily imply that they do not have access to a place, but only that they cannot claim it as a right. Conditional free access refers to the provision of ECEC services to parents free of charge, based on certain conditions, such as income and benefit entitlements. Unconditional free access refers to the provision free of charge for all children of the concerned age group. Here, "none" means that there is no regulation to ensure free access for some or all children of the concerned age group. This is independent of whether or not they have access to a place.

Early childhood education and care governance and organisation: some trends have emerged

The move towards integrated ECEC settings, i.e. the whole ECEC system administered under the responsibility of one ministry, is observed in several OECD countries.

Findings from the literature show that integrated ECEC systems administered under the responsibility of one ministry (or agency) are associated with better ECEC quality and help enhance universal entitlement, more affordable access, better qualified staff and smoother transitions (Bennett, 2008). A study conducted by Kaga, Bennett and Moss (2010) on five countries (Brazil, Jamaica, New Zealand, Slovenia, and Sweden) confirmed that the integration of ECEC systems from age 1 until entry to compulsory education had several positive effects: 1) it increased access and enrolment (particularly for programmes designed for children under the age of 3); 2) it improved staff working conditions and status; 3) it increased staff recruitment levels and training; and 4) it had a positive impact on pedagogical practices and curriculum development. Another study on New Zealand's integrated ECEC system shows that having one leading ministry that regulates funds and evaluates ECEC services has positive effects on quality (CCL, 2006). However, previous Starting Strong reports (OECD, 2012b and OECD, 2015) point out that to ensure these benefits, the ministry or agency responsible for ECEC needs to have a strong focus on children's development, learning and well-being. Research also shows that greater integration of ECEC services is particularly beneficial for disadvantaged children and their families (Wong and Sumsion, 2013).

The move towards integrated ECEC settings is observed in several OECD countries. In some countries, such as the Nordic countries, integrated ECEC systems have been the tradition for some decades as a way of responding to family and children's needs and holistically combining education and care. In these countries, full-day pedagogical provision also reduces the need for horizontal transitions for the child between pre-school and out of pre-school settings during the day. An increasing number of countries have moved towards or are discussing moving towards this kind of system, with recent examples being Luxembourg and Italy, as noted in Box 2.1. This reflects an emerging trend of emphasising the educational benefits of ECEC for children, in addition to the childcare services needed to support parents' participation in the labour force.

Nonetheless, the governance of the sector remains fragmented in many of the jurisdictions surveyed. Traditionally, a split or two-tier system often implies a focus on either "education" or "care" of certain services, which may lead to incoherent objectives, operational procedures, regulation, staff training and requirements (OECD, 2015). About half of the participating jurisdictions operate a split system, with different authorities in charge of different settings at the central level. The central level is understood to be the highest level of authority in a jurisdiction, such as the national government, or the governments of the Belgian Communities or of the countries of the United Kingdom (Table 2.3). Research shows that split systems have negative effects, in particular for childcare services, as they are less developed and less affordable, and staff are less qualified and have worse working conditions (Kaga, Bennett and Moss, 2010). An integrated system can create a favourable institutional environment for facilitating the transition from one ECEC service to another, as well as to primary school. As discussed below, the care-education divide has become less pronounced, even in split systems.

In all countries and jurisdictions with an integrated system, except Germany, the Ministry of Education is in charge of the entire ECEC age group at the central level. Germany is the sole country that concentrates responsibility for the entire ECEC age bracket in the welfare sector, under the auspices of the Federal Ministry of Family Affairs, Senior Citizens, Women and Youth (see Table 2.3). Countries and jurisdictions operating a split system attribute the provision for children from the age of 3 (in Ireland and the Netherlands from the age of 4) to the Ministry of Education, while younger children are typically under the authority of welfare and health authorities. In Ireland, early years services may cater for children aged 0 to 6, and are regulated and receive funding from the Department of Children and Youth Affairs and its agencies. Children may also begin the early stage of primary school (junior infants class) as early as 4 years. Primary schooling is the responsibility of the Department of Education.

Box 2.1. Integration of early childhood education and care governance

The case of Italy

In July 2015, law number 107 came into force, reforming the entire education system (*La Buona Scuola* or The Good School Reform). Within this reform, Paragraph 181 of Art. 1 is devoted to the integration of ECEC governance. A new decree implementing the new 0-6 Integrated ECEC System is currently being issued. For the first time in Italy, an integrated system of education and instruction from birth up to 6 years is being instituted.

With the new decree, ECEC services for younger children will transition from an assistance dimension centred on care to a broad educational dimension. The new ECEC system is meant to guarantee children "equal opportunities of education, instruction, care, relationships and play, overcoming territorial, economic, ethnic and cultural inequalities". Particular attention will be given to children with disabilities.

With the institution of the integrated system, ECEC services will be progressively extended, increased and qualified on the entire national territory. Such services will be organised within a clear and efficient legal framework of governance between all actors involved (state, regions, and local authorities). The new system will be supported by a specific annual fund that will provide resources to local authorities.

The decree is expected to launch a National Implementation Plan that will involve all actors, including families. On the basis of this governmental national plan, the Ministry of Education, University and Research (MIUR) is in charge of the co-ordination, direction and promotion of the new system, in tune with regions and local authorities.

The institution of "Infancy hubs" (*Poli per l'infanzia*) is foreseen, creating settings for children aged 0-6. These hubs can be hosted also within state comprehensive institutes and primary schools, in order to foster pedagogical and educational continuity. The hubs will be supported by specific funding for school building. Initial training of educators for children aged 0-3 is foreseen at the tertiary level in order to guarantee higher pedagogical quality in the system. For the first time, a maximum threshold for family contributions will be set.

Source: Case study provided by Cristina Stringher (INVALSI),based on MIUR press release of April 2017

The case of Luxembourg

In December 2013, a new government was formed by the Democratic Party, the Socialists and the Green Party. All responsibility for the departments concerning children and youth was concentrated in a single ministry, now called the Ministry of National Education, Children and Youth. Previously, all services providing non-formal education* for early childhood and school-aged children, including day care for families and day care centres, had been the responsibility of the Ministry of Family and Social Affairs.

The goal was to develop an integrated system to administer resources for children, to co-ordinate decision making, and to enhance quality and efficiency. At the local level, schools and non-formal education services are encouraged to co-operate more closely to ensure better co-ordination of actions and services. The government wants both sectors to collaborate in the interests of the children.

Both sectors have complementary but different fields of action, and different educational, pedagogical and methodological particularities. Since they were historically separated and developed apart from one another, it will be necessary to build bridges between the two sectors, both at the central level between the different ministerial departments, and at the operational level. The educational sector is highly centralised, teachers are state employees and resources are allocated by the ministry to the communes.

Non-formal education, such as family day care and day care centres, is offered by private actors. Settings are mostly run by non-governmental organisations, subsidised by the government, or even by private for-profit organisations (this mainly concerns the ECEC sector for children aged 0 to 3 or 4 years, until the start of compulsory education). The prevailing views of child development in the two sectors are very different, and efforts must be made to enhance an exchange of views and organise common continuous professional training to bring together the two groups of professionals, teachers, educators and social pedagogues.

Box 2.1. Integration of early childhood education and care governance *(continued)*

The government has instituted incentives to local schools and less formalised settings to work together to establish a common plan, with weekly schedules and activities designed to bring more coherence into the children's daily routines and ensure that their needs are better met. Efforts have also been made to invite professionals to share the facilities at their disposal and use them in different and more effective ways. New buildings are planned and services are organised with the children and their daily needs in mind, rather than the interests of the institution (e.g. school or out of school setting). Educational settings for children will be planned around a variety of functions and daytime activities that correspond to the children's needs, such as learning, playing, relaxing, moving, building and experimenting.

In Luxembourg, non-formal education takes place within an institutional educational setting (such as day care centres) for children aged 0 to 12, and is organised outside the established formal system (school). It has its own identifiable learning framework, learning areas and learning objectives, but does not lead to any formal qualification. Formal, non-formal and informal education complement each other and mutually reinforce the lifelong learning process.

Sources: OECD (2015), *Starting Strong IV: Monitoring Quality in Early Childhood Education and Care (ECEC)*, OECD Publishing, Paris, http://dx.doi.org/10.1787/9789264233515-en.

Case study submitted by the Luxembourg Ministry of Education, Children and Youth, edited by the OECD Secretariat.

Combining education and care is a widespread practice: as the divide between the 0-2 and 3-5 age groups has become less pronounced, so has the divide between education and care.

Today, most ECEC settings (ISCED 0 and other ECEC services) are framed as delivering both education and care. Thus, a separation between education and care is no longer observed in countries and jurisdictions such as Australia, the Flemish and the French Communities of Belgium, Chile, Finland, France, Germany, Ireland, Italy, Kazakhstan, Korea, New Zealand, Norway, Sweden and England (United Kingdom). However, the distinction of care and education-only settings is maintained in many jurisdictions. Care-only settings continue to exist, often for the youngest age group, in the Czech Republic (day nursery), Japan (nursery centres), Mexico (centre-based care for low socio-economic status 0-5 year-olds, SNDIF; federal home-based care for 0-3 year-olds of working parents, CONAFE; and federal social security centre-based care for 0-5 year-olds, IMSS), the Netherlands (childminding), Portugal (childminders and family crèches), the Slovak Republic (nurseries, mother centres and children centres) and Scotland (United Kingdom) (childminders).

Education-only centres are less common, and found only in Japan (kindergarten), Belgium (pre-primary education), Luxembourg (in its early childhood education programme and compulsory pre-school education), Mexico (mandatory pre-school) and Scotland (United Kingdom) (local authority nurseries). The traditional separation between less formal, care-only provision for younger children and more formal, education-oriented services for older children is still seen, but such differences have become less pronounced (OECD, 2015).

References

Bennett, J. (2008), "Early Childhood Education and Care Systems in the OECD Countries: the Issue of Tradition and Governance", *Encyclopedia on Early Childhood Development*, Centre of Excellence for Early Childhood Development and Strategic Knowledge Cluster on Early Child Development, Montreal, www.child-encyclopedia.com/pages/PDF/BennettANGxp.pdf.

CCL (2006), "Why is High-Quality Child Care Essential? The link between Quality Child Care and Early Learning", *Lessons in Learning*, Canadian Council on Learning, Ottawa.

EU (2014) *Statistics on Income and Living Conditions*, European Union, Brussels, http://ec.europa.eu/eurostat/web/income-and-living-conditions/overview.

European Commission/EACEA/Eurydice/Eurostat (2014), *Key Data on Early Childhood Education and Care in Europe: 2014 Edition,* Eurydice and Eurostat Report, Publications Office of the European Union, Luxembourg.

Kaga, Y., J. Bennett and P. Moss (2010), *Caring and Learning Together: A cross-national study on the integration of early childhood care and education within education*, UNESCO, Paris.

Magnuson, K., C. Lahaie and J. Waldfogel (2006), "Preschool and School Readiness of Children of Immigrants", *Social Science Quarterly*, Vol. 87, pp. 1241-1262.

OECD (2017a), *OECD Family Database*, OECD, Paris, www.oecd.org/els/family/database.htm.

OECD (2017b), *OECD Employment Database*, OECD, Paris, www.oecd.org/employment/emp/onlineoecdemploymentdatabase.htm.

OECD (2017c), "International migration database", *OECD International Migration Statistics (database)*, http://dx.doi.org/10.1787/data-00342-en, (accessed 24 April 2017).

OECD (2017d), *OECD online education database*, OECD, Paris, www.oecd.org/education/database.htm.

OECD (2016a), *International Migration Outlook 2016*, OECD Publishing, Paris, http://dx.doi.org/10.1787/migr_outlook-2016-en.

OECD (2016b), OECD historical data and projections (1950-2050), OECD, Paris, https://stats.oecd.org/Index.aspx?DataSetCode=POP_PROJ.

OECD (2015), *Starting Strong IV: Monitoring Quality in Early Childhood Education and Care (ECEC)*, OECD Publishing, Paris, http://dx.doi.org/10.1787/9789264233515-en.

OECD (2014), Trends Shaping Education 2014, Spotlight 6, Modern Families, OECD, Paris, http://www.oecd.org/edu/ceri/Spotlight6-Modern-Families.pdf.

OECD (2012a) Meeting of the OECD Council at Ministerial Level (Paris, 23-24 May 2012), *Gender Equality in Education, Employment and Entrepreneurship: Final Report to the MCM 2012,* https://www.oecd.org/employment/50423364.pdf.

OECD (2012b), *Starting Strong III: A Quality Toolbox for Early Childhood Education and Care*, OECD Publishing, Paris, http://dx.doi.org/10.1787/9789264123564-en.

OECD (2011), *Doing Better for Families,* OECD Publishing, Paris, http://dx.doi.org/10.1787/9789264098732-en.

OECD (2006), *Starting Strong II: Early Childhood Education and Care*, OECD Publishing, Paris, http://dx.doi.org/10.1787/9789264035461-en.

OECD (2003a), Babies and Bosses: Reconciling Work and Family Life, Vol. 2, OECD, Paris.

OECD/Eurostat/UNESCO Institute for Statistics (2015), ISCED 2011 Operational Manual: Guidelines for Classifying National Education Programmes and Related Qualifications, OECD Publishing, Paris, http://dx.doi.org/10.1787/9789264228368-en.

UNESCO institute for statistics, ISCED Mappings (2015), http://uis.unesco.org/en/isced-mappings

Wong and Sumsion (2013), "Integrated early years services: a thematic literature review", *Early Years,* Vol 33/4, http://dx.doi.org/10.1080/09575146.2013.841129.

Tables of Chapter 2

StatLink http://dx.doi.org/10.1787/9789264276116-en

Table 2.1. Coverage of early childhood education and care in OECD and partner countries (2017)

Early childhood education and care (ISCED 0) and other registered ECEC services

	Registered ECEC services (outside the scope of the ISCED 2011 Classification)				ISCED 01 - Early childhood development programmes			
	Typically aimed at very young children, aged 0-2.				Typically aimed at very young children, aged 0-2.			
	Name of the programme in national language	Name of the programme in English	Theoretical starting age	Theoretical duration of the programme (years)	Name of the programme in national language	Name of the programme in English	Theoretical starting age	Theoretical duration of the programme (years)
OECD countries								
Australia	Occasional care		0	5	Family day care and in-home care, Long-day care	Early childhood education	0	2 - 4
Austria1	Tageseltern/ Tagesmütter	regulated home-based care, which is ensured by day care parents/ mothers	0	5	Kinderkrippe	Crèche	0	3
Belgium (Fl.)	Gezinsopvang	Home-based settings	0	2.5-3 years	Kinderopvang van baby's en peuters	Child care of babies and toddlers	0	2.5-3 years
	Groepsopvang	Centre based settings.	0	2.5-3 years				
Belgium (Fr.)	Creches	Nursery	0	2	a			
	Acceuillante d'enfants	Childminder	0	2				
Canada	a				Early childhood development or equivalent	Pre-elementary education or equivalent - early childhood development	3 - 4	1 - 2
Chile	a				Educación parvularia (sala cuna y nivel medio menor); Salas Cuna (Nurseries) and Jardines Infantiles (Childcare Centres)	Pre-primary education (day care and lower middle level)	0 - 2	3
Czech Republic	Jesie	Day nursery	0	2	a			
	zařízení pro péči o děti do 3 let	centre-based but a small number of home-based settings	0	3				
Denmark	Dagpleje	Home-based provision	0	6	Aldersintegrerede institutioner	Age-integreted system	From 26 weeks	3
					Vuggestuer	Nursery school	0 - 2	3
Estonia	Childcare service (Lapsehoiuteenus)				Included with ISCED-02			

	Registered ECEC services (outside the scope of the ISCED 2011 Classification)				ISCED 01 - Early childhood development programmes			
	Name of the programme in national language	Name of the programme in English	Theoretical starting age	Theoretical duration of the programme (years)	Name of the programme in national language	Name of the programme in English	Theoretical starting age	Theoretical duration of the programme (years)
Finland	a				0-2-v. lapset päiväkodeissa	Kindergartens (0 to 2-year-old children), including special education programmes	0 - 2	1 - 3
					0-2-v. lapset perhepäivähoidossa	Family day care (0 to 2-year-old children), including special education programmes	0 - 2	1 - 3
France	Crèches collectives (EAJE), Assistant(e)s maternel(le)s	Family day care, community Creches	0	2	a			
	Jardin d'eveil	Discovery garden	2	1				
Germany	a				Krippen	Crèche, Day nursery	0	2 - 3
					Mixed-age settings or Kindertagespflege (the 3 last years are reported with ISCED 02)	Family day care	0	6
Greece	Paidikos stathmos	Child centre	2.5	2.5	Vrefonipiakos stathmos	Kindergarten Early childhood	0	1 - 3
Hungary	a				Gyógypedagógiai tanácsadás, korai fejlesztés, oktatás és gondozás	Special education consulting, early development, education and care	0	5
					Egységes óvoda-bölcsőde	Integrated kindergarten-infant nurseries	2	1
					Óvoda (3 év alatt)	Kindergarten (under 3 years)	2.5	0.5
Iceland	Home-Based provision (Dagforeldri)		0	2	Leikskóli I	Pre-primary schools I	0	1-3
Ireland	Private, community and voluntary interests settings (including crèches, nurseries, preschools and playgroups); childminding		0	3	a			

	Registered ECEC services (outside the scope of the ISCED 2011 Classification)				ISCED 01 - Early childhood development programmes			
	Name of the programme in national language	Name of the programme in English	Theoretical starting age	Theoretical duration of the programme (years)	Name of the programme in national language	Name of the programme in English	Theoretical starting age	Theoretical duration of the programme (years)
Israel	a				Hinuh be ganey misrad ha kalkala or harevacha	Early childhood education supervised by Ministry of Economy or by Ministry of Welfare	0	3
Italy	Nido d'infanzia; asilo familiare	Nursery /child care, Home-based provision	0	3	a			
Japan	Day-care centres	Day-care centres	0	3	a			
Korea	a				어린이집 (0-2세) (Eorinyijip, age 0-2)	Child care centre	0-2	1-3
Latvia	a				Pirmskolas izglitibas programmas (līdz 2 gadu vecumam)	Pre-primary education programmes (part of the programme up until the age of 2 years) (early childhood education)	0	1-2
Luxembourg	Assistants parentaux	Childminders	0	4	a			
	Crèches	Day care centres	0	9 months				
Mexico	m				Educación inicial	Early childhood education	0	3
Netherlands	• Private day-care centres (kinderdagverblijven): offer care for children between birth and four-years-old. These are primarily for working parents. • In-home care by childminders (gastouderopvang): offer care for children between birth and 12 years of age. The main aim is to support working parents. • Public pre-kindergarten facilities (peuterspeelzalen), or playgroups: offer a more formal type of ECEC for children 2-3 year-olds.				a			
New Zealand	a				New Zealand offers integrated programmes that include education and childcare services. There are five main types of ECEC settings, which are broadly split between centre-based provisions (including education and care services for 0-5 year-olds and kindergartens for 2-5 year-olds), playcentres for 0-5 year-olds, and home-based education and care for 0-5 year-olds. In addition, there are Māori language nests providing integrated ECEC in te reo Māori, the Māori language.			
Norway	a				Barnehage, 0-2 åringer	Kindergarten	0	2

	Registered ECEC services (outside the scope of the ISCED 2011 Classification)				ISCED 01 - Early childhood development programmes			
	Name of the programme in the national language	**Name of the programme in English**	**Theoretical starting age**	**Theoretical duration of the programme (years)**	**Name of the programme in national language**	**Name of the programme in English**	**Theoretical starting age**	**Theoretical duration of the programme (years)**
Poland	żłobki ; kluby dziecięce	Childcare	0.5-1	2	a			
Portugal	Creches, Ama	Day care, home-based provision, chilminder	0	2	a			
Slovak Republic	Detské jasle.	centre- or home-based	0	3	a			
Slovenia	Child care can be provided by childminders who are not qualified to provide an educational programme. They can only provide childminding services. However, they must be registered with the Ministry of Education. This home-care service caters a very small share of children from 11 month up (the starting age is not define) to the starting age for basic education.				Predšolska vzgoja (1.starostno obdobje)	Pre-school education (1st age period)	1	2
Spain	a				Educación infantil primer ciclo (0-2 años)	Early childhood education	0	3
Sweden	Pedagogisk omsorg	pedagogical care, which is run by registered childminders	0	6	Förskola för barn/elever under 3 år	Pre-school, for children/pupils younger than 3 years	0	0-2
Switzerland	Centre-based ECEC (in Kindertagesstätten or Krippen/Structures d'accueil collectif de jour or crèches/Strutture di custodia collettiva diurne) is available for children between 3.5 months up to age 4 (until the start of compulsory education). In some cantons, it is also available for children up to age 5 or 6 for additional hours of provision. There is also home-based ECEC (Tagesfamilie/Famille de jour/ Famiglia diurna) that usually caters for children between 3.5 months up to the start of compulsory education, but they are also open to older children				a			
Turkey	Kres	Crèche, day care centre	0	2	Erken çocukluk dönemi eğitimi (0-2 yaş)	Early childhood care and education (ages 0-2)	0-2	1-2
United Kingdom	Non-registered childminders and day nurseries				Children's centres (including Sure Start centres)	Children's centres (including Sure Start centres)	0	2
					Registered childminders	Registered childminders	0	2
					Day nurseries	Day nurseries	0	2
United States	m				a			

	Registered ECEC services (outside the scope of the ISCED 2011 Classification)				ISCED 01 - Early childhood development programmes			
	Name of the programme in national language	Name of the programme in English	Theoretical starting age	Theoretical duration of the programme (years)	Name of the programme in national language	Name of the programme in English	Theoretical starting age	Theoretical duration of the programme (years)
Partner countries								
Brazil			m		Educação infantil – crèche	Nursery schools/day-care centres	0	3
Colombia			m		Atención integral a la primera infnacia	Early childhood educational development	0	3
Kaskastan	a				In Kazakhstan, an integrated system for ECEC is in place whereby the same central authority is in charge of the different ECEC settings and age groups. All children aged 1-6 are under the responsibility of the Ministry of Education and Science. Children under the age of 1 are under the responsibility of the Ministry of Health Care and Social Development.			
Lithuania	a				Ikimokyklinio ugdymo programos	Early childhood educational development	0	1-2
Russian Federation	m				Программы развития детей младшего возраста	Early childhood educational development	0	2

	ISCED 02- Pre-primary education			
	Aimed at children in the years immediately prior to starting compulsory schooling, typically aged 3 5.			
	Name of the programme in national language	Name of the programme in English	Theoretical starting age	Theoretical duration of the programme (years)
OECD countries				
Australia	Pre-primary, preschool	Preschool programmes delivered in educational institution settings, family day care and in-home care or educational long-day care settings.	4	1
Austria1	Kindergarten	Kindergarten	3	3
	Vorschulstufe	Pre-primary stage (of primary school)	6	1
Belgium (Fl.)	Gewoon kleuteronderwijs	Regular nursery education	2.5 - 3	3
	Buitengewoon kleuteronderwijs	Special nursery education	2.5 - 3	3
Belgium (Fr.)	Enseignement maternel ordinaire	Regular pre-primary education	2.5 - 3	3
	Enseignement maternel spécialisé	Special pre-primary education	2.5 - 3	3
Canada	Kindergarten	Pre-elementary education or equivalent - kindergarten	4 - 5	1
Chile	Educación parvularia (nivel medio mayor, nivel de transición 1 y nivel de transición 2)	Pre-primary education (upper middle level, 1st transition level and 2nd transition level)	3 - 5	3
Czech Republic	Mateřská škola	Kindergarten	3	3
	Přípravné třídy pro děti se sociálním znevýhodněním	Preparatory classes for socially disadvantaged children	6	1
	Přípravný stupeň základní školy speciální	Preparatory stage of special basic school	6	3

	ISCED 02- Pre-primary education			
	Name of the programme in national language	**Name of the programme in English**	**Theoretical starting age**	**Theoretical duration of the programme (years)**
Denmark	Aldersintegrerede institutioner	Age-integreted system	3	3
	Børnehave	Kindergarten	3 - 5	2
Estonia	Alusharidus (alushariduse raamõppekava)	Pre-primary education (general study programme of pre-primary education)	0	6
Finland	3-5-v. lapset päiväkodeissa	Kindergartens (3 to 5-year-old children), including special education programmes	3 - 5	1 - 3
	6-v. lasten esiopetus	Pre-primary education for 6-year-old children in kindergartens and comprehensive schools, including special education programmes	6	1
	3-5-v. lapset perhepäivähoidossa	Family day care (3 to 5-year-old children), including special education programmes	3 - 5	1 - 3
France	Enseignement préélémentaire	Pre-elementary education	2 - 3	3
Germany	01 Kindergärten	Kindergarten	3	3
	02 Schulkindergärten	School kindergarten	6	1
	03 Vorklassen	Pre-school classes	5	1
Greece	Nipiagogio	Pre-primary	4 - 5	1 - 2
Hungary	Óvoda	Kindergarten (of which one year is pre-school education)	3	3
Iceland	Leikskóli II	Pre-primary schools II	3	0 to 3 years, variable
	5 ára bekkur	0. grade for 5 year-olds	5	1
Ireland	Early start	Early start	3 - 4	1
	Privately provided pre-primary education - Early Childhood Care and Education (ECCE) Scheme	Privately provided pre-primary education - Early Childhood Care and Education (ECCE) Scheme	3	1-2
Israel	Hinuh kdam yesody-ganey yeladim-ziburi (misrad ha kalkala, misrad ha revacha ve misrad ha hinuh)	Pre-primary education - public (supervised by Ministry of Economy , Ministry of Welfare or by MoE)	3	3
	Hinuh kdam yesody-ganey yeladim-prati	Pre-primary education - independent private	3	3
Italy	Scuola dell'infanzia	Pre-primary school	3	3
Japan	Yohorenkeigata-Nintei-Kodomo-En	Integrated centre for early childhood education and care	3-5	1-3
	Yochien	Kindergarten	3-5	1-3
	Tokubetsu-shien-gakko Yochi-bu	School for special needs education, kindergarten department	3-5	1-3
	Hoikusho	Day nursery	3-5	1-3
Korea	어린이집 (3-5세) (Eorinyijip, age 3-5)	Child care centre	3-5	1-3
	유치원 (Yuchiwon)	Kindergarten	3-5	1-3
Latvia	Pirmskolas izglītības programmas (no 3 gadu vecuma)	Pre-primary education programmes (part of the programme from the age of 3 years on)	3	1-4

	ISCED 02- Pre-primary education			
	Name of the programme in national language	**Name of the programme in English**	**Theoretical starting age**	**Theoretical duration of the programme (years)**
Luxembourg	Enseignement fondamental/cycle1- éducation précoce	Early maturity education	3	1
	Education précoce	Early maturity education (independent private institutions)	<4	1
	Enseignement fondamental/cycle1 - éducation préscolaire (Spillschoul)	Pre-primary education	4	2
	Education préscolaire	Pre-primary education (independent private institutions)	4	2
Mexico	Educación preescolar	Pre-primary education	3	2 - 3
Netherlands	Voorschools onderwijs	Pre-school education in day care centres and play groups	3	1
	Basisonderwijs en speciaal basisonderwijs, groep 1 en 2	Pre-primary education in school settings, including pre-primary special needs education group (class) 1 and 2	4	2
New Zealand	New Zealand offers integrated programmes that include education and childcare services. There are five main types of ECEC settings, which are broadly split between centre-based provisions (including education and care services for 0-5 year-olds and kindergartens for 2-5 year-olds), playcentres for 0-5 year-olds, and home-based education and care for 0-5 year-olds. In addition, there are Māori language nests providing integrated ECEC in te reo Māori, the Māori language.		0	5
Norway	Barnehage, 3-5 åringer	Kindergarten	3	3
Poland	Wychowanie przedszkolne	Pre-school education	3	4
	Wychowanie przedszkolne specjalne	Special pre-school education	3	4
Portugal	Educação pré-escolar	Pre-primary education	3 to 5	3
Slovak Republic	Materská škola	Kindergarten	3	3
	Špeciálna materská škola	Special kindergarten	3	3
	Prípravné triedy na základnej škole	Preparatory classes in basic school	6	1
	Prípravné triedy v špeciálnej škole	Preparatory classes in special school	6	1
Slovenia	Predšolska vzgoja (2. starostno obdobje)	Pre-school education (2nd age period)	3	3
Spain	Educación infantil segundo ciclo (3+ años)	Pre-primary education	3	3
Sweden	Förskola för barn/elever 3 år eller äldre	Pre-school, for children/pupils 3 years of age or older	3	3
	Förskoleklass	Pre-school classes	6	1
Switzerland	Vorschule, préscolarité, prescolarità	Kindergarten	4-6	2
	Besonderer Lehrplan, programme d'enseignement spécial, programma scolastico speciale	Special needs education programmes	4-6	2
Turkey	Okul öncesi eğitimi (3-5 yaş)	Pre-primary education (ages 3-5)	3-5	1-3
United Kingdom	Reception and nursery classes in schools	Reception and nursery classes in schools	3	1-2
	Preschool or pre-kindergarten	Preschool or pre-kindergarten	2-4	1-2
United States	Preschool or pre-kindergarten	Preschool or pre-kindergarten	2-4	1-2
	Kindergarten	Kindergarten	4-6	1
Brazil	Educação infantil - pré-escola	Preschool	4	2
Colombia	Pre-jardin (3-year-olds), Jardin (4-year-olds), and Transicicón (5-year-olds)	Pre-primary education	3-5	1-3

	ISCED 02- Pre-primary education			
	Name of the programme in national language	**Name of the programme in English**	**Theoretical starting age**	**Theoretical duration of the programme (years)**
Kaskastan	In Kazakhstan, an integrated system for ECEC is in place whereby the same central authority is in charge of the different ECEC settings and age groups. All children aged 1-6 are under the responsibility of the Ministry of Education and Science. Children under the age of 1 are under the responsibility of the Ministry of Health Care and Social Development.		0	6
Lithuania	Ikimokyklinio ir priešmokyklinio ugdymo programos	Pre-primary education	3	1-4
Russian Federation	Дошкольное образование	Pre-primary education	3	3

1. The names of institutions as well as minimum/maximum age limits for attendance vary across the different federal states.

Source: UNESCO institute for statistics, ISCED Mappings (2015), http://uis.unesco.org/en/isced-mappings; Starting Strong IV: Monitoring Quality in Early Childhood Education and Care (ECEC), OECD Publishing, Paris, http://dx.doi.org/10.1787/9789264233515-en

StatLink http://dx.doi.org/10.1787/888933487302

Table 2.2. Characteristics of legal access entitlement (2015)

Country	Type of ECEC setting	Age of children	Entitlement to a place in ECEC		Entitlement to free access		Comments
			Legal access entitlement	Hours/week of ECEC provision to which parents/children have a legal right	Free access entitlement	Hours/week the child has free access to ECEC	
Australia	m	m	M	m	m	m	In Australia, the starting age of compulsory schooling is 4 or 5, depending on the state/territory.
Austria	ISCED 02	5	universal	16-20	universal	16-20	Since 2010 (implementation of a mandatory year of kindergarten), 5-year-old children are obliged to attend kindergarten to a minimum extent of 16 to 20 hours per week, on a minimum of four days a week in the year preceding compulsory education. Mandatory attendance is free of charge. Additionally, most federal states offer free or publicly funded access to ECEC for other age groups.
Belgium-Flemish Community	ISCED 02	2.5-5	universal	23.33	unconditional	23.33	In Belgium, Flemish community children enter the compulsory school on 1 September of the calendar year in which the child is 6.
Belgium-French Community	ECEC settings outside ISCED 2011	0-2.5	targeted	m	conditional	m	
	ISCED 02	2.5-5	universal	28	unconditional	28	
Chile	ISCED 01 and ISCED 02	0-5	targeted	55/40	conditional	55/40	
	ISCED 01	0-2	targeted	55	conditional	55	
	ISCED 02	4-5	universal	22	unconditional	22	
Czech Republic	ISCED 02	5	universal	50	unconditional	≥40	In the Czech Republic, the average attendance time depends on the opening hours of the school facility. Free access is provided for 40 hours or more, depending on the opening hours of the facility.

Country	Type of ECEC setting	Age of children	Entitlement to a place in ECEC		Entitlement to free access		Comments
			Legal access entitlement	Hours/week of ECEC provision to which parents/children have a legal right	Free access entitlement	Hours/week the child has free access to ECEC	
Finland	ISCED 01 and ISCED 02	0-6	universal	50	conditional	50	In Finland, the number of hours is according to need and parents' choice, with a maximum of about 10 hours per day, but on a day with long shifts, it could be even more. The hours a week that 0-6 year-olds have free access to ECEC is capped at 10 hours per day in low-income families.
	ISCED 02	6	universal	20	unconditional	20	
France	ECEC settings outside ISCED 2011	0-2	none	a	conditional	40	
	ISCED 02	2.5-5	universal	24	unconditional	24	
Germany	ISCED 01	1-2	universal	m	differs across Länder	a	In Germany, the age for compulsory school entry varies between 5 and 6, depending on the Länder.
	ISCED 02	3-5	universal	m	differs across Länder	a	
Ireland	ECEC settings outside ISCED 2011 and ISCED 02	0-5	none	a	conditional	15-60	In Ireland, ECCE programme is free, unconditional access to pre-school (ISCED 02) for 15 hours per week. Other conditional funding mechanisms exist for ISCED 01 and ISCED 02 for children 0-5. Additionally, primary education may be accessed from age 4.
	ISCED 02	3-5	none	a	unconditional	15	
Italy	ISCED 02	3-5	universal	40	unconditional	40	
Japan	ECEC settings outside ISCED 2011	0-2	targeted	a	conditional	55	In Japan, low-income families have free access to 20 hours a week in kindergartens and 55 hours in nursery centres.
	ISCED 02	3-5	none	a	conditional	20/50	

Country	Type of ECEC setting	Age of children	Entitlement to a place in ECEC		Entitlement to free access		Comments
			Legal access entitlement	Hours/week of ECEC provision to which parents/children have a legal right	Free access entitlement	Hours/week the child has free access to ECEC	
Kazakhstan	ISCED 01 and ISCED 02	1-6	universal	50-60	unconditional	50-60	In Kazakhstan, as far as public preschool is concerned, preschool education is free, but parents must pay monthly for food. Sanatorium kindergartens and kindergartens for children with disabilities are totally free. Mini-centres are open 25-60 hours per week; all other ECEC settings 50-60 hours a week.
Korea	ISCED 01 and ISCED 02	0-5	none	a	unconditional	> 30-60	In Korea, the hours of infant care for 0-2 yeas old children were dualized in 2015. One is shortened program for 9am to 3-4pm and the other is full-time programme for 7:30am to 7:30pm on daily basis. The child care hours for 3-5 years-old chldren are full-time of 12 hours per day, but the actual time used varies depending on parental needs.
	ISCED 02	3-5	none	a	unconditional	20-25	The teaching hours of Nuri Curriculum in kindergartens are 4-5 hours per day, and after-school program is provided depending on parental needs.
Luxembourg	ECEC settings outside ISCED 2011	0-3	none	a	conditional	3	In Luxembourg, a legal entitlement to 36 weeks per year for children at school is provided (from 3-5 years-old).
	ISCED 02	3-5	universal	26	unconditional	≤26	
Mexico	ISCED 01	0-2	none	a	targeted	m	In Mexico, social security laws guarantee morning and evening shifts for children in early childhood. Refernce year: 2013/14.
	ISCED 02	3-5	universal	15-20	unconditional	15-20	
Netherlands	ISCED 0 and ECEC settings outside ISCED 2011	0-4	none	a	targeted	10	In the Netherlands, children of working parents of age 0 to 6 have access to child care, and children of 3 to 4 also have access to playgroups. Target group-specific programs for children from disadvantaged backgrounds (of age 3 to 4) are available in both childcare and playgroups. In some municipalities target group-specific programmes in playgroups are free. All children (of age 3 to 4) have access to play groups or child care, but not for free and not by legal entitlement. For child care, parents can receive an income-related tax allowance.

Country	Type of ECEC setting	Age of children	Entitlement to a place in ECEC		Entitlement to free access		Comments
			Legal access entitlement	Hours/week of ECEC provision to which parents/children have a legal right	Free access entitlement	Hours/week the child has free access to ECEC	
New Zealand	ISCED 02	3-5	none	a	unconditional	20	
Norway	ISCED 01 and ISCED 02	1-5	universal	41	Conditional	20	A measure to increase the participation of children from low-income families was introduced in August 2015, when children aged 4 and 5 were given the right to 20 hours free kindergarten per week. From August 2016 this was extended to 3-year-old children.
Portugal	ECEC settings outside ISCED 2011	0-2	none	a	conditional	m	
	ISCED 02	3-4	none	a	unconditional	25	
	ISCED 02	5	universal	40	unconditional	25	
Slovak Republic	ISCED 02	3-6	universal	m	unconditional	m	In Slovak Republic, children can stay at kindergarten according to opening hours. Child can be at kirdengarten whole day (6-8 hours, maximum to 10 hours every day a week) or half a day (3-4 hours every day) depending on parent´s decision.
Slovenia	ISCED 01 and ISCED 02	11 months-5 years	universal	45	conditional	45	In Slovenia, in kindergarten (as an integrated ECEC setting for 1-5 year-olds), the hours of legal entitlement vary depending on the length of the programme in which the child is participating. This calculation is based on the full-day programme (9 hours a day). For child minding of preschool children, parents can enrol a child younger than 11 months (the minimum age for kindergarten), but this is uncommon, since parental leave lasts until a child is 11 months old.
Sweden	ISCED 01	1-2	universal	15-50	none	a	In Sweden, the legal entitlement is unconditional from the autumn term in the year the child turns 3.
	ISCED 02	3-6	universal	15-50	unconditional	15	

Country	Type of ECEC setting	Age of children	Entitlement to a place in ECEC		Entitlement to free access		Comments
			Legal access entitlement	Hours/week of ECEC provision to which parents/children have a legal right	Free access entitlement	Hours/week the child has free access to ECEC	
United Kingdom-England	ISCED 01	2	none	a	conditional	15	In the United Kingdom-England, local authorities have a legal duty to secure, so far as is reasonably practicable, sufficient child care for working parents or parents who are studying or training for employment. This includes after-school/wrap-around care and holiday clubs. They must also assess that there is child care adequate to meet the needs of parents with children aged 0-14 or up to 18 for disabled children in their area. Conditions of entitlement for targeted free access to ECEC were changed in 2013 and 2014.
	ISCED 02	3-4	none	a	unconditional	15	
United Kingdom-Scotland	ISCED 02	3-4	universal	16	unconditional	12.5	In the United Kingdom-Scotland, 3-4 year-olds, and 2-year-olds from disadvantaged families, are entitled to 16 hours a week (600 hours/year), as of August 2014. Hours of free provision vary, but tend to be 12.5 hours per week.

Sources: OECD. Table 2.1 and OECD (2015), Starting Strong IV: Monitoring Quality in Early Childhood Education and Care (ECEC), OECD Publishing, Paris, http://dx.doi.org/10.1787/9789264233515-en.

StatLink http://dx.doi.org/10.1787/888933487310

Table 2.3. Distribution of responsibilities in early childhood education and care between national, regional and local levels, by topic (2013)

Responsibility for financing system of ECEC (F), minimum standard setting (S), curriculum development (C), monitoring of ECEC (M).

Country	System organisation at central level	National level	Regional/ state level	Local level
Australia	Integrated, but many responsibilities are decentralised	C	F, S, M	
Belgium-Flemish Community[1]	Split		F, S, C, M	
Belgium-French Community[1]	Split	S	F, S, C, M	F, M
Chile	Integrated	F, S, C, M		S
Czech Republic	Split	F, C, M		
Finland	Integrated	F, S, C	M	F, C, M
France	Split	F, S, C, M		F, S, C
Germany	Integrated, mainly decentralised		F, S, C, M	F, M
Ireland	Split	F, S, C, M		
Italy	Split	F, S, C, M	F, S, C, M	F, C, M
Japan	Split	F, S, C, M	F	F
Kazakhstan	Integrated	F, S, C, M	F,M	F, M
Korea	Split	F, S, C, M	F, M	M
Luxembourg	Integrated	F, S, C, M		F, C
Mexico	Split	F, S, C, M		M
Netherlands	Split	F, S, M	F	
New Zealand	Integrated	F, S, C, M		
Norway	Integrated	F, S, C, M		F, M
Portugal	Split	F, S, C, M		F, M
Slovak Republic	Split	F, S, C, M	M	F
Slovenia	Integrated	F, S, C, M		F, M
Sweden	Integrated	F, S, C, M		F, M
United Kingdom-England	Integrated		F, S, C, M	F, M
United Kingdom-Scotland[2]	Split		F, S, C, M	

1. Authority in charge at central level refers to the highest level of authority for ECEC for a country or jurisdiction. For countries, this refers to the national level, and for jurisdictions to the highest level of authority in that jurisdiction, whether regional, state or provincial. For the Flemish and French Communities of Belgium, the central level refers to the Flemish government and the government of the French Community of Belgium, respectively.

2. In United Kingdom-Scotland, for the school year 2013/14, the main practice guidance for those working with 0-3 year-olds was a document called "Building the Ambition".

Source: Starting Strong IV: Monitoring Quality in Early Childhood Education and Care (ECEC), OECD Publishing, Paris, http://dx.doi.org/10.1787/9789264233515-en.

StatLink http://dx.doi.org/10.1787/888933487322

Chapter 3.

Policy inputs into early childhood education and care: Financing, profile of teachers and working conditions

Sustained public funding is critical for supporting the growth and quality of early childhood education programmes. Appropriate funding helps to recruit professional staffs that are qualified to support children's cognitive, social and emotional development and to provide good working conditions. Investment in early childhood settings and materials also helps support the development of child-centred environments for well-being and learning. Teachers and pedagogical staff also play a crucial role in early childhood education and care (ECEC) systems – they are the front-line workers responsible for engaging children and promoting their well-being, development and learning. It is now widely accepted that within ECEC settings, teachers- and pedagogies are the most important factors that influence child well-being, development and learning. This chapter presents indicators of the resources that are invested into a system, such as the level and type of ECEC financing, the regulations of staff-child ratios, or some indicators on teaching workforce at ECEC level (e.g. level of qualification, teacher's salary or organisation of the working time of teachers).

The statistical data for Israel are supplied by and are under the responsibility of the relevant Israeli authorities. The use of such data by the OECD is without prejudice to the status of the Golan Heights, East Jerusalem and Israeli settlements in the West Bank under the terms of international law.

Key messages

Financing of early childhood education and care (ISCED 0)

International comparisons reveal some clear trends:

- Expenditure on ECEC (ISCED 0) accounts for an average of 0.8% of GDP, of which around three quarters go to pre-primary education (ISCED 02). While 0.2% or less of GDP is spent on ECEC (ISCED 0) in Japan, Ireland and Switzerland, more than 1.0% of GDP is spent in Chile, Denmark, Finland, Iceland, Israel, Norway, the Russian Federation, Slovenia and Sweden.
- Variations across countries in the duration of ECEC programmes have a strong impact on the level of expenditure allocated to ECEC. For instance, in some countries, such as Ireland and the United Kingdom, children typically enter primary education at age 5, while in Estonia, Finland, Latvia, Poland and Sweden, they typically enter at age 7. In all the other countries, children typical enter primary education at age 6.
- Annual expenditure per young child enrolled in early childhood educational development programmes (ISCED 01) is significantly higher than annual expenditure for pre-primary education (ISCED 02) in most countries. In pre-primary education, annual expenditure per child for both public and private settings averages USD 8 070 in OECD countries, while annual expenditure for early childhood educational development averages USD 12 501.
- In most OECD countries, there is substantial public investment in ECEC, and parental fees are often publicly subsidised. In early childhood educational development (ISCED 01), public sources account for an average of 69% of total expenditure, while in pre-primary education (ISCED 02), it amounts to 83%.
- Many governments delegate responsibilities for ECEC public funding to local authorities. As a result, public funding is more decentralised in early childhood education (ISCED 0) than at any other level of education. On average across OECD countries, only 41% of public funds for early childhood education come from the central government, before transfers. After transfers, this share drops to 34%.
- Similar levels of expenditure among countries can mask a variety of contrasting policy choices. This helps to explain why there is no simple relationship between overall spending on education and the quality of ECEC settings.

Teaching workforce

Research tells us that:

- Evidence from the literature shows that staff initial training level and duration are positively associated with the overall quality of ECEC.
- High staff qualifications also result in a more stimulating environment and high-quality pedagogical practices, which boost children's well-being and learning outcomes. This does not mean that all staff members need to have high levels of qualification. For example, there is evidence from the English Effective Provision of Pre-School Education (EPPE) study that less qualified staff improve their practices when working with highly trained colleagues.

- Research has indicated that staff job satisfaction and retention – and thereby the quality of ECEC environments – can be improved by: 1) low child-to-staff ratios and low group size; 2) competitive wages and other benefits; 3) reasonable schedule/workload; 4) low staff turnover; 5) good physical environment; and 6) a competent and supportive centre manager.
- Recent research shows that in pre-primary, the effects of specialised in-service training on process quality are larger than those of pre-service training, particularly on collaborative work, support for play, and support for early literacy, mathematics and science.

International comparisons reveal some clear trends:

- The highest proportions of women teachers are concentrated in the earlier years of schooling, and shrink at each successive level of education. On average across OECD countries, around 97% of teachers in pre-primary education are women. The lowest proportions are observed in the Netherlands, where 87% of pre-primary teachers are women, in Norway (91%), France (92%) and Spain (93%).
- The age distribution of teachers working in pre-primary education varies considerably across countries. In pre-primary education, 25% of teachers are at least 50-year-olds, on average across OECD countries. The proportion is equal or exceeds 35% in the Czech Republic, Estonia, Hungary, the Netherlands, Portugal and the Slovak Republic.
- The qualification awarded after successfully completing teacher training signals the level of knowledge and skills that the new teacher has acquired, and may even indicate the social status of teachers. The bachelor degree has become the minimum qualification required to be a teacher at the pre-primary level of education in 27 of the 37 countries. However, the duration and pedagogical component of initial teacher training vary significantly across countries.
- Teachers' salaries in pre-primary education vary widely across countries. For instance, the annual statutory salaries of pre-primary school teachers with 15 years of experience range from less than USD 20 000 in the Czech Republic, Hungary and the Slovak Republic, to more than USD 50 000 in Australia, the Netherlands and the United States, and exceed USD 100 000 in Luxembourg.
- Teachers' salaries in pre-primary education have been impacted by the economic crisis in one third of OECD countries. In 2014, teachers' salaries remained below those of other tertiary-educated workers in most countries. On average, pre-primary teachers in OECD countries earn only 74% of the average salary of a tertiary-educated, 25-64 year-old full-time, full-year worker.
- Teacher salaries and teaching time are not strongly correlated. Both teacher salaries and the number of teaching hours per year in pre-primary education vary considerably across countries. At the pre-primary level, 83% of teachers' statutory working time is spent, on average, on teaching, and the rest on non-teaching tasks.
- At the pre-primary level, there are 14 children for every teacher, on average across OECD countries. When considering all countries with available data, this number varies widely, and ranges from more than 20 children per teacher

in Chile, China, France and Mexico, to fewer than 10 children for every teacher in Australia, Iceland, New Zealand, Slovenia and Sweden.

- However, some countries make extensive use of teaching assistants at the pre-primary level. Twelve OECD countries (and three partner countries) reported smaller child-to-staff ratios than child-to-teacher ratios.
- Smaller child-to-teacher ratios are observed in early childhood development programmes ISCED 01). On average across the 12 OECD countries with available data for both programmes, there are 14 children for each pre-primary teacher working in pre-primary education, while the ratio is only 9 children per teacher in early childhood development programmes.

Financing of early childhood education and care

Without sufficient public spending, there is a greater risk that access to ECEC programmes will be restricted to affluent families, and that the quality of the programmes will vary.

Sustained public funding is critical for supporting the growth and quality of early childhood education programmes. Appropriate funding helps to recruit professional staff who are qualified to support children's cognitive, social and emotional development, and to provide good working conditions. Investment in early childhood settings and materials also helps support the development of child-centred environments for well-being and learning. In countries that do not channel sufficient public funding to cover quantity and quality, some parents may be more inclined to send their children to private ECEC services, which implies heavy financial burdens in most countries. Others may prefer to stay home, which can hinder parents' participation in the labour force (OECD, 2012).

Expenditure per child on ECEC settings

In most countries, expenditure per child on ECEC settings is higher for very young children (under the age of 3) and smaller for older children enrolled in pre-primary education.

One way to compare educational expenditure across different countries is to examine annual expenditure per child. Expenditure per child for both public and private settings is largely influenced by teachers' salaries, pension systems, number of contact hours of teachers with children, the cost of teaching and of pedagogical materials, maintenance costs and the number of children enrolled in the ECEC settings. Policies to attract new teachers, to reduce average group size or to change staffing patterns have also contributed to changes in expenditure per child over time (OECD, 2016: Education at a Glance 2016, indicator B1).

In pre-primary education, annual expenditure per child for both public and private settings averages USD 8 070 in OECD countries. It ranges from USD 4 000 or less in Turkey, to more than USD 14 000 in Luxembourg and Norway. Annual expenditure per child enrolled in early childhood educational development programmes (ISCED 01) is significantly higher than in pre-primary education (ISCED 02) in 10 out of the 13 OECD countries with available data for both programmes, and averages USD 12 501 (Figure 3.1).

Figure 3.1. Annual expenditure on early childhood education and care settings per child (2013)

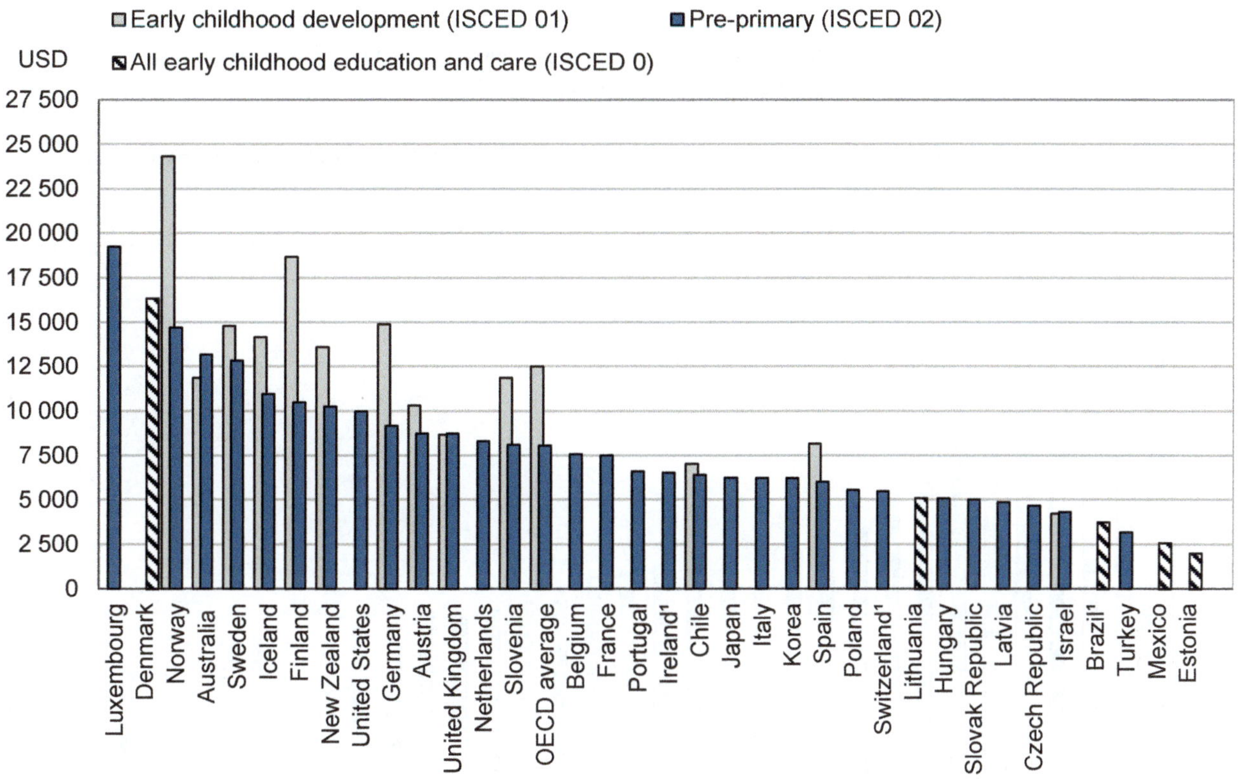

Note: Countries are ranked in descending order of annual expenditure per student by educational institutions for pre-primary education.

1. Public institutions only.

Source: OECD (2016), Education at a Glance 2016: OECD Indicators, Table C2.3, http://dx.doi.org/10.1787/eag-2016-en.

StatLink http://dx.doi.org/10.1787/888933487339

A smaller child-to-staff ratio observed in early childhood development programmes (ISCED 01) is the main explanation for this pattern (Figure 3.10). This is the result of policies implemented in most countries to reduce group size at that level. These policies are supported by research. There is evidence indicating that infants and toddlers especially benefit from low child-to-staff ratios, while too high child-to-staff ratios can be detrimental at these ages. Therefore, child-to-staff ratios have been regulated in many countries, with smaller ratios for the very young and higher ratios for older children (NICHD, 2002).

Expenditure on ECEC settings relative to GDP

Expenditure on ECEC (ISCED 0) accounts for an average of 0.8% of GDP, of which around three quarters go to pre-primary education (ISCED 02).

Another way to compare ECEC expenditure is to analyse expenditure on ECEC settings relative to a nation's wealth. National wealth is estimated based on GDP, and expenditure on ECEC settings includes spending by governments, enterprises and foundations and parents of children. There are large differences in the relative investment in provision of ECEC across OECD countries.

Figure 3.2. Expenditure on early childhood education and care (ISCED 0) as a percentage of GDP, public and private settings (2013)

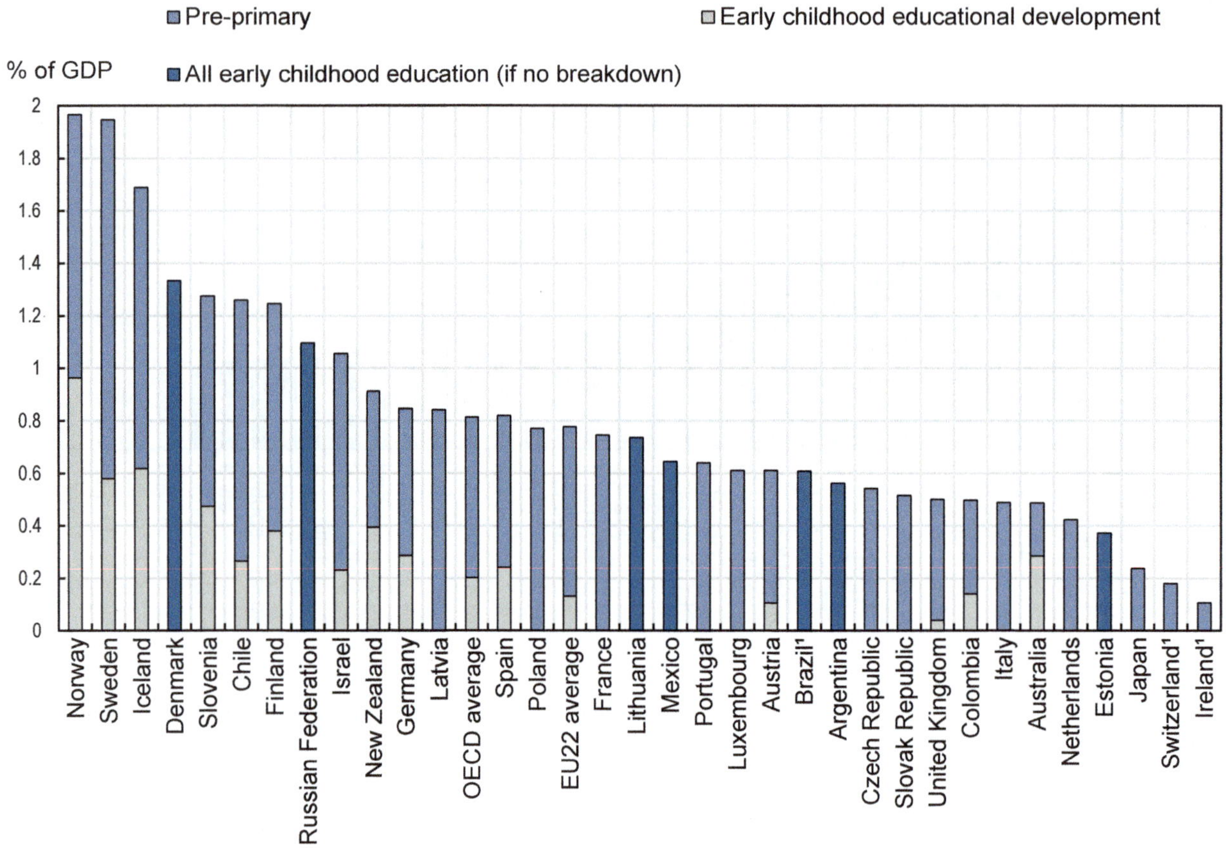

Note: Countries are ranked in descending order of public and private expenditure on educational institutions (2013).

1. Public institutions only.

Source: OECD (2016), Education at a Glance 2016: OECD Indicators, Table C2.3, http://dx.doi.org/10.1787/eag-2016-en.

StatLink http://dx.doi.org/10.1787/888933487340

Expenditure on ECEC (ISCED 0) accounts for an average of 0.8% of the collective GDP, of which 0.2% goes to early childhood educational development (ISCED 01), and 0.6% to pre-primary education (ISCED 02). Differences between countries are significant. For example, while 0.2% or less of GDP is spent on ECEC (ISCED 0) in Japan, Ireland and Switzerland, more than 1.0% is spent in Chile, Denmark, Finland, Iceland, Israel, Norway, the Russian Federation, Slovenia and Sweden (Figure 3.2).

However, significant variations across countries in the duration of ECEC programmes and in size of the young population have a strong impact on the level of expenditure allocated to ECEC.

These large variations are mainly explained by significant differences across countries in participation in ECEC services, in the mode of enrolment (full-time versus part-time), in teacher working conditions (e.g. salary and working time), in child-to-staff ratios, in the fees for parents and public support provided to families to enrol their children in ECEC settings, and in the duration of ECEC programmes. In some countries, such as Ireland and the United Kingdom, children typically leave pre-primary education at age 4, while in Estonia, Finland Latvia, Poland and Sweden, children typically enter primary education at age 7 (see Table C2.5 in Education at a Glance 2016, OECD, 2016). In all other countries, children typical enter primary education at age 6.

The duration of ECEC programmes, and the other factors included in the previous paragraph, have an impact on the level of expenditure allocated to ECEC (ISCED 0). For example, a shorter duration of pre-primary education as the result of an earlier transition to school, such as in Australia, Ireland and the United Kingdom, makes it difficult to compare different countries' total expenditure on ECEC as a percentage of GDP. These statistics should also be interpreted with caution, as expenditure is also influenced by the extent to which these indicators cover private settings and private expenditure, by the decision of some countries to consider some ECEC programmes outside the scope of the ISCED 2011 classification, or by the impossibility of providing reliable statistics to international organisations. For example, the absence of data on private expenditure and private institutions in Brazil and Switzerland is likely to understate the true level of expenditure and enrolment in early childhood education programmes (ISCED 0), and may affect the comparability of the data with other countries. Inferences on access to and quality of ECEC should therefore be made with caution.

As the ISCED 2011 classification has been newly introduced in international educational statistics (in 2015), the decision to allocate some ECEC programmes to the ISCED 01 category is still subject to discussion in some countries, especially those where younger children are typically under the authority of welfare and health authorities. Consequently, early childhood educational development programmes (ISCED 01) are not reported in some OECD countries, namely Belgium (French Community), the Czech Republic, France, Ireland, Italy, Japan, Luxembourg, the Netherlands, Poland, Portugal, the Slovak Republic, and Switzerland; or data are missing in some countries, such as the Flemish community of Belgium and the United States. In these countries, other settings exist for children under the age of 3, but ECEC provision is currently considered as outside the scope of ISCED 2011 (see ISCED mappings in Table 2.1). For instance, public spending on childcare (for children under 3 years) is over 0.4% of GDP in France, Luxembourg and the Netherlands, but the ECEC arrangements proposed to families are outside the scope of ISCED 2011 in these countries (OECD, 2017b).

Salary cost of teachers per child

Similar levels of expenditure among countries can mask a variety of contrasting policy choices. This helps to explain why there is no simple relationship between overall spending on education and the level of performance reached.

Governments seek to provide more and better education (including for the ECEC sector) for their population, while ensuring that public funding is used efficiently, particularly when public budgets are tight. Teacher compensation usually constitutes the largest part of current expenditure, and therefore of expenditure on ECEC. As a result, the level of teacher compensation divided by the number of children (referred to here as "salary cost of teachers per child") is the largest share of expenditure per child. Four main factors influence the salary cost of teachers per child enrolled in pre-primary education

(ISCED 02): 1) time children spend on intentional pedagogical or educational activities; 2) contact time of teachers with children; 3) teachers' salaries; and 4) estimated group size.

Specific levels of the salary cost of teachers per child may result from different combinations of these four factors. Consequently, a given level of salary cost of teachers per child may result from different combinations of these four factors. Similarly, a reform (or structural change) to one of these factors (all of the other factors remaining the same) has a direct impact on the level of expenditure: 1) increasing teachers' salaries leads to an increase in the public budget; 2) decreasing estimated group size implies a need for additional teachers, thus increasing the public budget; 3) increasing the number of hours children spend on intentional or pedagogical activities, or decreasing the number of teachers' contact hours with children, results in a need for additional teachers, thus increasing the public budget.

The salary cost of teachers per child indicator examines the choices countries make when investing their resources in pre-primary education. Some of these choices do not reflect policy decisions, but rather demographic changes that have led to a change in the number of children. For example, in countries where enrolment has been declining in recent years, estimated group size will also shrink (assuming all other factors remain constant), unless there was also a simultaneous drop in the number of teachers.

Higher levels of expenditure on ECEC cannot automatically be equated with better performance by ECEC systems. This is not surprising, as countries spending similar amounts on education do not necessarily have similar education policies and practices. For example, at the pre-primary level, the Netherlands and Norway had very similar levels of salary costs of teachers per children in 2014, both slightly above the OECD average. In Norway, this can be explained by an above OECD average time children spent on intentional pedagogical or educational activities, above-average contact time of teachers with children, average level of teacher salaries, and below-average estimated group size. In the Netherlands, there were above-average teacher salaries, average contact time of teachers with children, and small estimated group size compared to the average, however, these were more than offset by a significant below-average amount of time children spent on intentional pedagogical or educational activities (Figure 3.3).

Comparing the relative salary cost of teachers per child using this analysis affects the ranking of some countries when compared to measuring in USD. For example, because of Luxembourg's high USD salaries, it has by far the highest salary cost in pre-primary education: at USD 9 729, it is over triple many countries shown in Figure 3.3. However, when differences in countries' wealth are considered, Luxembourg is still in first position, but the differences with other countries are significantly smaller.

Alongside such contrasts, there are also striking similarities in countries' policy choices, even if these similarities can result in different levels of salary cost of teachers per child. For example, in Luxembourg and the Netherlands, an above-average teacher's salary and a small estimated class size acts to increase the salary cost of teachers per children relative to the OECD average. In contrast, in Chile, Greece, and Mexico, and to a lesser extent in France and Italy, a below-average teacher's salary and a bigger estimated group size acts to decrease the salary cost of teachers per children relative to the OECD average (Figure 3.3).

Figure 3.3. Contribution (in USD) of various factors to salary cost of teachers per child, pre-primary education (2014)

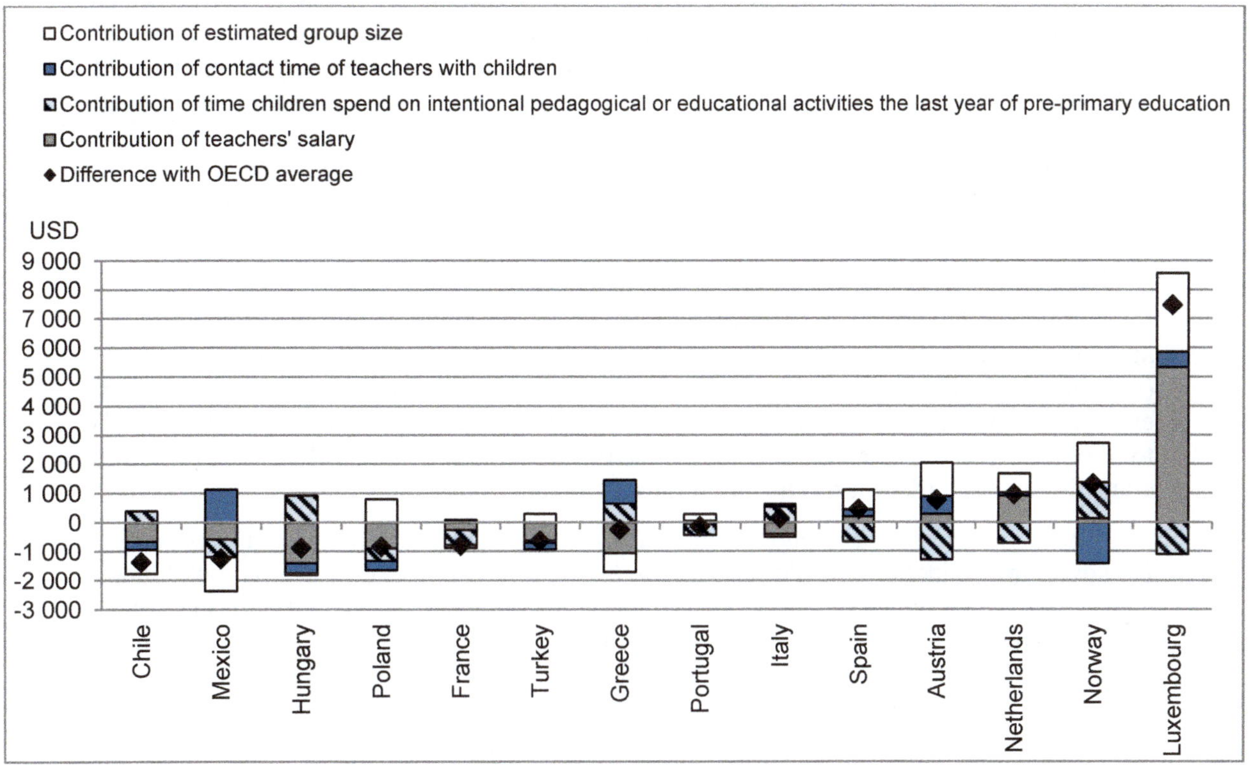

Notes: This chart shows the contribution (in USD) of the factors influencing the difference between salary cost of teachers per child in the country and the OECD average. For example, in Hungary, the salary cost of teachers per child is USD 877 lower than the OECD average. This is because Hungary has lower teachers' salaries (- USD 1 392) than the OECD average, above-average time children spend on intentional pedagogical or educational activities the last year of pre-primary education (+ USD 921), above-average contact time of teachers with children (- USD 357), and slightly above-average estimated group size (- USD 49).

Countries are ranked in ascending order of the difference between the salary cost of teachers per student and the OECD average.

Source: OECD (2017a), OECD Online education database, OECD, Paris, www.oecd.org/education/database.htm.

StatLink http://dx.doi.org/10.1787/888933487356

Distribution of public and private expenditure on ECEC settings in pre-primary education

In most OECD countries, there is substantial public investment in ECEC systems, especially for pre-primary education. Parental fees are also publicly subsidised in an increasing number of countries.

Publicly funded pre-primary education tends to be more strongly developed in the European countries of the OECD than in the non-European countries. In Europe, the concept of universal access to education for 3-6 year-olds is generally accepted. Many countries in this region provide all children with at least two years of free, publicly funded pre-primary education before they begin primary education.

Ireland was not in this category in the past, but the establishment of the Early Childhood Care and Education (ECCE) scheme in 2010, which entitled children aged between 3 and 5 to one year of free pre-school education, was expanded. Thus, since September 2016, children have been eligible to start free pre-school once they turn 3 years of age, and can continue until they start primary school (once the child is not older than 5 years and 6 months at the end of the relevant pre-school year i.e. end June). In addition, families have traditionally benefited from 38 weeks of free pre-school. However, with the expansion of the ECCE programme, this has now been increased to 61 weeks, on average. Additional funding of €85 million was allocated to the Department of Children and Youth Affairs in 2016 for early years care and education, an increase of 30% on the 2015 allocation.

With the exception of the Netherlands, access is generally a statutory right from the age of 3, and even before in some countries with integrated ECEC systems (see Chapter 1). However, in the Netherlands, almost all children from age 4 have a legal entitlement to free access to pre-primary education in school settings (age 4 corresponds to the first year of enrolment in these settings, children are enrolled in pre-school education in day care centres and playgroups at age 3).

There is substantial public investment in ECEC across OECD countries. However, a distinction should be drawn between pre-primary and early childhood educational development (ISCED 01). A general pattern emerges when both programmes are compared, with the share of public spending tending to be smaller in early childhood educational development (ISCED 01) in 9 out of the 14 countries with available data for both categories. On average, in early childhood educational development (ISCED 01), public sources account for 69% of total expenditure, while in pre-primary education (ISCED 02), the share of public expenditure is 83% of the total.

In countries such as Australia, Colombia and Israel, the share of public expenditure in the funding of early childhood development programmes (ISCED 01) is lower than 25%, while in Finland, Norway and Sweden, more than 90% of expenditure comes from public sources. At the pre-primary level, 90% or more of expenditure comes from public funds in 11 out of the 32 countries with available data for pre-primary education (Figure 3.4). In the case of Australia, much of the private funding is actually subsidised by the government in the form of subsidies to families. In Australia, 61% of funding for early childhood educational development programmes (ISCED 01) comes from Australian Government subsidies to families, 4% comes directly from other levels of government, and the rest from families' out-of-pocket expenses (OECD, 2016: Education at a Glance 2016, Table C2.3).

In pre-primary education, Australia and Japan are the only countries where private sources account for more than 50% of total expenditure. In the case of Australia, much of the private funding is actually subsidised by the government in the form of subsidies to families. This expenditure is treated as a transfer to the private sector and is therefore reported as 'private expenditure', which has the effect of understating the level of public funding for ECEC in Australia. Although these grants are used as private funding for early childhood programmes, their initial source is from government subsidies.

In Japan, the high cost of pre-primary education is shared between households, foundations and the business sector. Thus, the proportion of expenditure covered by private businesses and foundations represents 19% of total expenditure, while household expenditure represents 37% of the total (Figure 3.4). The Second Basic Plan for the Promotion of Education (2013-17) in Japan stipulates the introduction of free-of-charge and universal ECEC for all children. The Japanese government is examining potential revenue sources to fund this new initiative. In addition, at a conference to discuss implementation of the new policy, the government and the ruling parties set the main policy objectives as follows: 1) eliminate tuition fees so that every child can access high-quality early childhood education; 2) start providing free early childhood education to 5-year-olds incrementally as of 2014; 3) introduce free-of-charge early childhood education at kindergarten for children whose parents are welfare recipients; 4) alleviate financial obligations for large families starting in 2014; and, 5) increase financial support for children whose parents get municipal tax exemption, starting in 2015.

Figure 3.4. Distribution of public and private expenditure on early childhood education and care settings in pre-primary education (2013)

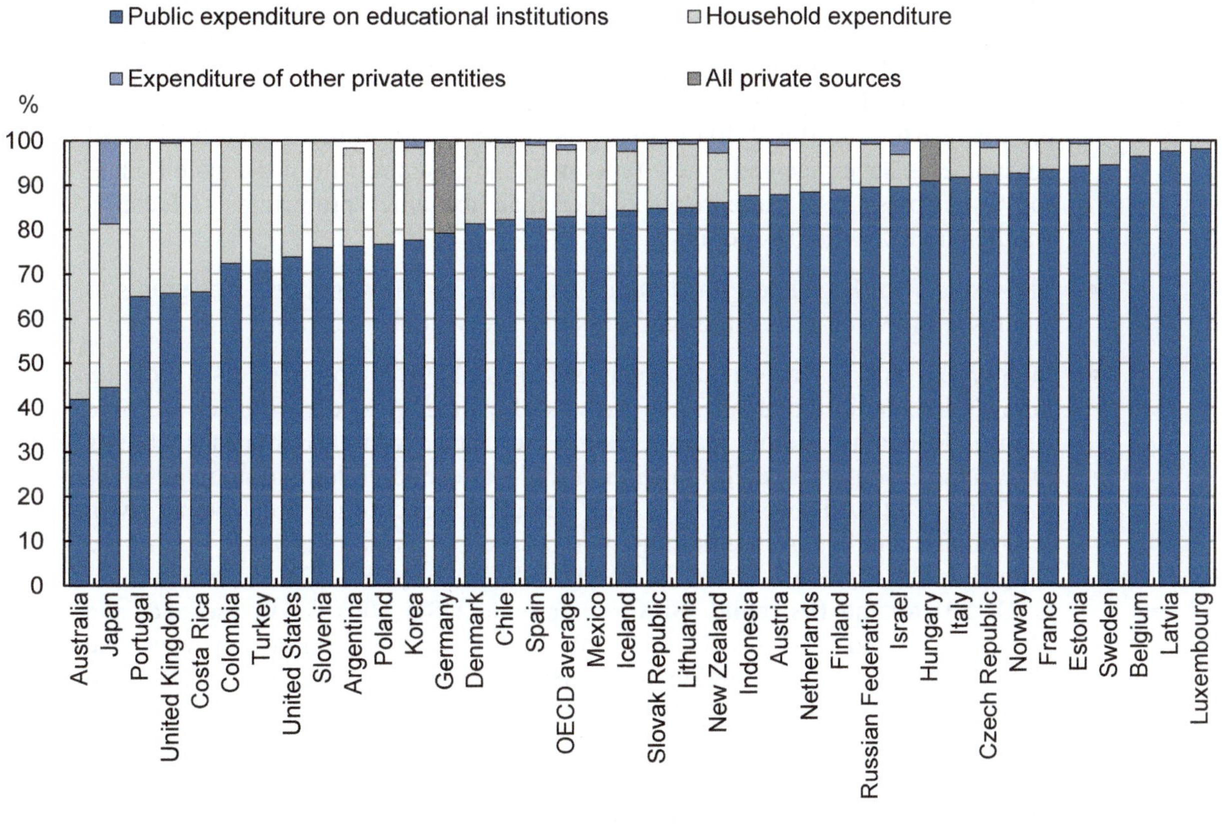

Notes: All Private sources include subsidies attributable to payments to educational institutions received from public sources.

Countries are ranked in descending order of the proportion of private expenditure on educational institutions in pre-primary education

Source: OECD (2017a), OECD Online education database, OECD, Paris, www.oecd.org/education/database.htm.

StatLink http://dx.doi.org/10.1787/888933487365

Many countries have recently reformed their ECEC system to make it more affordable for disadvantaged children at younger ages and for the entire cohort enrolled in pre-primary education. This is not surprising as the affordability of ECEC is a major criterion for universal access. Some countries have taken the following initiatives (OECD, 2015b):

- Parents in Denmark pay a contribution for operating costs (with a discount for a sibling), and the local council must only grant financial aid to eligible parents.
- Norway introduced the regulation of maximum parental fees across all kindergartens, both public and private (see case studies in Box 3.1).
- Parliament in Poland amended the School Education Act (Ustawa o systemie oświaty, 2013) to limit the fee paid by parents for each hour of pre-primary education, beyond the minimum five free compulsory hours, to a maximum of Polish Złoty (PLN) 1 (USD 0.30), with earmarked grants to local governments from the state budget to cover additional costs. In order to support higher numbers of children in kindergartens, the government increased the subsidy per child for the year 2016 from PLN 1 305 to PLN 1 370. Moreover, from January 2017, local governments have received a new type of financial support from the state budget for 6-year-olds. It is three times higher than for other pre-primary education children, at PLN 4 300 per child.
- The Exercise of Rights to Public Funds Act (2012) in Slovenia provides grants to parents with two or more children enrolled in pre-school education.
- In Sweden, policy states that parents should only have to spend 1-3% of the family's income on childcare (i.e. pre-school, pedagogical care and leisure time centre), depending on how many children they have, with a discount for siblings (maximum 3% for first child, maximum 2% for second child, and maximum 1% for third child). However, fees are calculated according to income, with low-income families paying nothing, while the costs for more affluent parents are capped. In 2017, the maximum fee is Swedish Krona (SEK) 1 362/month (around USD 150) for the first child, SEK 908 (around USD 100) for the second, and SEK 404 (around USD 45) for the third child. From the autumn term when the child reaches the age of 3, and up to the time when school starts, there is a right to 525 hours free of charge per year. The fee covers most activities, including food. This means childcare costs for families in Sweden are a fraction of those in other nations. Fees make up about 8% of the total costs of a place in pre-school. Pre-school is granted to all children above the age of 1, to the extent that is needed regarding parents' work or studies, or to the needs of the child itself. Children whose parents are unemployed or on parental leave with a younger sibling are entitled to at least 15 hours/week (or 3 hours/day) in pre-school.

Box 3.1. Policy reform: Changes in parental fees in kindergartens in Norway

As part of the kindergarten reform 2004-2009, Norway introduced the regulation of maximum parental fees across all kindergartens, both public and private. This was achieved through increased public funding, which reduced the parental contribution to running costs from 37% in 2002 to 15% in 2012. From 2005 to 2014, the real cost of a place in kindergarten for parents has reduced by 35% (Norway's background report 2015).

Kindergartens in Norway provide ECEC for children between (0)1 to 5 years of age. Most children and families have a full-time place (over 41 hours per week), which allows flexibility for families and the possibility to combine work and family life. From 2004, parental fees are fixed with a yearly cap decided in the national budget. According to the regulation, siblings attending kindergartens should have reduced fees, regardless of whether they attend different kindergartens or even kindergartens with different owners. The reduction for the second child should be a minimum of 30%, and for the third child and any subsequent children 50%.

In addition, municipalities were obliged to have reduced fees or free provision for families in need. Despite the overall reduction in parental fees between 2004 and 2014, distribution among different income groups was uneven, and for low-income families, parental fees still seemed to be a disincentive for participation in ECEC (Moafi and Bjørkli, 2011). To better target low-income families, a regulation was introduced in 2015 stating that the maximum annual fee shall not exceed 6% of the family income, replacing the general rule that municipalities were obliged to have reduced fees for families in need. In 2016, this meant that families with an income below 19 800 USD had reduced fees. Families with higher income paid the maximum fee decided in the national budget. The municipality is responsible for ensuring that this is applied in all kindergartens, both public and private (they will refund private providers).

Another measure to increase the participation of children from low-income families was introduced in August 2015, when children aged 4 and 5 were given the right to 20 hours free kindergarten per week. From August 2016 this was extended to 3-year-old children. In addition, from 2016 the general grant to municipalities was increased by 118 000 USD for reach out measures to families with low socio-economic and minority backgrounds to increase participation in ECEC (kindergartens).

Changes in parental fees and the introduction of 20 free hours of kindergarten (core time) for children in low-income families will be analysed and evaluated. The main report is expected in the second half of 2018, with some aspects published in a report in October 2017. However, Norwegian research (Bråthen et al., 2014; Drange, 2015) on free kindergarten in targeted areas have shown that the number of years in kindergarten affects the propensity to score low on literacy tests in first grade. Among children that have been at least four years in kindergarten only 15% scored low, compared to nearly 40% of children with only 0-2 years of experience. The availability of free core time (20 hours per week) increased the participation of minority-language children by 15% and led to better results on mapping tests in the first and second grade compared to areas with no intervention (i.e. free core time).

Sources: Department of Early Childhood Education and Care, Ministry of Education and Research, Norway;

Drange, Nina (2016) Gratis kjernetid i barnehage i Oslo Rapport 1: Oppfølging av barna på tredje trinn, Reports 2016/36, Statistics Norway, www.udir.no/globalassets/filer/tall-og-forskning/rapporter/2016/gratis-kjernetid-i-barnehager-i-oslo.pdf;

Drange, Nina (2015) "Gratis barnehagetid – et vellykket forsøk?" SSB, Samfunnsspeilet 2/2015, www.ssb.no/utdanning/artikler-og-publikasjoner/_attachment/232072?_ts=14e1ae312f0;

Beret Bråten (2014) Gratis kjernetid i barnehager Sluttrapport. FAFO-rapport 2014: 44, FAFO, Oslo, www.fafo.no/images/pub/2014/20391.pdf;

Moafi, H. & Bjørkli, E.S. (2011): Barnefamiliers tilsynsordninger høsten 2010. Rapporter 34/2011, Statistisk sentralbyrå.

The majority of private expenditure on pre-primary education comes from households. However, private business and non-profit organisations contribute to the cost of pre-primary education in a small number of countries.

To maximise constrained resources, the main cost of providing ECEC is usually shared among different levels of government (national, regional, and local), parents, and sometimes business. However, the majority of private expenditure on pre-primary education comes from households via parental fees.

On average across the OECD, household expenditure accounts for 93% of expenditure from private sources in pre-primary education, and is the biggest source of private funds in most countries. However, in Austria, the Czech Republic, Estonia, Germany, Iceland, Israel and Japan, more than 9% of all private funding comes from other private entities (e.g. private businesses and non-profit organisations, religious organisations, charitable organisations, and business and labour associations). In these countries, encouraging private foundations and community engagement to support ECEC centres is increasingly seen as an important policy lever and a potential source of additional resources. This type of funding can act as a "connector" between families and ECEC services, as well as other services for children; a "social network" to support parents in reducing stress and making smart choices, especially for disadvantaged families; and an "environment" to promote social cohesion.

In Germany, providers contribute the most to private expenditure on ECEC. However, some foundations may also contribute to the financing of ECEC settings. Private foundations can act as "source or resources". For example, the Haus der kleinen Forscher (Little Scientist's House) association promotes nationwide early childhood education in the natural sciences and technology. Its goal is to promote interest in natural phenomena among 3-6 year-olds. The foundation develops workshops and teaching materials for educators, hosts annual promotion days and provides comprehensive background information and experiments on the Internet. To offer workshops throughout Germany, the foundation established local networks.

Similar initiatives exist in other countries. For example, in Japan, Sony established the Sony Foundation for Education. Its Early Development Activity Centre conducts an extensive programme of activities in its quest to make science widely known among the public, to foster well-balanced personality development in young individuals and to educate the general public about the importance of building a healthy relationship between parents and children. The achievements of the various programmes and the lessons learned about child rearing are shared in various ways with parents, the community and childcare workers. The Foundation gives awards to ECEC centres to stimulate excellent practices, and supports teachers through booklets and posting information, experiences and lessons learned on the Internet (OECD (2015b), *OECD* Education Policy Outlook, Making Reform Happen: Lessons from OECD Countries).

Share of public funding, by level of government

Many governments delegate responsibility for ECEC public funding to local authorities. As a result, public funding is more decentralised in early childhood education (ISCED 0) than at any other level of education.

All government sources of expenditure on education (apart from international sources) are classified in three different levels of government: central, regional and local. In some countries, the funding of education is centralised, while in others, funding can be decentralised after transfers among the different levels of government (OECD, 2016: Education at a Glance 2016, Indicator B4).

In 2013, many countries had ECEC settings organised as autonomous and decentralised organisations. ECEC settings have also become more accountable to children, parents and the public at large for their outcomes. Public funding is more decentralised in early childhood education (ISCED 0) than at higher levels of education. In 2013, on average across OECD countries, only 41% of public funds for early childhood education came from the central government, before transfers. After transfers, this share dropped to 34%, and the share of local funds rose from 45% to 54%. Central government is the source of over 80% of funds after transfers only in Australia, Colombia, Ireland and New Zealand (Figure 3.5).

There is great variation among countries, particularly in terms of the share of funds managed by regional governments. Although 17 countries do not have regional governments, in countries that do, such as Austria, Belgium, the Czech Republic, Japan, Spain and Switzerland, over half of initial and final funds in early childhood education comes from regional governments. Local government is the source of over 90% of funds after transfers in 11 countries: Brazil, Estonia, Finland, Iceland, Latvia, Lithuania, Norway, Poland, the Slovak Republic, Slovenia and the United Kingdom. In these countries, central authorities can delegate responsibility to ECEC settings to manage a variety of tasks, including implementation, monitoring, evaluation and reporting. Local authorities can better co-ordinate with parents and communities to determine the appropriateness of national ECEC goals (Mahon, 2011).

The devolution of tasks in the early childhood field may be necessary to concretely acknowledge the rights of local communities, and for reasons of practical management. Numerous providers and fragmented provision patterns in the early childhood field can make it difficult for central governments to ensure quality and the appropriate provision of services, especially in the absence of devolved local management.

A shift towards more devolution can also be motivated by the desire to bring decision making and delivery closer to the families being served, and to adapt services to meet local needs and circumstances. Thus, central authorities can delegate responsibility to ECEC settings to manage a variety of tasks, including implementation, monitoring, evaluation and reporting. Local authorities can better co-ordinate with parents and communities to determine the appropriateness of national ECEC goals (Mahon, 2011).

However, the devolution of powers and responsibilities may also widen differences of access and quality between regions. In the devolution process, it seems important to ensure that early childhood services are part of a well-conceptualised national policy, with devolved powers to local authorities on the one hand, and a national approach to goal setting, legislation and regulation, financing, staffing criteria, quality monitoring and programme standards on the other. It also seems important that in the devolution or federalising process, a role should be retained for the responsible central government ministry.

Figure 3.5. Distribution of initial sources of public funds for education by level of government in early childhood education (ISCED 0), 2013

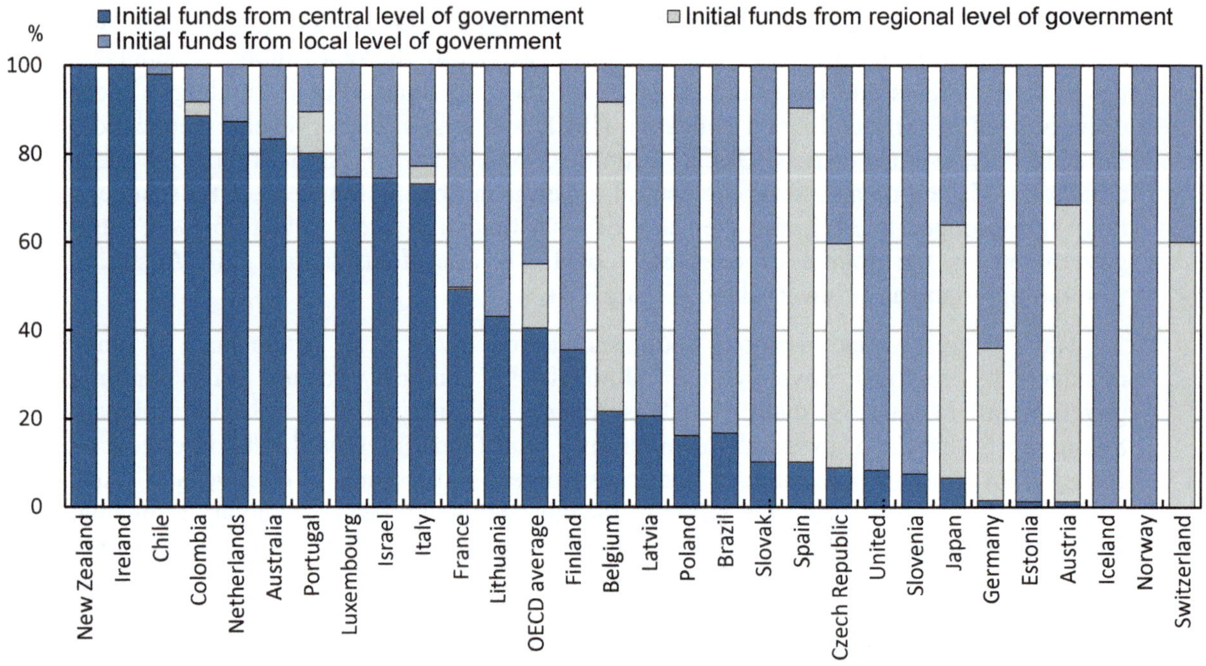

Changes in the proportion of educational funds received from the different levels of government between initial and final purchasers of educational resources

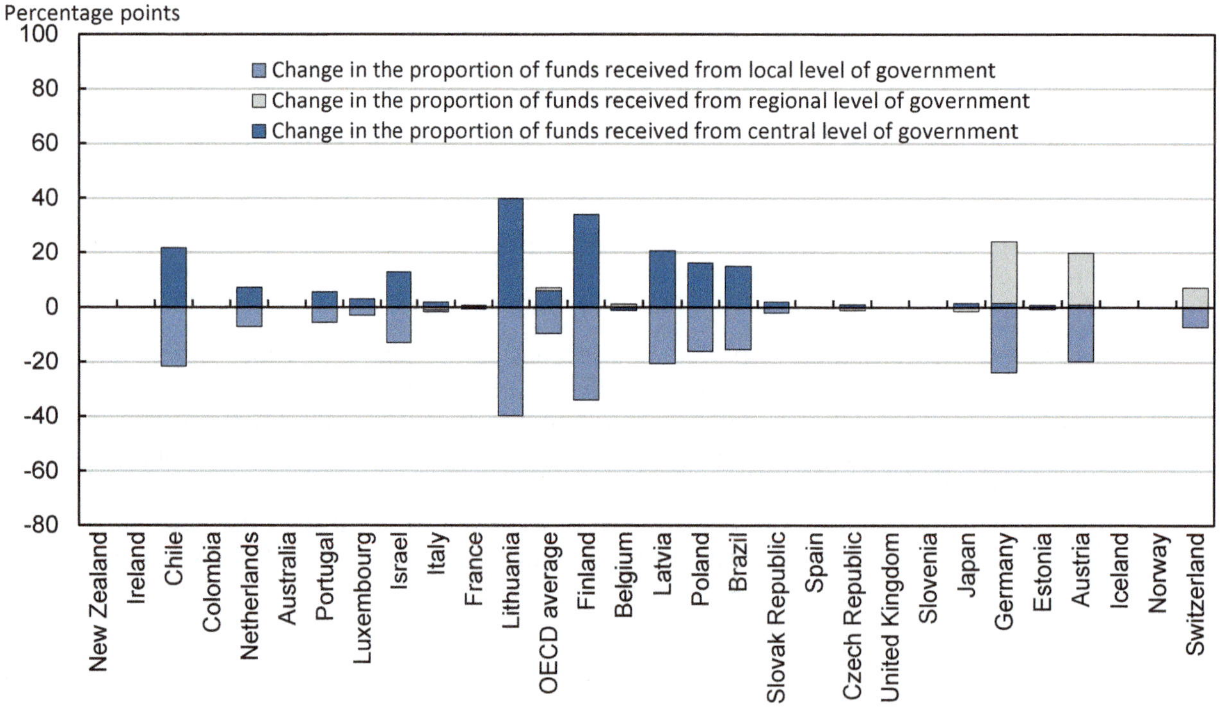

Note: Countries are ranked in descending order of the share of initial sources of funds from the central level of government.

Source: OECD (2017a), OECD Online education database, OECD, Paris, www.oecd.org/education/database.htm.

StatLink http://dx.doi.org/10.1787/888933487374

Teaching workforce

Teachers and pedagogical staff play a crucial role in ECEC systems as they are the front-line workers responsible for engaging children and promoting their well-being, development and learning. It is now widely accepted that within ECEC settings, teachers and pedagogical staff are the most important factors that influence child well-being, development and learning (e.g. Darling-Hammond, 2000; Konstantopoulos, 2006; Rivkin, Hanushek and Kain, 2005; Rockoff, 2004; Scheerens, Vermeulen and Pelgrum, 1989; Scheerens, 1993; Willms, 2000). As such, countries are especially interested in learning more about their own teaching and ECEC workforce, and making comparisons with other countries to develop more effective policies to improve teaching and learning (OECD, 2014b).

There are a variety of categories of professionals working in ECEC systems, such as pre-primary school teachers, pedagogues, care workers, educators and counsellors. Broadly speaking, the following categories can be distinguished:

- Teachers and comparable practitioners: Pre-primary education teachers have the most responsibility for a group of children at the class or playroom level. They may also be called pedagogue, educator, childcare practitioner or pedagogical staff in pre-primary education, while the term teacher is almost universally used at the primary level. Data sourced from the OECD's Education at a Glance Indicators exclusively covers this category.
- Assistants: Assistants support the teacher in a group of children or class. Assistants are more common in pre-primary education than in primary education. They usually have lower qualification requirements than teachers, which may range from no formal requirements to, for instance, vocational education and training. This category is only included in the indicator on child-to-staff ratio.
- Staff for individual children: These staff members work with some children only, for example, children with special educational needs or those who do not speak the language of the centre or school. They may be in the setting or play/classroom every day, or only for selected time slots or lessons.
- Advisors or counsellors: Professionals who work across classes and/or playgroups and provide additional guidance and support to teachers, other staff or children, either generally or specific to transitions. This category only appears in a few countries.

Few international indicators currently exist on the three last categories. Most indicators shown in this section will be based on the first category. However, the OECD is in the process of "filling in the gap" and collecting indicators on all four categories of ECEC staff (except counsellors). For example, **the Teaching and Learning International Survey (TALIS) Starting Strong Survey**, is an international survey of ECEC staff that aims to collect data on staff characteristics, pre-service and in-service education, pedagogical practices and beliefs, organisation and management, and working conditions in order to give countries an internationally framed assessment of what actually happens in their ECEC settings, i.e. the quality of the learning and well-being environment children experience (instrument development and pilot study in 2015/16, main study in 2018 and reporting in 2019).

Age distribution of teachers and proportion of women

The age distribution of teachers working in pre-primary education varies considerably across countries, and around 97% are women.

The level of formal education needed to become a teacher is a key issue across OECD countries; therefore, the demographic and gender characteristics of teachers are of interest to policy makers and researchers. The potential impacts of gender imbalance in the teaching workforce on issues such as student achievement, student motivation, teacher retention represent policy concerns in a number of countries where very few men are attracted to the profession (Drudy, 2008; OECD, 2005, 2009). This gender imbalance seems to be common in many regions of the world. It is most prominent in pre-primary education (ISCED 02), although differences persist well into primary and secondary education in many countries (OECD, 2016: Education at a Glance 2016, Indicator D5).

Gaining information about the age distribution of the teaching workforce is also valuable to policy makers. Some countries face significant challenges related to their ageing teacher workforce, with a high proportion of teachers nearing retirement age. The age of teachers is also related to teacher attrition in schools: attrition rates tend to be higher in the first few years of teaching, and decline the longer that teachers are in the profession (Ingersoll, 2001).

The age distribution of teachers varies considerably across countries and can be affected by a variety of factors, such as the size and age distribution of the population (see Chapter 1), the number of years of tertiary education needed to obtain a teacher qualification, and teachers' salaries and working conditions (see next sections). Declining birth rates, for example, may drive down the demand for new teachers, and longer tertiary education can delay the entrance of teachers to the labour market. The ageing of teachers increases school costs, which limits the resources available to implement other initiatives at the school level (OECD, 2016: Education at a Glance 2016, indicator D5).

In pre-primary education (ISCED 02), 25% of teachers are at least 50-years-old, on average across OECD countries. The proportion is equal or more than 35% in the Czech Republic, Estonia, Hungary, the Netherlands, Portugal and the Slovak Republic. At the other end of the spectrum, in most countries with available data, 20% of pre-primary teachers are under the age of 30. Only in Australia, Korea, Japan, New Zealand, Turkey and the United Kingdom does the proportion of pre-primary teachers under the age of 30 equal or exceed 25% (Figure 3.6).

The age distribution of teachers varies widely across OECD countries. However, a common pattern emerges when the gender of teachers is analysed. The highest proportions of women teachers are concentrated in the earlier years of schooling, and shrink at each successive level of education. On average across OECD countries, around 97% of teachers in pre-primary education are women; the average drops to 43% at the tertiary level. In 35 out of the 39 OECD and partner countries with available data, 93% or more of pre-primary teachers are women. The exceptions are France, where 92% of pre-primary teachers are women, the Netherlands (87%), Norway (91%) and Spain (93%) (see Table 1.1).

Figure 3.6. Age distribution of teachers (full-time and part-time) in pre-primary education (2014)

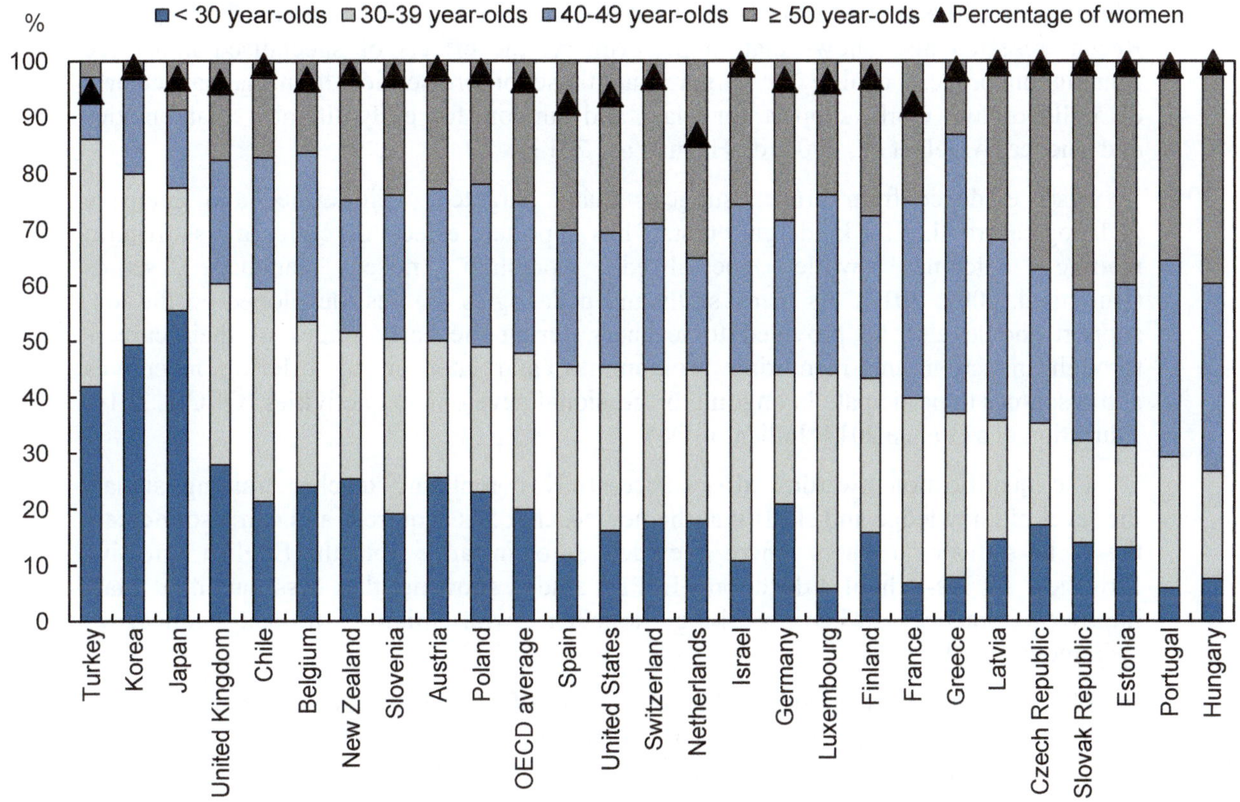

Note: Countries are ranked in ascending order of the percentage of teachers aged 40 years or older at the pre-primary level.

Source: OECD (2017a), OECD Online education database, OECD, Paris, www.oecd.org/education/database.htm.

StatLink http://dx.doi.org/10.1787/888933487386

Level of qualification of pre-primary teachers

In most countries, pre-primary teachers have a bachelor degree or equivalent (ISCED level 6). However, the duration of teacher training for pre-primary education varies more than for any other level of education.

Prospective teachers should be provided with high-quality initial training. The types of qualification, the duration of training and the programme content provided can influence the extent to which initial teacher education prepares teachers for their role. Evidence from the literature shows that staff initial training level and duration are positively associated with ECEC overall quality (Burchinal et al., 2002; Manning et al., 2017; Faour, 2010; Montie, Xiang and Schweinhart, 2006; Early et al., 2007; Howes, Whitebook and Phillips, 1992). High staff qualifications result in a more stimulating environment and high-quality pedagogical practices, which boost children's well-being and learning outcomes (Litjens and Taguma, 2010; Early et al., 2007; Fontaine et al., 2006; Phillipsen et al., 1997).

However, no matter how high the quality of pre-service training, initial training cannot be expected to prepare teachers for all the challenges they will face throughout their careers. Given the changes in student demographics, the length of the careers that many teachers have, and the need to update knowledge and competencies, initial teacher education must be viewed as only the starting point for teachers' ongoing development. Recent research also shows that in pre-primary, the effects of specialised in-service training on process quality are larger than those of pre-service training, particularly on collaborative work, support for play, and support for early literacy, mathematics and science (Assel, et al., 2007; de Haan et al., 2013).

Also, evidence from France suggests that a targeted, well-defined and intensive pedagogical training for kindergarten staff has important effects on children's short-term reading outcomes while specialised workshop raised language scores (Burchinal, 2002; 2012). As many skills and pedagogies are best developed on the job, support should also be provided to teachers during the early stages of their careers through induction and mentoring programmes, and later on by offering incentives and resources to participate in ongoing professional development activities (OECD, 2014: Education at a Glance 2014, Indicator D6).

The qualification awarded after successfully completing teacher training signals the level of knowledge and skills that the new teacher has acquired, and can also indicate the social status of teachers. There is evidence, for instance from the English Effective Provision of Pre-School Education (EPPE) study, showing that less qualified staff improves practices when working together with highly trained colleagues (Sammons, 2010).

The qualification awarded at the completion of a teacher training programme for almost all pre-primary teachers is a tertiary qualification. In 27 out of the 37 countries with available data, an individual can teach at the pre-primary level of education after earning a bachelor's degree or equivalent (ISCED level 6) at the end of initial teacher education. However, there are some exceptions. In the Slovak Republic, pre-primary teachers can start teaching with an upper secondary diploma, but an increasing number of teachers have now a bachelor or a master degree; in Germany and Ireland, they can begin teaching after graduating from a post-secondary vocational programme; in Austria, they typically start initial teacher training at age 14 when they enter upper secondary education, and graduate at ISCED level 5 after two years of a short tertiary cycle programme (e.g. higher technical and vocational college). At the other end of spectrum, only in England, France, Iceland, Italy, Poland and Portugal is a master's degree or equivalent (ISCED level 7) required of pre-primary school teachers (see Table 1.1).

As a consequence, the duration of initial teacher training for pre-primary teachers ranges widely among the 37 countries with relevant data: from two years for basic certification in Japan and two years of college for kindergarten teachers and high school graduates and one year training for childcare teachers in Korea; to five years in Austria, Chile, France, Iceland and Italy (OECD, 2014: Education at a Glance 2014, Indicator D6, and UNESCO institute for statistics, ISCED Mappings, 2015).

Education programmes for pre-primary are typically organised according to the concurrent model, in which pedagogical and practical training are provided at the same time as courses in specific subject matters.

There are two models of teacher education: concurrent and consecutive. Education programmes for prospective pre-primary teachers in OECD and partner countries are typically organised according to the concurrent model, in which pedagogical and practical training are provided at the same time as courses in subject matter. This is the case in 23 out of the 35 countries with available data for prospective pre-primary teachers. Only in Brazil, England and France is initial teacher education for pre-primary teachers mainly organised according to the consecutive model, i.e. pedagogical and practical training follow courses in subject matter. Among these countries, France implemented a reform in 2013, and initial teacher training now follows the concurrent model.

The content areas of initial teacher education differ little between the different levels of education, except regarding academic subjects. For pre-primary school teachers, academic subjects are mandatory in only 20 out of the 33 countries with available data. In addition, courses in academic subjects are specific to prospective teachers at the pre-primary level in around two-thirds of countries (OECD, 2014: Education at a Glance 2014, Indicator D6).

Teachers' salaries

Teachers' salaries and career pay progression in pre-primary education vary significantly between countries.

Competitive salaries and good working conditions may attract qualified young people to teaching in some countries (Manlove and Guzell, 1997), and help retain effective teachers in the profession in others (Huntsman, 2008). Wages not only affect job satisfaction, they also have an effect on teacher effectiveness (Huntsman, 2008; Moon and Burbank, 2004; Murnane and Olsen, 1990). In addition to prompting recruitment and training efforts to replace retiring teachers, the ageing of the teacher workforce also has budgetary implications. In most school systems, there is a link between teachers' salaries and years of teaching experience.

Teachers' salaries represent the largest single cost in formal education and have a direct impact on the attractiveness of the teaching workforce. Salaries influence decisions to enrol in teacher education, become a teacher after graduation (as graduates' career choices are associated with relative earnings in teaching and non-teaching occupations and their likely growth over time), return to the teaching workforce after a career interruption, and/or remain a teacher (in general, the higher the salaries, the fewer people choose to leave the profession).

Teachers' salaries are one component of teachers' total compensation. Other benefits, such as regional allowances for teaching in remote areas, family allowances, reduced rates on public transport, and tax allowances on the purchase of instructional materials, may also form part of teachers' total remuneration. There are large differences in taxation and social benefit systems in OECD countries, which should be borne in mind when comparing statutory salaries across countries.

Teachers' salaries in pre-primary education (ISCED 02) vary widely across countries. For instance, the annual statutory salary of pre-primary school teachers with 15 years of experience (before taxes and converted into USD using purchasing power parity) ranges from less than USD 20 000 in the Czech Republic, Hungary and the Slovak Republic, to more than USD 50 000 in Australia, the Netherlands and the United States, and exceeds USD 100 000 in Luxembourg (Figure 3.7).

Pre-primary systems differ not only in how much they pay teachers, but in the structure of their pay scales. Increases from starting salary to the top of the salary scale are, on average, 65%, but wide variations are observed across countries. For instance, some countries, such as Australia, Colombia, the Czech Republic, Hungary, Italy, the Nordic countries, the Slovak Republic and Turkey, concentrate salary increases early on in a teacher's career. Others, such as Chile, Colombia, France, Israel, Korea, Luxembourg and Mexico, offer higher rewards to more experienced teachers, while in other countries, teachers' pay increases steadily throughout their career (Figure 3.7).

Figure 3.7. Annual statutory teachers' salaries in pre-primary education (2014)

Based on typical qualifications, in public settings, in equivalent USD converted using PPPs

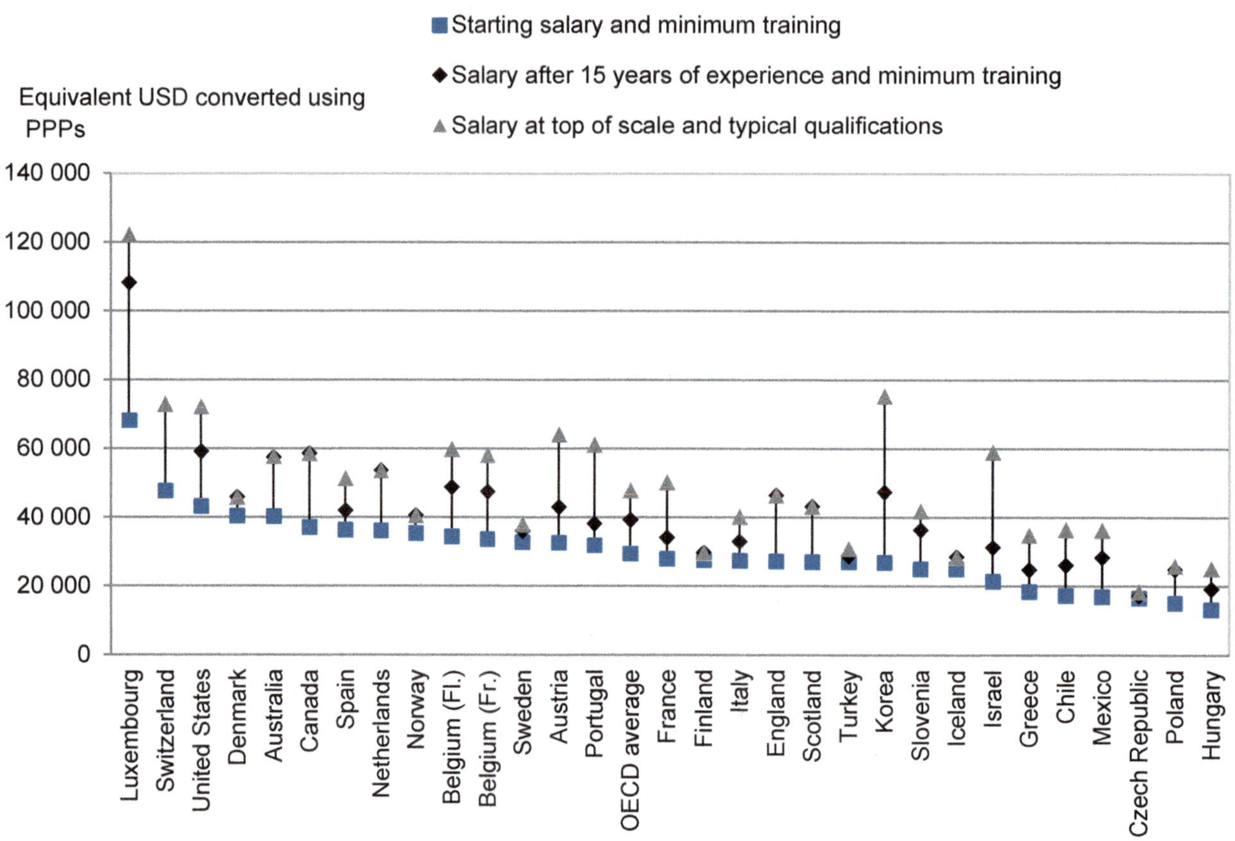

Note: Countries are ranked in descending order of starting salaries for pre-primary teachers with minimum qualifications.

Source: OECD (2016), Education at a Glance 2016: OECD Indicators, Indicator D3, http://dx.doi.org/10.1787/eag-2016-en.

StatLink http://dx.doi.org/10.1787/888933487391

Teachers' salaries in pre-primary education have been impacted by the economic crisis in one third of OECD countries. In 2014, teachers' salaries in pre-primary education were significantly below the salaries of other tertiary graduates in most countries.

Between 2005 and 2014, the statutory salaries of teachers (with typical qualifications and 15 years of experience) increased in real terms by 6% at the pre-primary level, on average across OECD countries. However, the financial and economic crisis that hit the world economy in 2008 significantly affected salaries for civil servants and public sector workers in general. Teachers' salaries were either frozen or cut in 8 out of the 21 OECD countries with available data on pre-primary education over the period

2010-2014. The decrease reached more than 5% in England (UK), Italy, Portugal, Scotland (UK) and Spain, and up to 30% in Greece (Figure 3.8).

Figure 3.8. Change in pre-primary teachers' statutory salaries (2005, 2010 and 2014)

Index of change between 2005 and 2014 (constant prices), for statutory salaries of teachers with 15 years of experience and typical qualifications

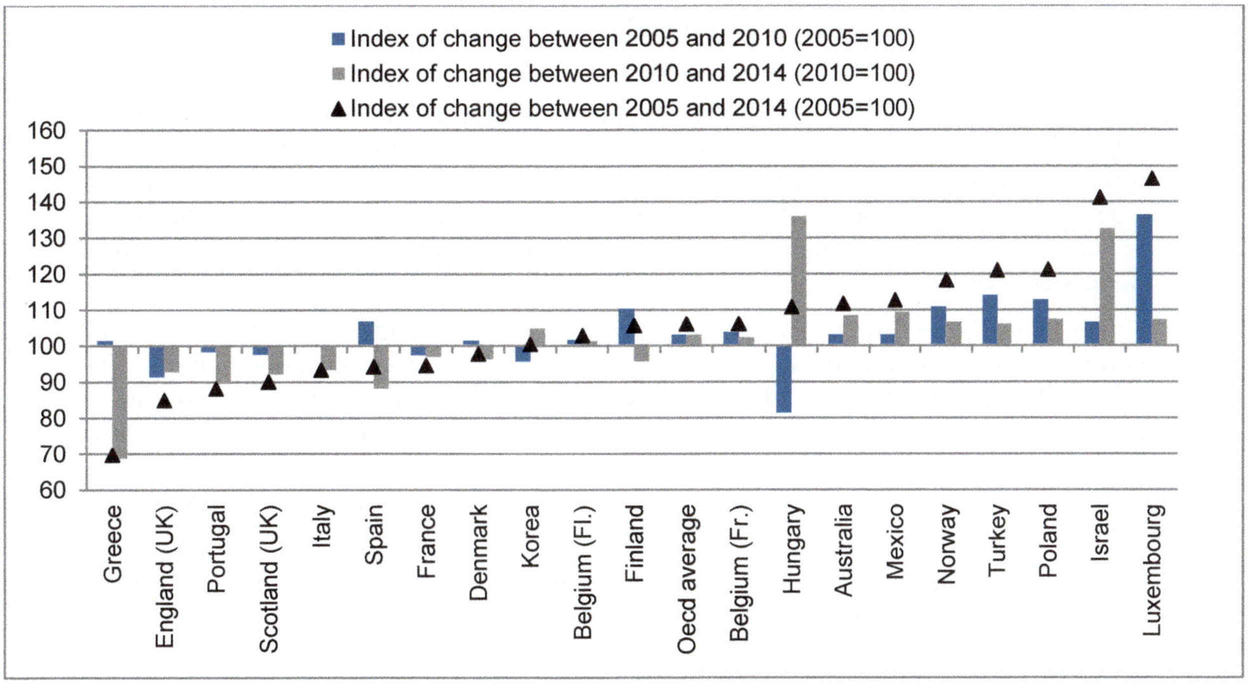

Note: Countries and economies are ranked in ascending order of Index of change between 2005 and 2014.

Source: OECD (2016), Education at a Glance 2016: OECD Indicators, Indicator D3, http://dx.doi.org/10.1787/eag-2016-en.

StatLink http://dx.doi.org/10.1787/888933487401

In Greece, various reductions in teachers' benefits and allowances affected teachers' salaries in 2010, 2011 and 2012. As a result, gross salaries fell by around 30% in real terms between 2010 and 2014. In Portugal in 2011, using a method defined in a new law and as part of a reform package, salaries higher than EUR 1 500 were reduced. They fell again in 2012 as civil servants were paid salaries covering 12 rather than months, as had previously been the case. In England, teachers' salaries were frozen between 2011 and 2012 at all levels of education, followed by a below inflation increase of 1% in following years for the public sector as a whole. These reductions were all due to the financial crisis. Similarly, the Scottish Negotiating Committee for Teachers (SNCT) agreed to freeze teachers' pay from April 2011 until March 2013. In Italy, teachers' salaries have been frozen since 2011 (OECD, 2015a: Education at a Glance 2015, Indicator D3).

The economic downturn may also have influenced the supply of teachers. In general, when the economy is weak and there is high unemployment among graduates and low graduate earnings, teaching might seem a more attractive job choice than other occupations. In 2014, teachers' salaries remained below those of other tertiary-educated workers in most countries. On average, pre-primary teachers in OECD countries earn only 74% of the average salary of a tertiary-educated, 25-64 year-old full-time, full-year worker. Relative salaries for pre-primary teachers are highest only in Luxembourg, where they are at least 8% higher than those of similarly educated workers (OECD, 2016: Education at a Glance 2016, Indicator D3).

Organisation of teaching time over the year in pre-primary education

Countries vary considerably in the number of contact hours with children per year required of the average ECEC teacher.

In order to attract the best candidates to the teaching workforce, countries need to not only offer adequate pay, which is evidence that teachers are valued by society, but also provide an environment where teachers are given the autonomy to work as professionals and are given a direct role in school improvement. In this respect, statutory working hours and the child-to-staff ratio are two important system-level indicators to assess the quality of the school environment.

Heavy workloads are associated with stressed staff. Workload refers to the number of working hours, indicating the extent to which staff schedules are compatible with family life and the physical demands of the job. Large group sizes, low staff-child ratios and a heavy workload are potential stressors for ECEC practitioners. Some research findings show the effects of workload on ECEC quality, indicating that practitioners with a heavy workload perform less well than colleagues with lighter schedules (De Schipper et al., 2007).

Although statutory working hours and contact hours with children only partly determine teachers' actual workload, they do offer a valuable insight into the demands placed on teachers in different countries. Contact hours with children and the extent of non-teaching duties may also affect the attractiveness of the teaching workforce.

At the pre-primary level of education, countries vary considerably in the number of contact hours with children per year required of the average ECEC teacher working in a public setting. Required contact time with children at the pre-primary level in public ECEC settings varies more across countries than it does at any other level of education. The number of teaching days ranges from 162 in France to more than 220 in Iceland and Norway. Annual contact time of teachers with children ranges from less than 700 hours in Greece, Korea and Mexico to more than 1 450 hours in Iceland and Norway. On average across OECD countries, teachers at this level of education are required to be in contact with children 1 005 hours per year, spread over 40 weeks or 190 days of teaching (Figure 3.9).

Translated into hours per day, teachers are required to be in contact with children between 4 and 6 hours a day in 17 out of 25 countries with available data. The main exceptions are Germany, Hungary and Norway, where teachers are in contact with children more than 6.5 hours per day in pre-primary education, and England (UK), Korea and Mexico, where they are in contact with children fewer than 4 hours per day. There is no set rule on how contact time is distributed throughout the year across OECD countries. In Poland, for example, pre-primary teachers must teach 1 137 hours per year, about 130 hours more than the OECD average. However, those contact hours with children are spread over 25 more days of instruction than the OECD average. As a result, pre-primary teachers in Poland teach an average of 5.3 hours per day, which is the same number of hours per day as the OECD average (Figure 3.9).

Figure 3.9. Organisation of teaching time over the year in pre-primary education (2014)

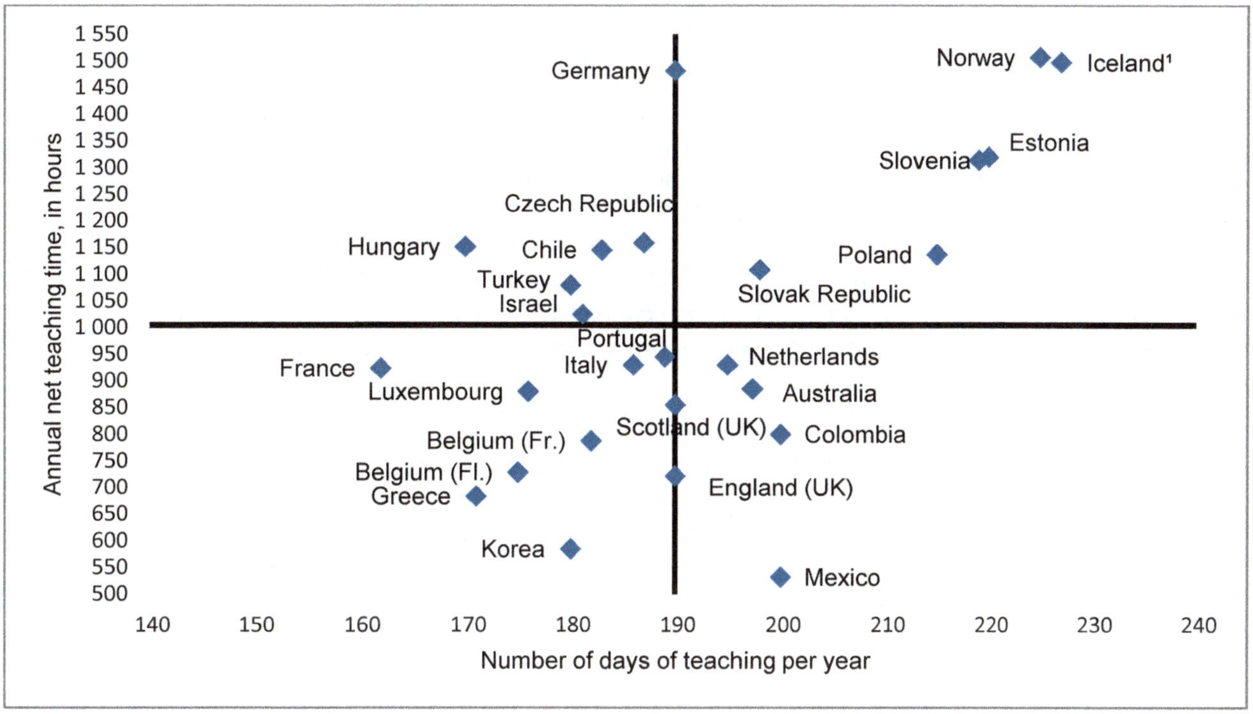

1. Year of reference 2013.

Source: OECD (2016), Education at a Glance 2016: OECD Indicators, Indicator D4, http://dx.doi.org/10.1787/eag-2016-en.

StatLink http://dx.doi.org/10.1787/888933487418

In most countries, teachers' working time is determined by the statutory teaching time specified in working regulations, and teachers are formally required to work a specific number of hours per year. This may be specified as the number of hours teachers must be available at the setting for teaching and non-teaching activities. It corresponds to official working hours as specified in contractual agreements. On average across countries with data for both teaching and total working time in settings for pre-primary teachers, 83% of teachers' working time is spent on teaching, with the proportion ranging from less than 65% in Colombia, Chile, England (UK) and Greece, to more than 90% in France, Hungary, Israel and Turkey.

While the proportion of working time spent teaching increases with the annual number of teaching hours, there are significant variations between countries. For example, the Flemish Community of Belgium and England (UK) have a similar number of teaching hours (729 hours in the Flemish Community of Belgium and 722 hours in England), but 80% of working time is spent on teaching in the Flemish Community of Belgium, compared to only 57% in England (UK) (OECD, 2016: Education at a Glance 2016, Indicator D4).

Child-to-teacher ratios

At the pre-primary level, there are 14 children for every teacher, on average in OECD countries. This number varies widely across all countries with available data.

A low child-to-staff ratio impacts staff working conditions, alongside other factors such as reasonable hours or workload and salary levels. These affect job satisfaction and staff retention, and through this, contribute to the quality of ECEC services (Clarke-Stewart et al., 2002; Burchinal et al., 2002; Huntsman, 2008). Smaller ratios are often seen as beneficial because they allow staff to focus more on the needs of individual students, and reduce the amount of class time needed to deal with disruptions. Staff effectiveness is also affected by the size of the groups; smaller groups are beneficial for enhancing process quality (De Schipper et al., 2007; Burchinal et al., 2002; Huntsman, 2008).

The child-staff ratio is one of the key variables that policy makers can use to control spending on education. It is therefore an important indicator of the resources invested in ECEC, and of the quality of these services. At the pre-primary level, there are 14 children for every teacher, on average across OECD countries. This number varies widely across countries with available data, ranging from more than 20 children per teacher in Chile, China, France and Mexico, to fewer than 10 children for every teacher in Australia, Iceland, New Zealand, Slovenia and Sweden.

However, some countries make extensive use of teaching assistants at the pre-primary level. Twelve OECD countries (and three partner countries) reported smaller child-to-staff ratios than child-to-teacher ratios. Among these countries, few have large numbers of teaching assistants. As a result, the child-to-staff ratios are substantially lower than child-to-teacher ratios (at least three children or fewer) only in Chile, China, France, Norway (for the whole ECEC sector) and the United Kingdom (Figure 3.10).

The difference is particularly large in Chile, where there are at least 10 fewer pupils per contact staff than per teacher. Regulations of the child-to-teacher ratio require that in pre-kindergarten (programme classified in pre-primary education) there is one early childhood educator and one pre-school technician for every 35 children. However, if there are fewer than 11 children, the pre-school technician is not required. Similarly, for kindergarten (programme also classified in pre-primary education), regulations state that there should be one early childhood educator and one pre-school technician for every 45 children. If there are fewer than 16 pupils, the pre-school technician is not required (Chilean Education Decree n° 315).

Wide variations are also observed between early childhood development programmes (ISCED 01) and pre-primary education (ISCED 02), although a common pattern has emerged. In most countries with available data for both programmes, the ratios of children to contact staff (and of children to teacher) are smaller in early childhood development programmes (ISCED 01) than in pre-primary education (ISCED 02). On average across the 12 OECD countries with available data for both programmes, there are 14 children for each pre-primary teacher working in pre-primary education, while the ratio is only 9 children per teacher in early childhood development programmes. When other staff are taken into account, the ratio of children to contact staff is equal or exceeds 7 only in Austria, Brazil, Mexico and the United Kingdom.

Figure 3.10. Ratio of children to teaching staff in early childhood education (2014)

Public and private institutions, calculation based on full-time equivalents

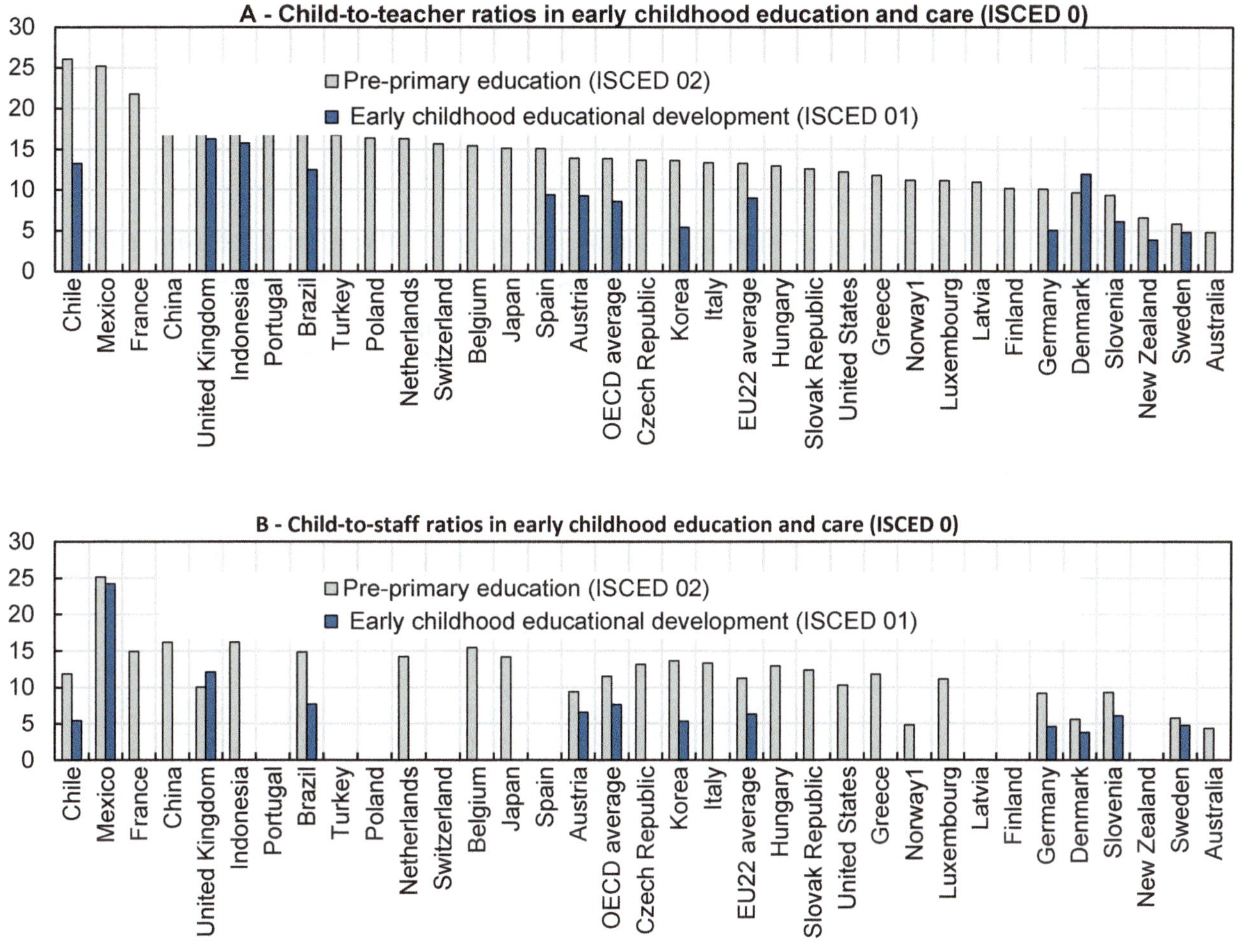

1. Including early childhood development (ISCED 01).

Note: Countries are ranked in descending order of children to teacher ratios in pre-primary education.

Sources: OECD (2016), Education at a Glance 2016: OECD Indicators, Table C2.2, http://dx.doi.org/10.1787/eag-2016-en.

StatLink http://dx.doi.org/10.1787/888933487425

References

Assel, M.A., et al (2007), "An evaluation of curriculum, setting, and mentoring of children enrolled in pre-kindergarten", *Reading and Writing*, Vol. 20, pp. 463–494.

Bråten B.et al (2014) Gratis kjernetid i barnehager Sluttrapport. FAFO-rapport 2014, Vol. 44, Norwegian Research Center (FAFO), Oslo, www.fafo.no/images/pub/2014/20391.pdf

Burchinal, M.R., D. Cryer, R.M. Clifford and C. Howes (2002), "Caregiver training and classroom quality in child care centers", *Applied Developmental Science*, Vol. 6/1, pp. 2-11.

Burchinal M.R., E. Peisner-Feinberg, R. Pianta and C. Howes (2002), "Development of academic skills from preschool through second grade: Family and classroom predictors of developmental trajectories", *Journal of School Psychology*, Vol. 40, pp. 415–436.

Clarke-Stewart, K.A., et al. (2002), "Do regulable features of childcare homes affect children's development?", *Early Childhood Research Quarterly*, Vol. 17, pp. 52-86.

Darling-Hammond, L. (2000), Teacher quality and student achievement: A review of state policy evidence, *Journal of Education Policy Analysis*, Vol. 8/1.

De Haan, A., et al. (2013), "Targeted versus mixed preschool and kindergartners: Effects of classroom composition and teacher managed activities on disadvantaged children's emergent academic skills", *School Effectiveness and School Improvement*, Vol. 24, pp. 177–194

De Schipper, E.J., M.J. Riksen-Walraven and S.A. Geurts (2007), "Multiple determinants of caregiver behavior in child care centers", *Early Childhood Research Quarterly*, Vol. 22, pp. 312-326.

Drange, Nina (2016) *Gratis kjernetid i barnehage i Oslo Rapport 1: Oppfølging av barna på tredje trinn*. Reports 2016/36. Statistics Norway, www.udir.no/globalassets /filer/tall-og-forskning/rapporter/2016/gratis-kjernetid-i-barnehager-i-oslo.pdf.

Drange, Nina (2015) "Gratis barnehagetid – et vellykket forsøk?" SSB, Samfunnsspeilet 2/2015,www.ssb.no/utdanning/artikler-og-publikasjoner/_attachment/232072?_ts=14 e1ae312f0.

Drudy, S. (2008), "Gender Balance/Gender Bias: The Teaching Profession and the Impact of Feminisation", *Gender and Education*, Vol. 20/4, pp. 309-323.

Early, D. et al. (2007), "Teachers' Education, Classroom Quality, and Young Children's Academic Skills: Results From Seven Studies of Preschool Programs", *Child Development*, Vol. 78/2, pp. 558-580.

Faour, B. (2010), Early Childhood in the Arab Countries: Status and Challenges (Regional report No. WCECCE/Ref.7), Early Childhood Care and Education Regional Reports, UNESCO, WCECCE.

Fontaine, N.S., et al. (2006), "Increasing Quality in Early Care and Learning Environments." *Early Child Development and Care 176*, pp. 157–169. http://dx.doi.org/10.1080/0300443042000302690.

Howes, C., M. Whitebook, D. Phillips (1992), "Teacher characteristics and effective teaching in child care: Findings from the National Child Care Staffing Study", *Child and Youth Care Forum*, Vol. 21/6, pp. 399-414, Kluwer Academic Publishers-Human Sciences Press.

Huntsman, L. (2008), *Determinants of quality in child care: A review of the research evidence*, Centre for Parenting and Research, NSW Department of Community Services.

Ingersoll, R.M. (2001), "Teacher turnover and teacher shortages: An organizational analysis", *American Educational Research Journal*, Vol. 38/3, pp. 499–534.

Konstantopoulos, S. (2006), "Trends of school effects on student achievement: Evidence from NLS:72, HSB:82, and NELS:92", *Teacher College Record,* Vol. 108/12, pp. 2550-2581.

Litjens, I. and M. Taguma (2010), *Literature overview for the 7th meeting of the OECD Network on Early Childhood Education and Care*, OECD, Paris.

Mahon, R. (2011), "Child Care Policy: A Comparative Perspective", *Encyclopedia on Early Childhood Development,* Centre of Excellence for Early Childhood Development and Strategic Knowledge Cluster on Early Child Development, Montreal, www.child-encyclopedia.com/pages/PDF/MahonANGxp2.pdf.

Manlove, E.E., and J.R. Guzell (1997), "Intention to leave, anticipated reasons for leaving, and 12 Month turnover of child care centre staff", *Early Childhood Research Quarterly*, Vol. 12/2, pp. 145-167.

Manning, M., S. Garvis, C. Fleming and G.T. Wong (2017), *The relationship between teacher qualification and the quality of the early childhood care and learning environment*, Campbell Systematic Reviews.

Montie, J.E., Z. Xiang and L.J. Schweinhart (2006), "Preschool experience in 10 countries: Cognitive and language performance at age 7", *Early Childhood Research Quarterly*, Vol. 21/3, pp. 313-331.

Moon, J. and J. Burbank (2004), "The early childhood education and wage ladder; a model for improving quality in early learning and care programs", *Policy Brief*, Economic opportunity Institute, Seattle WA.

Murnane, R.J. and R.J. Olsen (1990), "The effects of salaries and opportunity costs on length of stay in teaching: Evidence from North Carolina", *Journal of Human Resources*, pp. 106-124.

NICHD (2002), "Child Care Structure>Process>Outcome: Direct and indirect effects of caregiving quality on young children's development", *Psychological Science*, Vol. 13, pp. 199-206.

OECD (2017a), OECD online education database, www.oecd.org/education/database.htm

OECD (2017b), *OECD Family Database*, OECD, Paris, www.oecd.org/els/family/database.htm.

OECD (2016), *Education at a Glance 2016: OECD Indicators,* OECD Publishing, Paris, http://dx.doi.org/10.1787/eag-2016-en.

OECD (2015a), *Education at a Glance 2015: OECD Indicators*, OECD Publishing, Paris, http://dx.doi.org/10.1787/eag-2015-en.

OECD (2015b), *OECD Education Policy Outlook 2015, Making Reform Happen: Lessons from OECD Countries*, OECD, Paris, http://dx.doi.org/10.1787/9789264225442-en.

OECD (2015c), *Starting Strong IV: Monitoring Quality in Early Childhood Education and Care (ECEC)*, OECD Publishing, Paris, http://dx.doi.org/10.1787/9789264233515-en.

OECD (2014a), *Education at a Glance 2014: OECD Indicators*, OECD Publishing, Paris, http://dx.doi.org/10.1787/eag-2014-en.

OECD (2014b), TALIS 2013 Results: An International Perspective on Teaching and Learning, OECD Publishing, Paris, http://dx.doi.org/10.1787/9789264196261-en.

OECD (2012), *Starting Strong III: A Quality Toolbox for Early Childhood Education and Care*, OECD Publishing, Paris, http://dx.doi.org/10.1787/9789264123564-en.

OECD (2009), Creating Effective Teaching and Learning Environments: First Results from TALIS, OECD Publishing, Paris, http://dx.doi.org/10.1787/9789264072992-en.

OECD (2005), *Teachers Matter: Attracting, Developing and Retaining Effective Teachers, Education and Training Policy*, OECD Publishing, Paris, http://dx.doi.org/10.1787/9789264018044-en.

Phillipsen, L.C., M.R. Burchinal, C. Howes and D. Cryer (1997), "The prediction of process quality from structural features of child care", *Early Childhood Research Quarterly,* Vol. 12, pp. 281–303.

Rivkin, S., E. Hanushek and J. Kain (2005), "Teachers, schools, and academic achievement", *Econometrica,* Vol. 73/2, pp. 417-458.

Rockoff, J.E. (2004), "The impact of individual teachers on students' achievement: Evidence from panel data", *American Economic Review*, Vol. 94/2, pp. 247-252.

Sammons, P. (2010), "The EPPE Research Design: an educational effectiveness focus" in: Sylva et al. (eds.), *Early Childhood Matters: Evidence from the Effective Pre-school and Primary Education project*, Routledge, London/New York.

Scheerens, J. (1993), "Basic school effectiveness research: Items for a research agenda", *School Effectiveness and School Improvement*, Vol. 4/1, pp. 17-36.

Scheerens, J., C.J.A.J. Vermeulen and W.J. Pelgrum (1989), "Generalizability of instructional and school effectiveness indicators across nations", *International Journal of Educational Research*, Vol. 13/7, pp. 789-799.

UNESCO institute for statistics, ISCED Mappings (2015), http://uis.unesco.org/en/isced-mappings

Willms, J.D. (2000), "Monitoring school performance for standards-based reform", *Evaluation and Research in Education*, Vol. 14, pp. 237-253.

Tables of Chapter 3

StatLink http://dx.doi.org/10.1787/9789264276116-en

WEB Table 3.1 (Web only). Expenditure on early childhood education and care settings (2013).

WEB Table 3.2 (Web only). Annual statutory teachers' salaries in pre-primary education (2014).

WEB Table 3.3 (Web only). Organisation of teachers' teaching time over the year in pre-primary education (2014) WEB Table 3.4 (Web only). Ratio of children to teaching staff in early childhood education (2014).

Chapter 4.

Policy outputs of early childhood education and care: Access, participation intensity and curriculum frameworks

The share of children under the age of 3 enrolled in early childhood education and care (ECEC) settings is on the rise in the great majority of countries. Moreover, the concept of services for the children under the age of 3 is broadening in many countries from a labour market perspective to the inclusion of quality objectives, especially in integrated systems. Increases in the access to ECEC are not limited to children under the age of 3 and pre-primary education now begins for most children well before they are 5 years-old. However, universal access is not a guarantee for high-quality ECEC and inequities still persist in many countries. Therefore, curriculum frameworks can play a pivotal role in ensuring the quality of ECEC services. This chapter includes indicators that are the result of the policy inputs put in place, such as enrolment rates by age and type of institutions, intensity of participation, duration of early childhood education or content areas of curriculum frameworks.

The statistical data for Israel are supplied by and are under the responsibility of the relevant Israeli authorities. The use of such data by the OECD is without prejudice to the status of the Golan Heights, East Jerusalem and Israeli settlements in the West Bank under the terms of international law.

Key messages

Access to ECEC for younger children

International comparisons reveal some clear trends:

- The concept of services for children under the age of 3 is broadening in many countries from a labour market perspective to the inclusion of quality objectives, especially in integrated systems.
- The share of children under the age of 3 enrolled in formal childcare (ISCED 0 and other registered ECEC services outside ISCED 2011) is on the rise in most countries. On average across OECD countries, enrolment rates of children under the age of 3 increased by over eight percentage points between 2005 and 2014, from 26% to 34%.
- However, this proportion hides wide variations across countries. Enrolment rates in formal childcare range from less than 10% in the Czech Republic, Mexico and the Slovak Republic, to more than 45% in all Nordic countries, except Finland, in "Benelux" OECD countries (Belgium, Luxembourg and the Netherlands) and in France and Portugal.
- The move towards better provision in many European countries has also been the result of further stimulus by the 2010 objectives set by the European Union at its 2002 Barcelona meeting.
- Countries often offer a mix of part-time (less than 30 hours per week) and full-time (30 hours or more) provision, with strong variations across countries and across different settings within countries. On average, a child attended ECEC services for an average of 30 hours per week in 2014, which corresponds to full-time care.
- Part-time attendance for children under the age of 3 is widespread in countries such as Austria, Ireland, the Netherlands, New Zealand, Spain, Switzerland and the United Kingdom.
- When participation rates and average hours during a usual week are analysed together, different patterns emerge, reflecting policy choices made by countries. For example, ECEC settings in some countries, such as Estonia, Finland, Greece, Hungary, Latvia and Poland, provide long hours per week to a small proportion of children under the age of 3. The opposite is observed in the Netherlands and New Zealand, where fewer hours per week are provided to an above-average proportion of children under the age of 3.
- The proportion of young children enrolled in private early childhood educational settings (ISCED 01) is considerably larger than for pre-primary education (ISCED 02) in 15 out of 17 countries with available data for both levels. On average, 58% of children enrolled in early childhood development programmes (ISCED 01) attend private ECEC settings. This percentage exceeds 50% in around two thirds of countries. This can result in heavy financial burdens for parents, even when government subsidies are provided.

Access to ECEC for older children

International comparisons reveal some clear trends:

- Enrolment rates in pre-primary education at age 3 have risen over the last decade in most OECD countries, and pre-primary education for most children now begins well before they are 5-years-old.
- The enrolment of 3-year-olds in pre-primary education increased by more than eight percentage points on average in the OECD between 2005 and 2014: from 62% in 2005 to 70% in 2014. Similarly, rates for 4-year-olds increased from 73% in 2005 to 85% in 2014.
- Many countries have recently increased the number of free hours of ECEC entitlements, or shifted from half-day to full-day kindergartens, to increase the participation of children in ECEC, in particular those from disadvantaged backgrounds. These initiatives are often associated with other reforms that aim to improve the quality of ECEC settings and better align the structure of ECEC with that of primary school, as children may often spend longer hours in primary school than in ECEC.

Curriculum frameworks can play a pivotal role in ensuring the quality of ECEC services

Research tells us that:

- According to recent research, a balanced curriculum with roughly equal emphasis on play, self-regulation and pre-academic activities is related to the highest observed quality of staff-child interactions. Unfortunately, large-scale studies of ECEC suggest that too few adults have the necessary skills to provide optimal learning and emotional support for young children's intellectual growth, particularly in the curriculum areas of science, mathematics and numeracy.

International comparisons reveal some clear trends:

- Access is not a guarantee of high-quality ECEC. Curriculum frameworks can play a pivotal role in ensuring the quality of ECEC services. Therefore, in many countries, the curriculum framework in pre-primary education has been recently extended to enhance ECEC quality, and to ensure a better transition between pre-primary and primary education.
- In 2015, as in 2011, most of the 24 OECD countries and jurisdictions with data for both reference years still placed a high importance on literacy, numeracy, physical education, and science in their curriculum framework designed for pre-primary education. In 2015, play time was embedded into other content areas in order to stimulate learning in such areas through play.
- A significantly higher proportion of respondent countries included newly emerging subject matters in their pre-primary curriculum between 2011 and 2015, which responds to changing needs in present-day society, such as ICT skills, learning foreign languages, developing ethics and citizenship values, learning religion, and ensuring health and well-being for children. The increase between 2011 and 2015 is particularly marked for ICT, with around 40% of respondent countries citing ICT as a content area of their curriculum framework in 2015.
- The content of curriculum is still widely discussed across OECD countries. Some countries have introduced broad curriculum reforms that include ECEC.

For example, Finland and Korea introduced curricula to strengthen the quality of provision, while Denmark is reflecting on how to enhance the quality of ECEC services through a strengthened curriculum. Others, such as New Zealand and Norway, will launch their new ECEC curriculum frameworks in 2017.

Number of years of early childhood education and care and performance at age 15, by school socio-economic profile

Across OECD countries, 15-year-olds students attended, on average, three years of early childhood education (ISCED 0). However, this average time of early childhood education and care (ECEC) attendance masks wide variations between and within countries.

Whether and for how long students are enrolled in pre-primary education is an important aspect of the resources invested in education. Many of the inequalities observed in school systems are already present when children first enter formal schooling, and persist, and even widen, as they progress through education (Berlinski, Galiani and Gertler, 2009; Entwisle, Alexander and Olson, 1997; Mistry et al., 2010). Because research shows that inequalities tend to grow when children are not attending school (Downey, Von Hippel and Broh, 2004), earlier entry into formal childcare (ISCED 0) and other registered ECEC services may reduce inequalities in education. This will only be the case if disadvantaged children have the same chances as others to attend early childhood education, and if the learning opportunities across early childhood education are of high-quality and relatively homogeneous between ECEC settings.

Data from the Programme for International Student Assessment (PISA) 2015 relies on retrospective self-reporting from 15-year-olds (e.g. PISA students who entered ECEC 10-15 years ago, between 2000 and 2005). The PISA 2015 questionnaire found that across OECD countries, the average time spent in early childhood education (ISCED 0) by 15-year-old students was three years, but around 8% of 15-year-old students declared that they had not attended early childhood education at all, or that they were enrolled for less than one year. In contrast, 53% of 15-year-old students declared that they had attended early childhood education (ISCED 0) when they were younger for at least three years. Although most 15-year-old students in all education systems reported in 2015 that they had attended pre-primary education, in China (Beijing, Shanghai, Jiangsu, and Guangdong), Croatia, Lithuania, Montenegro and the United States, more than 17% of students – and in Turkey, almost half of students – reported that they had never attended early childhood education (Chapter 5). Among these countries, several have implemented policies during the last decade to improve access (see at the end of Chapter 4), suggesting that these high proportions will be smaller in the next PISA survey (OECD, 2016a).

Inequities in access to early childhood education (ISCED 0) persist in some countries. On average, student enrolled in socio-economically advantaged schools at age 15 had attended about four months more of early childhood education than students of the same age enrolled in disadvantaged schools.

PISA 2015 data show that across OECD countries, students enrolled at age 15 in socio-economically advantaged schools had spent four months more in early childhood education (ISCED 0) compared to students of the same age enrolled at age 15 in disadvantaged schools. This difference in time of exposure is particularly marked in China (Beijing, Shanghai, Jiangsu, and Guangdong), Croatia, Lithuania and Russia, where the difference is over one year. There is no country/economy where students enrolled in disadvantaged schools at age 15 had spent significantly more time in early childhood education compared to those enrolled in advantaged schools. However, students enrolled at age 15 in disadvantaged and advantaged schools show similar rates in Belgium, the Czech Republic, Germany, Hong Kong (China), Iceland, Italy, Japan, Korea, Macao (China), New Zealand, Switzerland and Chinese Taipei (Figure 4.1 and Table 4.1 on the web only).

Similar inequities exist when rural schools and urban schools, or public and private schools are compared, or when the comparison by socio-economic background is made at the level of students. Thus, across OECD countries, 15-year-old students in urban schools had spent two months more in early childhood education than students enrolled in rural schools, while 15-year-olds students enrolled in private schools had also spent two months more in early childhood education (ISCED 0) than students of the same age enrolled in public schools (OECD, 2016a: PISA 2015, Volume 2). Additionally, as shown in Figure 5.7, an average of 72% of disadvantaged compared to 82% of advantaged students at age 15 had attended early childhood education for at least two years (Table 4.1 on the web only).

Figure 4.1. Number of years 15-year-old students spent in early childhood education (ISCED 0), by school socio-economic profile (PISA 2015)

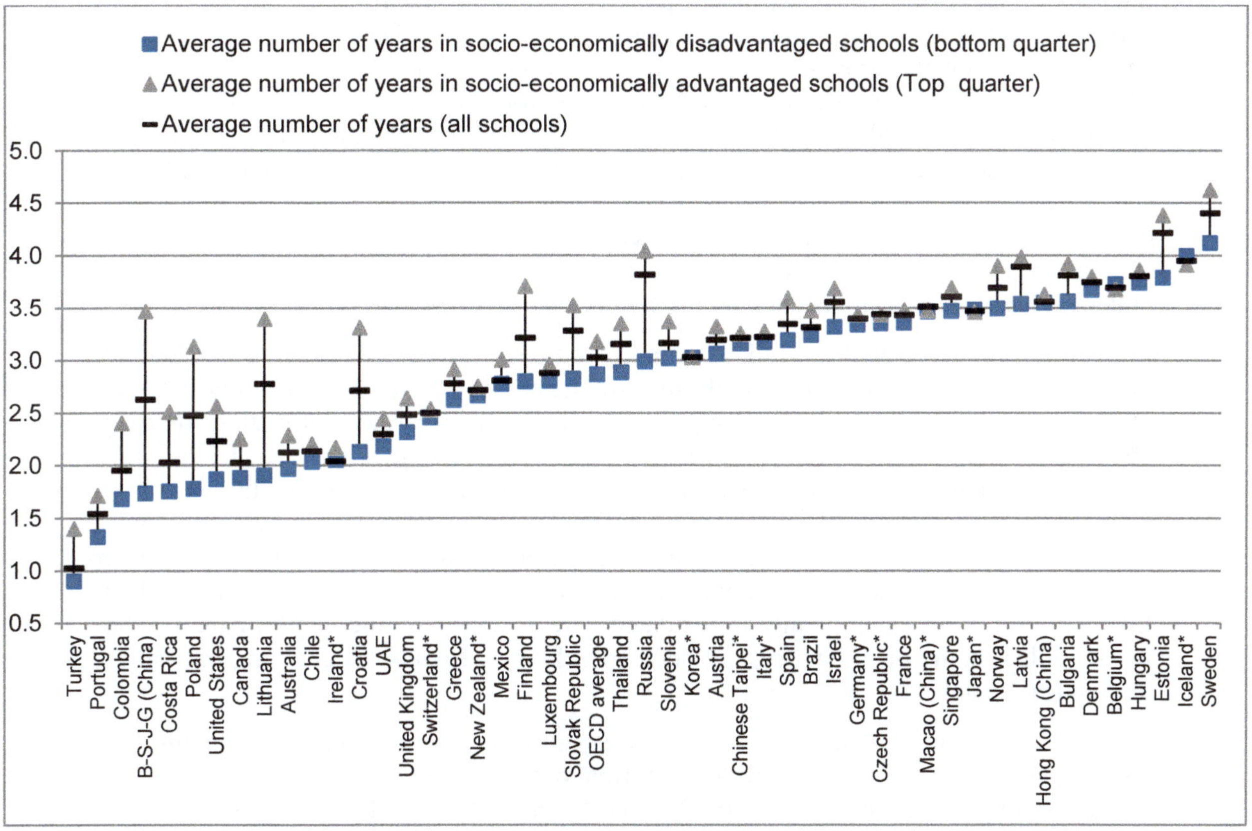

Notes: Countries where the difference between top and bottom quarters is not significant are marked with an "*".

Countries are ranked in descending order of the number of years in early childhood education (ISCED 0) among 15-year-olds pupils being enrolled at age 15 in socio-economically disadvantaged schools.

Source: OECD (2016a), PISA 2015 Results (Volume II): Policies and Practices for Successful Schools, PISA, OECD Publishing, Paris. http://dx.doi.org/10.1787/9789264267510-en.

StatLink http://dx.doi.org/10.1787/888933487434

Access and intensity of participation to early childhood education and care for younger children

On average, around one third of children under the age of 3 are enrolled in formal childcare (ISCED 0 and other registered ECEC services). However, this proportion hides wide variations across countries.

Early access to ECEC can play a significant role in the development of children. While primary and lower secondary enrolment patterns are similar throughout OECD countries, there is significant variation in ECEC among OECD and other G20 countries. This includes the overall level of participation in programmes, the number of hours in a usual ECEC week, the typical starting age for children, financing, programme length, and the type of settings providing ECEC services.

There is also a range of different approaches to identifying the boundary between early childhood education and childcare. Globally, ECEC settings can be classified in two categories: those in adherence with the criteria defined in the ISCED 2011 classification (adequate intentional educational or pedagogical properties delivered by qualified staff members that take place in an institutionalised setting and meet a minimum intensity/duration of at least two hours per day, a duration of at least 100 days a year, and are targeted at children from age 0 until entry into ISCED level 1), and the other ECEC arrangements providing care and education for children under compulsory school age (OECD/Eurostat/UNESCO Institute for Statistics, 2015: ISCED 2011 Operational Manual and Table 2.1*)*. However, as the ISCED 2011 classification has been newly introduced in international educational statistics (2015), the decision to allocate some ECEC programmes to the ISCED 01 category is still subject to discussion, especially in countries where younger children are typically under the authority of welfare and health authorities. The definition of formal childcare for children under the age of 3 used in this indicator is broader than the ISCED 2011 definition.

Formal childcare includes all early childhood education programmes covered by the ISCED 2011 classification, and all arrangements providing care only or care and education for children under compulsory school age, regardless of setting, funding, opening hours or programme content (see full classification in Table 2.1). This means that settings considered an integral part of countries' ECEC provision (e.g. registered settings), but not covered by the ISCED classification, still fall under the terminology of ECEC. Figure 4.2 and all the indicators showing enrolment under the age of 3 make the distinction between these two categories explicit. Informal care services (generally unregulated care arranged by the child's parent either in the child's home or elsewhere, provided by relatives, friends, neighbours, babysitters or nannies) do not enter this nomenclature.

Figure 4.2 shows that, on average across OECD countries, around one third of children under the age of 3 are enrolled in formal childcare (ISCED 0 and other registered ECEC settings outside ISCED 2011). Enrolment rates in formal childcare vary significantly across countries, ranging from less than 10% in the Czech Republic, Mexico and the Slovak Republic, to more than 50% in all Nordic countries, except Sweden, in "Benelux" OECD countries (Belgium, Luxembourg and the Netherlands) and in France (see Figure 4.2). Outside Europe, New Zealand (at 40%) has the highest enrolment rate in formal childcare among children under the age of 3 (Figure 4.2 and Table 4.2 on the web only). In a small number of OECD countries (Belgium, France, Italy, Luxembourg, Portugal), some 2-year-old children are already enrolled in pre-primary education

(ISCED 02). In all other countries, 2-year-old children are enrolled in early childhood development programmes (ISCED 01) or in other ECEC registered settings outside ISCED 2011. However, in integrated systems, children attending the same institutions, or even the same groups within an ECEC setting, are classified differently, but are exposed to the same programme/learning opportunities as those enrolled in pre-primary education at age 2 (Figure 4.2 and Table 2.1).

Figure 4.2. Enrolment rates of children under the age of 3 in formal childcare (ISCED 0 and other registered early childhood education and care settings outside ISCED 2011), 2005 and 2014

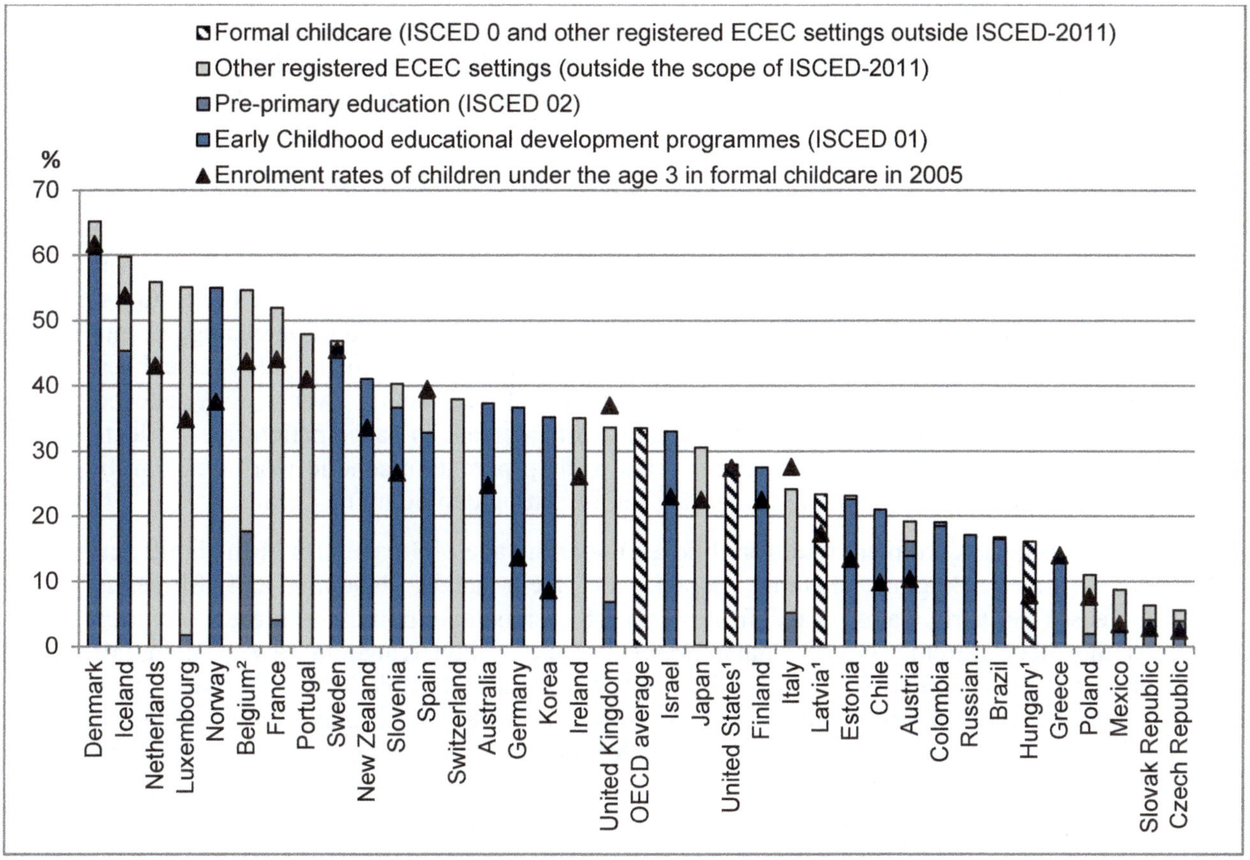

1. Data cannot be split between ISCED 01, ISCED 02 and other registered ECEC services.

2. Data for Flemish community on ISCED 01 were missing in 2014.

Note: Countries are ranked in descending order of the enrolment rates of children under the age of 3 in formal childcare in 2014.

Sources: OECD (2017a), OECD online education database, http://www.oecd.org/education/database.htm and OECD (2017b), OECD Family Database, OECD, Paris, http://www.oecd.org/els/family/database.htm and Table 4.2.

StatLink http://dx.doi.org/10.1787/888933487446

ECEC settings that enrol children under the age of 3 in OECD countries can also be organised differently. In some countries, such as Australia, Estonia, Finland, Germany, New Zealand, Norway, Slovenia and Sweden, the ECEC settings enrolling most children under and above the age of 3 are administered under the responsibility of one ministry, or have integrated curricula. In all these countries with integrated settings, except Germany, the Ministry of Education is in charge of the entire ECEC age group at the central level.

In other countries, such as Belgium, France, Israel, Italy, Luxembourg, the Netherlands, Portugal and Switzerland, ECEC settings that enrol children under the age of 3 are officially registered, but are provided in a distinct structure to what is provided for older children (consecutive model). These settings are not necessary in adherence with all ISCED criteria and are often under the authority of the Ministry of Social Affairs, while the settings providing ECEC for older children are under the authority of the Ministry of Education. In these countries, different standards are often set for different ECEC settings or for different age groups of children. In contrast, in the first group of countries, the same standards are applied to any ECEC setting.

Finally, some countries, such as Austria, Denmark, Iceland and the United Kingdom, have both systems, and families can choose between the integrated or the consecutive model. However, in all of these countries, the majority of children under 3 are enrolled in integrated settings (Figure 4.2 and Table 2.1).

The share of children under the age of 3 enrolled in ECEC settings is on the rise in most countries.

Across OECD countries, the share of children enrolled in ECEC services is on the rise, especially for children under the age of 3. On average across OECD countries, enrolment rates of children under the age of 3 increased by over eight percentage points between 2005 and 2014, from 26% to 34%. Increases in enrolment rates have been particularly pronounced in Germany, Korea and Luxembourg, where they exceed 20 percentage points (Figure 4.2). In Germany, this increase in participation rates reflects efforts the country has made in recent years to help parents reconcile work and family life, with the aim of boosting fertility rates and offsetting demographic ageing.

Increases in enrolment rates for children under the age of 3 have also been significant in Australia, Belgium, Estonia, Israel, the Netherlands, Norway and Slovenia. Increases in participation vary from 9 to 18 percentage points in these countries. At the other extreme, Greece, Italy, Spain and the United Kingdom saw a slight fall in enrolment rates between 2005 and 2014 (Figure 4.2 and Table 4.2 on the web only). Among these countries, Spain has recently implemented a plan, called Educa3, to increase the number of ECEC places for 0-3 year-olds and promote the quality of materials and workforce in ECEC (see more details in section "Recent initiatives to increase access and enhance quality to ECEC services").

This overall development over the last decade is partly supported by extended legal entitlements to a place in ECEC observed in several OECD countries, and efforts to ensure free access, at least for some ages and selected population groups. For instance, Belgium (Flemish community) recently prioritised its goal to increase the use of childcare by all children, including target groups, by making day care less expensive for parents through increasing the number of places with a means-tested fee. Other examples across OECD countries include Estonia, where the recent amendment to the Pre-school Act of 2000 (2010) (covering children from 1.5 to 7 years of age) introduced an obligation for local governments to provide childcare services where there is a shortage of places in municipal care centres. A legal right to a place in ECEC for each child over 1 came into force in 2009 in Norway, and in 2013 in Germany. Ireland implemented the National Childcare Investment Programme between 2006 and 2010 which aimed to create 50 000 new childcare places and help parents access affordable, quality childcare (see more details in section "Recent initiatives to increase access and enhance quality to ECEC services").

This move towards better provision in many European countries has also been the result of a further stimulus by the 2010 objectives set by the European Union (EU) at its Barcelona meeting in 2002, where one of the targets aimed to encourage EU member countries to supply subsidised full-day places for one-third of children under the age of 3. In 2014, about 14 EU and European Economic Area (EEA) countries – Belgium, Denmark, France, Germany, Iceland, Ireland, Luxembourg, the Netherlands, Norway, Portugal, Slovenia, Spain, Sweden and the United Kingdom – had reached the Barcelona targets for children under the age of 3, although at different levels of quality and different levels of intensity of participation (Figure 4.2).

When the enrolment rates of children under the age of 3 in formal childcare and intensity of participation during a usual week are analysed together, different patterns emerged, reflecting policy choices made by countries.

While participation rates by age provide a proxy of how long children are enrolled in ECEC over their childhood (in years), they do not provide any information about the intensity of participation in childcare services, i.e. whether children participate only for a few hours per day or full-time. The intensity of participation varies considerably across and within countries. Some countries offer a mix of part-time and full-time provision, understood as fewer than 30 hours per week versus 30 hours and more, with variations across countries and across different settings within countries.

Figure 4.3. Access to early childhood services versus intensity of participation (2014)

Enrolment rates in formal childcare (ISCED 0 and other registered ECEC settings outside ISCED 2011) of children under the age of 3, and intensity of participation in these services during a usual week

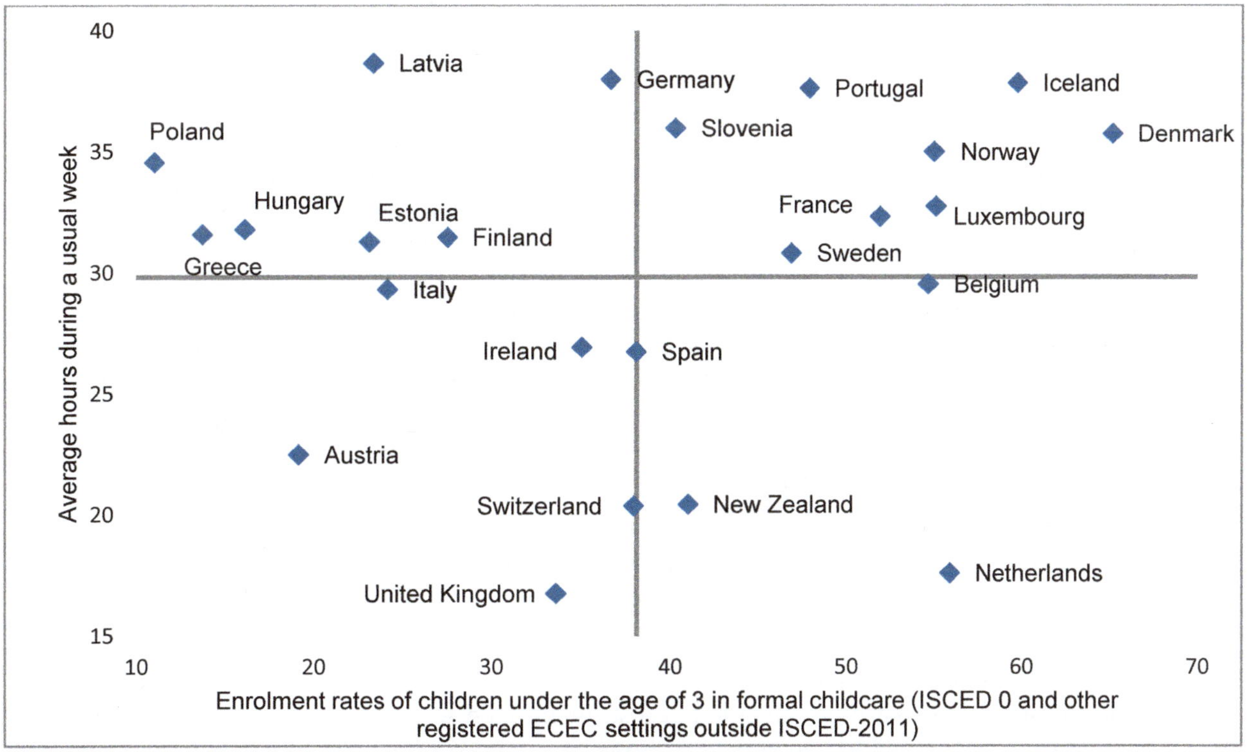

Sources: OECD (2017a), OECD online education database, www.oecd.org/education/database.htm and OECD (2017b), OECD Family Database, OECD, Paris, www.oecd.org/els/family/database.htm.

StatLink http://dx.doi.org/10.1787/888933487459

Child development research on the benefits of full-time compared to part-time programmes is less conclusive than evidence regarding the benefits of a longer period of participation. However, from a labour market perspective, the availability of full-day ECEC services is a crucial factor allowing parents of young children, especially mothers, to take up near full-time employment and secure higher earnings (OECD, 2012 and OECD, 2015b). On average, a child attended ECEC services for an average of 30 hours per week in 2014, which is equivalent to the 30 hours corresponding to full-time care. Figure 4.3 shows that part-time attendance for children under the age of 3 is widespread in countries such as Austria, Ireland, the Netherlands, New Zealand, Spain, Switzerland and the United Kingdom. However, in the remaining countries with available data, children under 3 years of age participated on average in ECEC for 30 hours per week or more (Figure 4.3 and OECD, 2017b).

When participation rates and average hours during a usual week are analysed together, different patterns emerge, reflecting policy choices made by countries. For example, ECEC settings in countries such as Estonia, Finland, Greece, Hungary, Latvia and Poland provide long hours per week to a small proportion of children under the age of 3. The opposite is observed in the Netherlands and New Zealand, where fewer hours per week are provided to an above-average proportion of children under the age of 3. Participation and intensity of participation are high in all Nordic countries, except Finland, and in France, Luxembourg, Slovenia and Portugal. In these countries, ECEC settings provide long average weekly hours to 40% or more of children under the age of 3. Austria, and to a lesser extent Ireland and the United Kingdom, are the only three countries with available data where participation rates and intensity of participation are both below the OECD average (Figure 4.3 and Table 4.2 on the web only).

Below-average enrolment rates of children under the age of 3 in formal childcare, or a low intensity of participation (in hours per week), imply greater participation in informal care (generally unregulated care arranged by the child's parent either in the child's home or elsewhere, provided by relatives, friends, neighbours, babysitters or nannies) in many countries. For example, more than 50% of children under the age of 3 are involved in informal childcare arrangements in Greece and the Netherlands (highest proportion among OECD countries with available data). Greece has one of the lowest participation rates in formal childcare, while the Netherlands is among the group of countries with the lowest intensity of participation in hours per week. However, exceptions exist, for example, Portugal cumulates high participation rates of children under the age of 3 in formal childcare and an intensity of participation above the OECD average, while more than 35% of children under the age of 3 benefit from informal childcare arrangements. Similarly, in 2014, the share of Finnish children using informal childcare arrangements was notably low (only 2% of children under the age of 3) despite low participation rates in formal childcare (OECD, 2017b).

The concept of services for children under the age of 3 is broadening in many countries from a labour market perspective to include quality objectives, especially in integrated systems.

Across countries and jurisdictions, enrolment rates in ECEC, especially for children under 3, are rising, but more attention is also being paid to the quality and educational content of care. A trend has emerged towards integrating services and ECEC governance across different age groups (see scoreboard in Chapter 1 and Chapter 2). In order to match progress towards access and enrolment targets with policies to ensure continuous and holistic child development, a growing number of OECD countries (or regional jurisdictions in federal systems) have started to refine the framework for early learning (e.g. curriculum and learning standards, administration and financing, staff qualifications, starting age of schooling). Learning frameworks and curricula increasingly include children from age 0 or 1 through to compulsory schooling. Moving beyond the simple insight that "ECEC matters", there is a growing recognition that the magnitude of the benefits of ECEC for children's future learning and cognitive and non-cognitive development depends on "quality". Furthermore, it is being acknowledged that many of the benefits may be lost unless the gains from quality ECEC are sustained by quality primary schooling, especially in the earliest years (OECD, 2015b).

Across OECD countries, this new understanding of young children can be seen in the national curricula of several countries, such as Australia, Chile, Finland, Germany, Ireland, Norway, Slovenia and Sweden, which make little distinction between the learning capacities of infants/toddlers and older children, and which consider that there is a need for care and well-being throughout education. In these countries, the issue of disturbing transitions from childcare to early education does not arise because a common curriculum across the age range 1-6 years is generally employed. For instance, in Australia, a nationally consistent system of quality rating and minimum standards, the National Quality Framework (NQF) for ECEC, aligns regulatory requirements for all ECEC services across the country and has been in use since 2012 in each state and territory. The National Quality Standard (NQS) is a key aspect of the NQF and sets a high national benchmark for ECEC and outside school hours care services in Australia (OECD, 2016c).

In contrast, discrepancies in goals and means can characterise the "childcare" and "early education" sectors in countries operating split or two-tiered early childhood systems, such as France, Italy, Luxembourg, the Netherlands, Portugal and Switzerland. The result can be a lack of coherence for children and families, with a confusing variation in objectives, funding streams, operational procedures, regulatory frameworks, staff training and qualifications. Initiatives to provide continuity when children move from the childcare sector into early education seem to be few, unless the ECEC sector has been integrated or a common pedagogical approach is used in both sectors. Among these countries, the situation in Italy is expected to change due to reform law 107/2015 (OECD, 2015b).

Access to early childhood education and care for older children

Enrolment rates in pre-primary education at age 3 have risen over the last decade in most OECD countries.

Enrolment rates in ECEC (ISCED 0) have also significantly increased for children aged 3 and above. As Figure 4.4 shows, the enrolment of 3-year-olds in pre-primary education increased by more than eight percentage points on average in the OECD between 2005 and 2014: from 62% in 2005 to 70% in 2014. Similarly, rates for 4-year-olds increased from 73% in 2005 to 85% in 2014.

Figure 4.4. Enrolment rates at age 3 in pre-primary education (2005 and 2014)

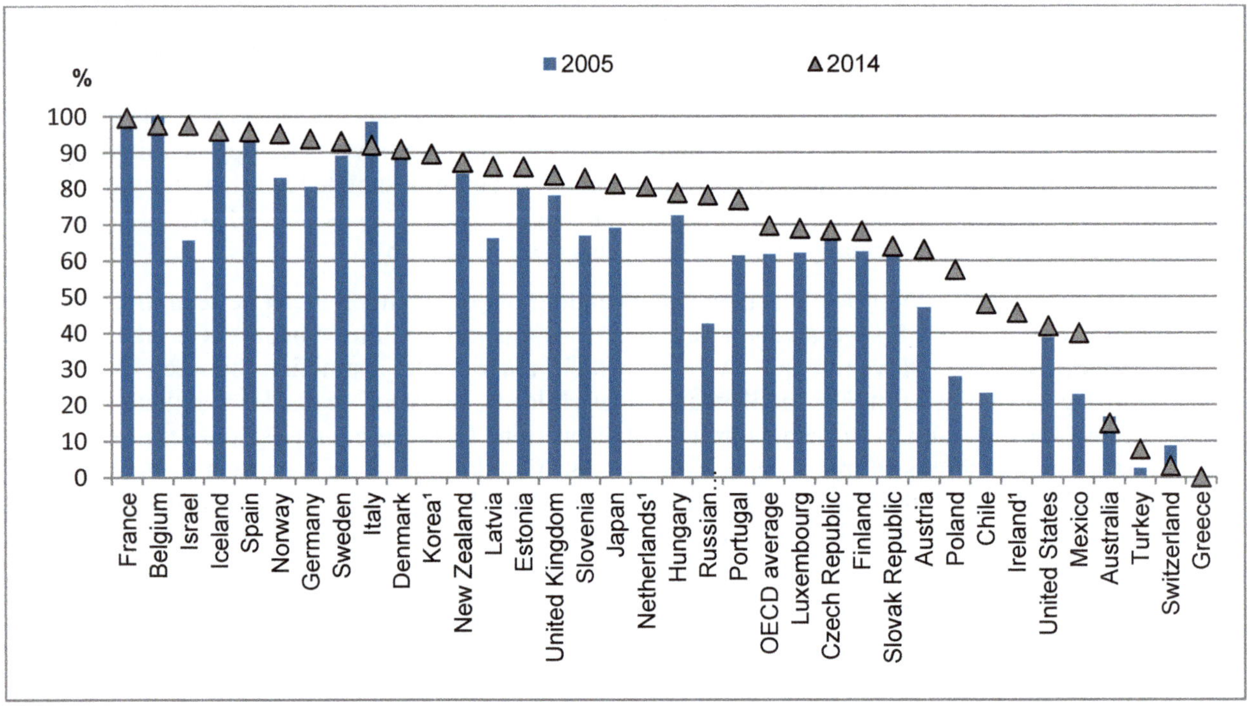

Note: Countries are ranked in descending order of the enrolment rates of 3-year-olds in pre-primary education (ISCED 02).

1. Data for reference year 2005 are missing.

Source: OECD (2016b), Education at a Glance 2016: OECD Indicators, Indicator C2, http://dx.doi.org/10.1787/eag-2016-en.

StatLink http://dx.doi.org/10.1787/888933487460

Increases in enrolment rates of 3-year-olds in pre-primary education exceeded 15 percentage points between 2005 and 2014 in a group of countries, including Austria, Chile, Israel, Latvia, Mexico, Poland, Portugal, the Russian Federation and Slovenia. Across OECD countries, the enrolment of 3-year-olds in pre-primary education ranged in 2014 from 20% or less in Australia, Greece, Switzerland and Turkey, to 95% or more in Belgium, France, Iceland, Norway and Spain (Figure 4.4). This data may even underestimate enrolments, as OECD countries might provide formal childcare beyond pre-primary education, or because some 4-year-olds are already enrolled in primary education. For instance, 54% of 3-year-olds are enrolled in early childhood development programmes (ISCED 01) in Australia, while 36% of 4-year-olds in Ireland are already enrolled in primary education (Figure 4.5 and OECD, 2016b)

Pre-primary education now begins for most children well before they are 5-years-old.

In the majority of OECD countries, most children enter pre-primary education well before the age of 5, and almost nine out of ten 4-year-olds are enrolled in pre-primary (or primary education) across OECD countries. In the OECD countries that are part of the European Union, 89% of 4-year-olds are enrolled at these levels. Additionally, 11 of the EU countries that are part of the OECD have already reached the target of the Education and Training 2020 strategy, which aims to ensure pre-primary education for at least 95% of children aged between 4 and the age of compulsory education. Overall, across OECD countries, enrolment rates of 4-year-olds in pre-primary and primary education vary from 95% or more in Belgium, Denmark, France, Germany, Israel, Italy, Japan, Luxembourg, the Netherlands, Norway, Spain, Sweden and the United Kingdom, to less than 60% in Greece, Switzerland and Turkey (Figure 4.5, Table 4.3 on the web only and OECD, 2016b).

Figure 4.5. Enrolment rates at age 3 and 4 in early childhood and primary education (2014)

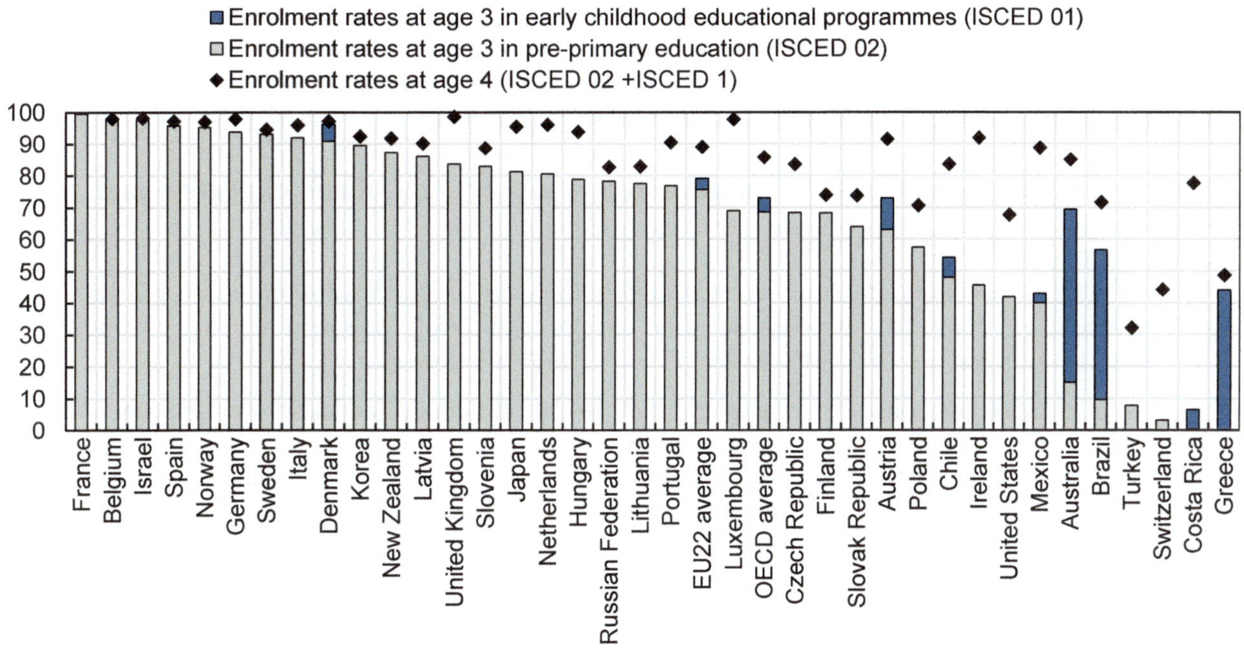

Note: Countries are ranked in descending order of the enrolment rates of 3-year-olds in pre-primary programmes.
Source: OECD (2016b), Education at a Glance 2016: OECD Indicators, Indicator C2, http://dx.doi.org/10.1787/eag-2016-en.

StatLink http://dx.doi.org/10.1787/888933487477

By 2014, 85% of 4-year-olds were enrolled in early childhood education, and 1% in primary education, while 81% of 5-year-olds were enrolled in early childhood education and 14% in primary education. This implies a trend toward universal ECEC (ISCED 0) in many countries, with 95% or more of 5-year-olds enrolled in France, Germany, Japan, the Netherlands and Norway, among others. In other countries, such as Australia, Ireland, New Zealand and the United Kingdom, 83 or more of children in this age group already attend primary school (OECD, 2016b). While the starting age of compulsory education is, on average, 6 years in the OECD, many countries use younger starting ages as a tool to ensure participation in education at an early age. For example, compulsory education starts at the age of 5 in the Netherlands, at age 4 in Luxembourg, and, since recently, at age 3 in Mexico (Figure 4.5 and Table 4.3 on the web only).

These trends are the results of policy initiatives across OECD countries that aim to increase access to ECEC services, as well as simultaneously improving the quality of early childhood education.

As illustrated at the end of this chapter, the heightened attention to the ECEC sector is not only motivated by concerns about parents' participation in the labour force, it is also increasingly justified by the important contribution that ECEC can make to children's development and educational progress. As a result, most recent reforms to improve access to ECEC services for children aged 3 and above, as well as for children under the age of 3, have often been accompanied by reforms to improve the quality of ECEC settings and to ensure consistency between the services offered to younger and older children. To respond to these challenges, expanding or consolidating the provision and quality delivery of ECEC are policy options that many countries are adopting. OECD countries have introduced comprehensive policies encompassing broad general strategies and structures, content-related policies that aim to strengthen the curriculum, and targeted policies that focus on the assessment of language development. Countries have also aimed to improve quality and access in ECEC through funding policies (see Box 3.1).

Proportion of children enrolled in public and private early childhood education and care settings

The proportion of children enrolled in private early childhood development settings (ISCED 01) is considerably larger than for pre-primary education (ISCED 02), and exceeds 50% in two thirds of OECD countries.

As countries continue to expand their early childhood education programmes, it will be important to consider parents' needs and expectations regarding accessibility, cost, programme and staff quality, and accountability. When parents' needs for quality, accessibility or accountability are not met in public institutions, some may be more inclined to send their children to private pre-primary institutions (Shin, Yung and Park, 2009).

When analysing private settings, a distinction needs to be made between government-dependent and independent private settings, according to the degree of dependence on government funding. Figure 4.6 includes three categories: 1) independent private ECEC settings controlled by a non-government organisation, or with a governing board not selected by a government agency, that receives less than 50% of core funding from government agencies: 2) government-dependent private ECEC settings controlled by a non-government organisation, or with a governing board not selected by a government agency, that receives more than 50% of core funding from government agencies; and 3) public ECEC settings controlled and managed by a public education authority or agency.

Figure 4.6 shows that not all privately managed ECEC settings are privately funded and generally more expensive than publicly managed settings, as often assumed. In Australia, Belgium, Chile, Korea and New Zealand, more than 50% of the child population attend pre-primary ECEC settings controlled by a non-government organisation, but largely funded by public money. In contrast, on average among OECD countries, only 10% of all children attended independent private ECEC settings in pre-primary education. This proportion exceeds 20% only in Brazil, Japan, the Netherlands, Italy and the United States.

The proportion of children enrolled in private early childhood educational settings (ISCED 01) is considerably larger than for pre-primary education (ISCED 02) in 15 out of 17 countries with available data for both levels. On average, 58% of children enrolled in early childhood development programmes (ISCED 01) attend private ECEC settings, and this percentage exceeds 50% in around two thirds of countries with available data on early childhood development programmes (ISCED 01). This can result in heavy financial burdens for parents, even when government subsidies are provided. On the other hand, in countries such as Finland, Iceland, Slovenia and Sweden, over 80% of children at this level are enrolled in public ECEC settings (OECD, 2016b).

The development of independent private settings can bring challenges, as well as benefits, for policy makers, as the leverage of public policy over unsubsidised private providers is limited for data collection and quality control. When the private market delivers a significant proportion of ECEC services, it helps provide access to ECEC services to an increasing number of children, but caution is needed for cases of "market failure" (OECD, 2006). Actions have been taken in some OECD countries through regulation, incentives and monitoring. For instance, to ensure an equal level of quality across public and government-dependent private settings in the Nordic countries, including Finland, Norway and Sweden, private providers must meet the same quality standards as publicly run institutions. The requirements are stated in the legislation and financing mechanisms.

Figure 4.6. Percentage of pupils enrolled in private settings in early childhood development and in pre-primary education (2014)

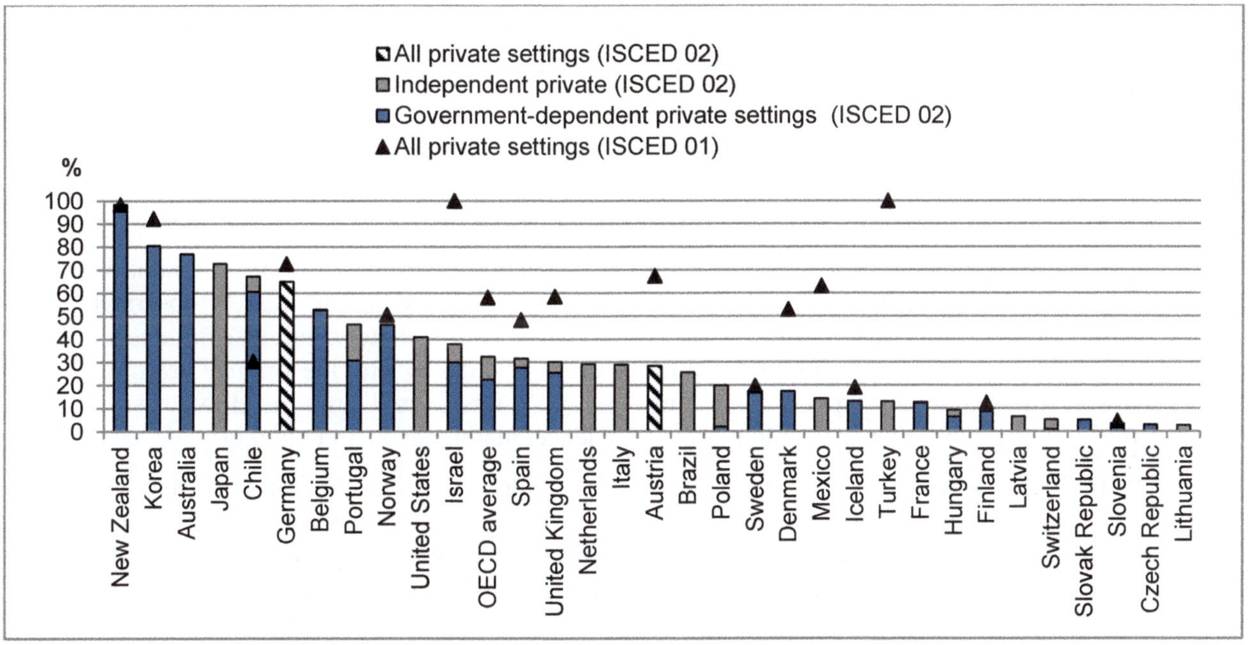

Note: Countries are ranked in descending order of the percentage of pupils enrolled in private settings in pre-primary education.

Source: OECD (2016b), Education at a Glance 2016: OECD Indicators, Indicator C2, http://dx.doi.org/10.1787/eag-2016-en.

StatLink http://dx.doi.org/10.1787/888933487485

Curriculum frameworks

Access is not a guarantee of high-quality ECEC. Curriculum frameworks can play a pivotal role in ensuring the quality of ECEC services.

The resources invested in education, the school environment and the overall quality of the teaching workforce are key determinants of quality, but are not the only variables that can influence the quality of learning. Curriculum frameworks can also play a pivotal role in ensuring the quality of ECEC services (Frede, 1998). Curriculum frameworks may ensure more consistent service provision within countries and jurisdictions, and establish common learning priorities and goals for educators and centres. It is crucial that curricula are well planned and co-ordinated (Bertrand, 2007; Ahtola et al., 2011), and that they reflect the visions and needs of all actors concerned by ECEC, including children (Bennett, 2011; Siraj-Blatchford and Woodhead, 2009).

Almost all OECD countries have some form of curriculum or framework in place - either in the form of a curriculum or learning standards - to guide ECEC staff and ensure an even level of quality across different settings. While the age groups covered may differ, curricula aligned with those of primary schooling or beyond also facilitate transition to the next level of education (Eurydice, 2009; Kagan and Kauerz., 2006). An aligned curriculum contributes to avoiding the fade-out effects of ECEC (Pianta et al., 2009).

Curriculum frameworks show that most countries and jurisdictions have created a learning framework for children in the older age bracket of ECEC: from around age 2.5/3 to compulsory schooling (see Chapter 4 in OECD, 2017b). Some countries have parallel frameworks for childcare (from age 0 to compulsory schooling) and for early education (from age 3 to compulsory schooling), such as Japan and Korea. Many countries aiming to deliver "integrated" services use a framework that covers age 0 or 1 to compulsory schooling (e.g. Australia, New Zealand, Nordic Countries, Slovenia and Prince Edward Island [Canada]).

In many countries, the curriculum framework in pre-primary education has been recently extended to enhance ECEC quality, and to ensure better transition between pre-primary and primary education.

According to a recent research, a balanced curriculum with roughly equal emphasis on play, self-regulation and pre-academic activities is related to the highest observed quality of staff-child interactions (Slot et al., 2016). Unfortunately, large-scale studies of ECEC suggest too few adults have the necessary skills to provide optimal learning support and emotional support for young children's intellectual growth (Howes et al., 2008), particularly in the curriculum areas of science, mathematics and numeracy.

In 2015, as in 2011, most of the 24 OECD countries and jurisdictions with data for both reference years still placed a high importance on arts, literacy, music, numeracy, physical education and science in their curriculum frameworks designed for pre-primary education. In contrast, practical skills were slightly less common content areas of the frameworks/guidelines in 2015 than in 2011, while the importance in the curriculum frameworks given by countries to social sciences significantly decreased between 2011 and 2015. No comparable data on "unguided playtime" were collected in 2011 and 2015. However, countries place importance on "unguided playtime" in 2015. In addition, as mentioned by several of them, this field is now being embedded into other content areas to stimulate learning through play (Figure 4.7; OECD, 2012 and OECD, 2017c).

As a result, some content areas (e.g. ICT, ethics and citizenship, foreign languages and, to a lesser extent, religion and health and well-being) have higher importance in the curriculum framework in 2015 compared to 2011.

A significantly higher proportion of respondent countries have included newly emerging subject matters in their pre-primary curriculum that respond to changing needs in present-day society, such as ICT skills, learning foreign languages, developing ethics and citizenship values, learning religion or ensuring health and well-being for children. The increase between 2011 and 2015 is particularly marked for ICT skills, with around

40% of respondent countries (Chile, Finland, Greece, Italy, Korea, Mexico, New Zealand, Norway, Portugal, Slovak Republic, Spain, Sweden, some provinces in Canada and some regions in Germany) citing ICT skills as a content area of their curriculum framework (OECD, 2017c). This result is not surprising, especially as an increasing number of countries have recently equipped their ECEC settings with IT tools. This digital trend was already observed a decade ago in the home environment. PISA 2015 data showed that a large majority of 15-year-old students, even among the most disadvantaged, had used computers before the age of 6 and were already familiar with IT tools when they began pre-primary education (ISCED 02).

Figure 4.7. Content areas included in early childhood education and care curriculum (2011 and 2015)

Proportion of countries and jurisdictions which declared in 2011 and 2015 that the following content areas are included in their ECEC curriculum framework

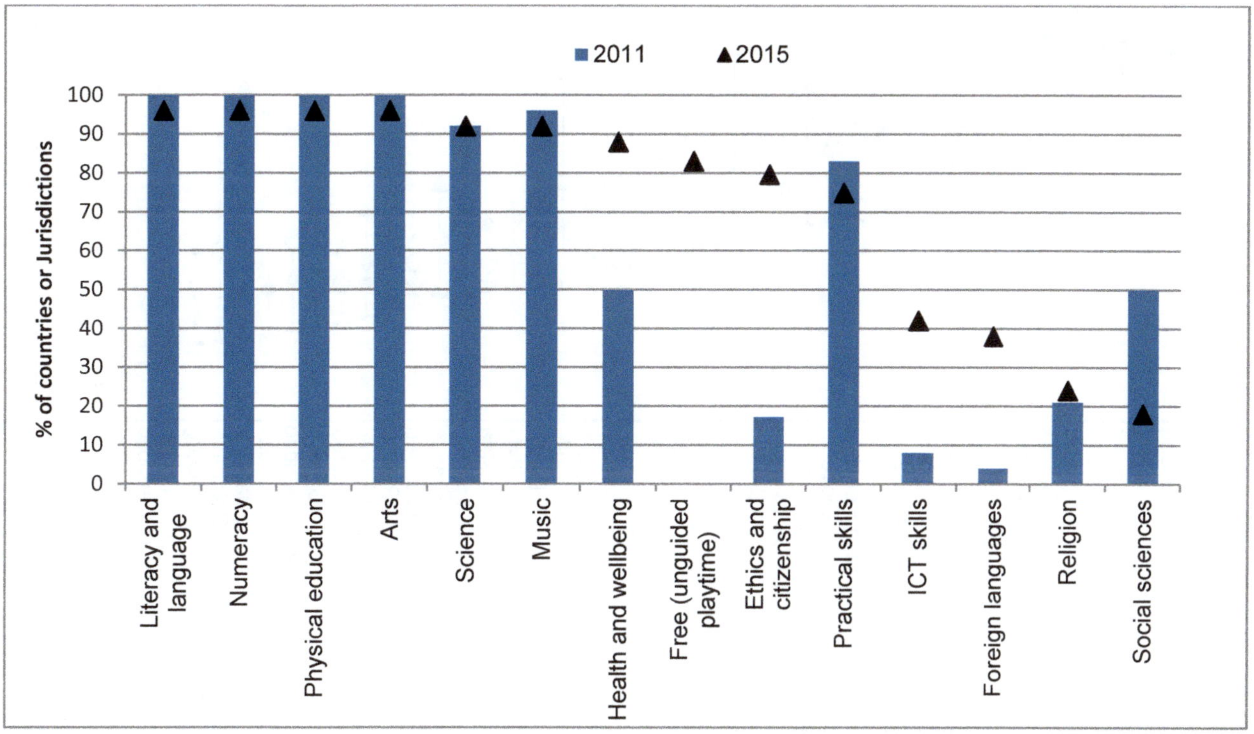

Notes: The figures are reported in percentage of total number of answers. The chart includes only the 24 countries and jurisdictions that participated in the survey in 2011 and 2015. Data on Free (unguided playtime) for 2011 are missing.

Countries are ranked in descending of order of the percentage of countries and jurisdictions declaring that the following content areas are included in their ECEC curriculum framework in 2015.

Sources: OECD (2017c), Starting Strong V, http://dx.doi.org/10.1787/9789264276253-en and OECD (2012), Starting Strong III: A quality toolbox for ECEC, http://dx.doi.org/10.1787/9789264123564-en.

StatLink http://dx.doi.org/10.1787/888933487492

Since, in many countries, the gap in access closed only recently, disadvantaged 15-year-old students may have less experience using computers than their more advantaged peers. On average across OECD countries, only 25% of disadvantaged 15-year-olds students assessed in the PISA 2015 survey had started using computers at the age of 6 or before (e.g. before 2005), compared to 38% of advantaged students. A significant difference between the two socio-economic groups is observed in all countries except Iceland; this is also where the largest proportion of disadvantaged students, almost one in two, started using a computer at pre-school age. Finland, Denmark, Sweden and Israel are the only other countries where more than 40% of students belonging to the lowest quarter of socio-economic started using computer at age 6 or before (Figure 4.8).

Figure 4.8. Early exposure to computers, by student socio-economic status (PISA 2015)

Percentage of 15-year-old students who first used a computer when they were 6 years or younger

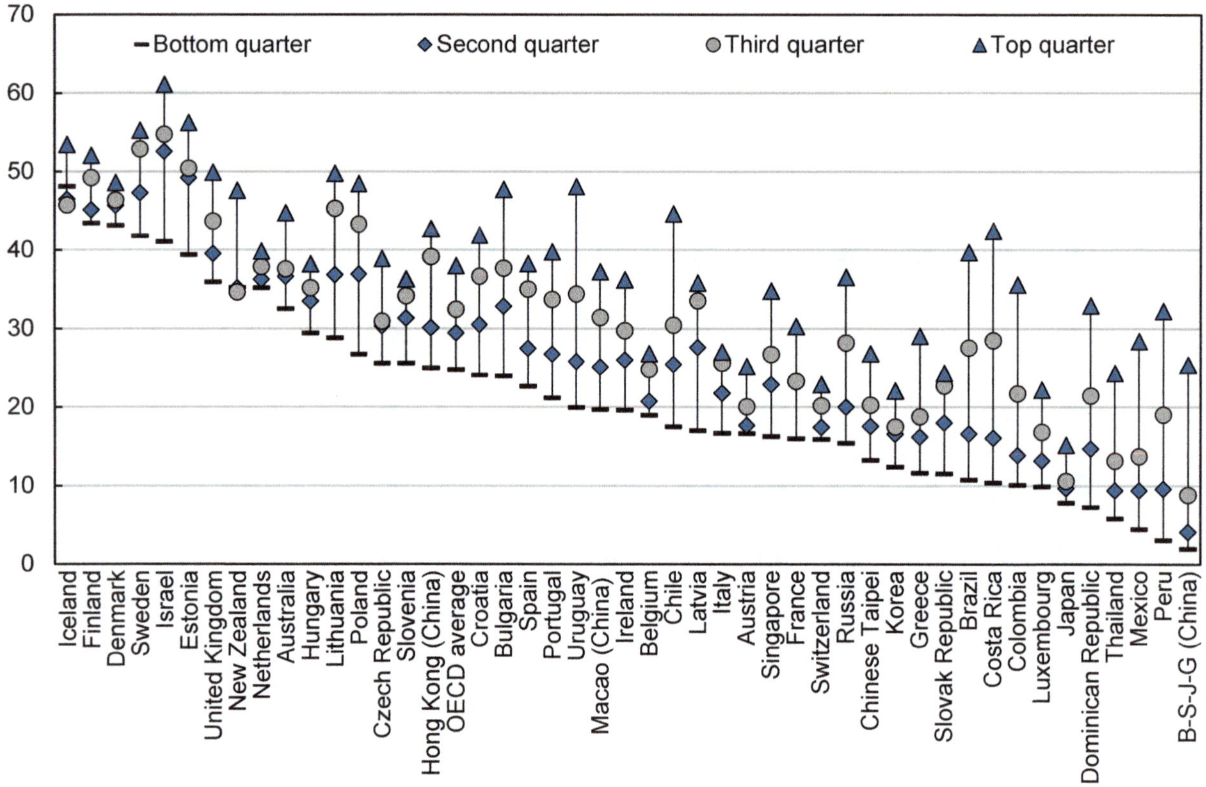

Notes: Differences between the top and the bottom quarter of the PISA Index of economic, social and cultural status (ESCS) are statistically significant in all countries and economies.

Countries and economies are ranked in descending order of the percentage of students in the bottom quarter of the PISA Index of economic, social and cultural status (ESCS) who first used a computer when they were 6 years or younger.

Source: OECD (2016a), PISA 2015 Results (Volume II): Policies and Practices for Successful Schools, PISA, OECD Publishing, Paris. http://dx.doi.org/10.1787/9789264267510-en.

StatLink http://dx.doi.org/10.1787/888933487507

As confirmation of the trends observed in Figure 4.7, the content of curriculum is still widely discussed across OECD countries. Some countries have introduced broad curriculum reforms that include ECEC. For example, Finland and Korea introduced curricula to strengthen the quality of provision, while Denmark is reflecting on how to enhance the quality of ECEC services through a strengthened curriculum. Some others, such as New Zealand and Norway, will launch their updated ECEC curriculum frameworks in 2017 (OECD, 2015a). Box 4.1 describes reforms of the content of curricula implemented in recent years.

Box 4.1. Reforms of the content of curricula implemented in recent years

Czech Republic: The Innovation of the Framework for Educational Programme of Pre-primary education was implemented in 2012.

Iceland: National curriculum guidelines for pre-primary were implemented in 2011.

Finland: A Core Curriculum for Pre-School Education (2000) was established from 2001, and renewed in 2010 with National Curriculum Guidelines on ECEC (2003, renewed in 2005) for the design of local curricula. In addition, legislation on early childhood education and the development of uniform pre-primary education instruction are in progress to ensure that all children have equal pre-requisites. Finland is currently developing a broader curriculum reform that includes pre-primary as well as primary and secondary education.

Italy: The National Curriculum for ECEC was revised in 2012 and included implementation of the European Framework of key competencies for lifelong learning.

Japan: Japan revised its National Curriculum of Day Care Centre Works in March 2008, clarifying the enhancement of staff quality and the expertise of all staff.

Korea: In 2012, Korea introduced the Nuri Curriculum, an integrated curriculum for early childhood kindergarten and nursery centres for 3-5 year-olds. It aims to promote the holistic development of children and establish overarching principles for becoming responsible citizens through the provision of key objectives and with financial support for tuition for all children, regardless of household income.

Mexico: Recent efforts to improve quality and coverage in ECEC include the creation of a framework syllabus to help ECEC institutions develop a curriculum that meets their specific needs.

New Zealand: The early childhood curriculum, Te Whāriki, has been updated to reflect changes in early learning contexts, theory and pedagogy since its original publication in 1996. Its original aspiration for children and bicultural framing have been retained and strengthened through the publication of two pathways – one for early childhood education services and one for kōhanga reo (an indigenous Māori curriculum model). Te Whāriki (2017) will be implemented from 2017 onwards.

Norway: Norway is in the process of revising the Framework Plan for the Content and Tasks of Kindergartens. It will be implemented in August 2017.

Sweden: Improved curriculum for pre-primary education implemented in 2011.

Recent initiatives to increase access and enhance quality to early childhood education and care services

For the past two decades, many countries have taken initiatives to increase access to ECEC services, especially for disadvantaged children (OECD, 2015a). These initiatives are often associated with other reforms aimed at improving the quality of ECEC settings and are the following:

- **Australia:** The participation of 3-4 year-olds in pre-primary education (ISCED 02) is close to the OECD average. Participation rates at age 4 have risen dramatically since 2005, from 53% in 2005, to 85% in 2014, representing the fourth highest increase in the OECD. To strengthen performance and support disadvantaged and indigenous populations, Australia has developed a number of strategies, including the National Partnership Agreement on Universal Access to Early Childhood Education, which aims to maintain universal access to quality early childhood education programmes for all children in the year before full-time school for 600 hours per year, delivered by a qualified early childhood teacher who meets National Quality Framework requirements.

- **Brazil:** Enrolment rates in ECEC are below the OECD average for ages 3 to 5. However, recent initiatives have been implemented. The Constitutional Amendment No. 59 (2009) increased the duration of compulsory education from 9 to 14 years (4-17 year-olds), and Law No. 12 796 (April 2013) made the enrolment of 4-year-olds in ECEC compulsory. All states and municipalities had until 2016 to comply with these policies. The programme Brazil Carinhoso (2012) provides financial incentives to municipalities and the Federal District to increase the number of places for disadvantaged children from 0-48 months in public or government-dependent day care centres. The second phase of the National Programme for the Restructuring and Acquisition of Equipment for the Public Early Education School Network began in 2011 to improve access to ECEC through investment in infrastructure and equipment.

- **Canada:** Access to ECEC in Canada varies depending on the jurisdiction. Enrolment rates in ECEC meet the OECD average at age 5. In 2016, the Government of Canada started to develop, with provinces and territories, a new Early Learning and Child Care Framework as a first step towards delivering affordable, high-quality, flexible and fully inclusive child care. In 2014, the Council of Ministers of Education, Canada (CMEC), through its CMEC Early Childhood Learning and Development Working Group, released the CMEC Early Learning and Development Framework. The framework presents a pan-Canadian vision for early learning to be adapted to the needs of each province and territory. It is designed to serve as a resource to support the development of policies and initiatives by ministries and departments of education and their partners to enhance the quality and continuity of the learning experience in the early years and beyond. Through intergovernmental agreements, the Government of Canada supports the work of provinces and territories to improve outcomes for indigenous populations and official-language minorities through the provision of programmes and subsidies to support learning environments.

- **Chile:** Enrolment rates in ECEC are significantly below the average at age 3, but only slightly below at ages 4 and 5. To strengthen performance and support disadvantaged pupils, a financial incentive, the *Ley de Subvención Escolar Preferencial*, 2008 (Law on Preferential Subsidies) was introduced. It increases funding for schools that serve disadvantaged pupils from early childhood through secondary education, while offering more support to these pupils and their schools. Pre-primary education is offered through a mix of public and government-subsidised private providers; quality assurance mechanisms are new and still in a pilot phase. Improvement in both access and quality of pre-primary education will promote the system's long-term performance and equity.

- **Denmark:** Enrolment rates in ECEC are high compared to the OECD average. In Denmark, children have guaranteed access to day care, as local councils must ensure the necessary number of places for children in their municipality. An assessment of language development (2010) was introduced for 3-year-olds to diagnose possible language problems before they start school. The assessment only applies if staff finds that the child is lagging behind in language development. If needed, children can receive support through additional language stimulation in their day care facility. Children not enrolled in an early childhood education and care programme, but who need support can also receive help, and parents are required by law to accept the offer. Early childhood education and care institutions are financed by local authorities through subsidies received from the central government.

- **Estonia:** The recent amendment to the Pre-school Act of 2000 (2010) (covering children from 1.5 to 7 years of age) introduces an obligation for local governments to provide childcare services where there is a shortage of places in municipal care centres.

- **Finland:** Enrolment in ECEC is comparatively high at age 2 compared to the OECD average, but enrolment rates at age 3, 4 and 5 are lower than the OECD average. However, the government target is to ensure that all children participate in pre-primary education, including children living in remote areas and children with an immigrant background. ECEC has been the object of different reforms. The administration and steering of ECEC services were transferred from the Ministry of Social Affairs and Health to the Ministry of Education and Culture in 2013.

- **France:** Enrolment rates in ECEC are above the OECD average. However, efforts related to pre-primary education are being pursued. An objective of the 2013 reform seeks to mobilise the different actors involved in education, social and family policies at local levels to increase the numbers of children under 3 attending quality early childhood education, especially in disadvantaged areas.

- **Germany**: Participation in ECEC is above the OECD average. Children aged 3-6 have been entitled to a place in ECEC since 1999, and since August 2013, parents have a right to a place in ECEC from their child's first birthday. This has already led to increased ECEC provision by local authorities, which are responsible for planning and implementing ECEC services at the local level, and are also responsible for the major part of the funding of these services. To boost the number of ECEC places, the federal government provided an extra budget to support the regions and local authorities, which also indicated a policy shift. The increase in participation rates (from 28% in 2012 to 33% in 2016) reflects the efforts Germany has made in recent years to help parents reconcile work and family life, with the aim of boosting fertility rates and offsetting demographic ageing.

- **Hungary:** Participation in ECEC is relatively high compared to the OECD average, especially at age 4. The government's updated Decree on the Basic National Programme of Kindergarten Education (363/2012(XII.17) came into force in 2013, outlining the principles and tasks of kindergarten education. Starting in 2015, participation in ECEC became mandatory from age 3, with minimum attendance of four hours per day.

- **Iceland:** has broad participation in ECEC, with pre-primary education that usually starts at age 2 and almost universal enrolment of 3-4 year-olds. Public pre-schools are open to all children, with priority access for children with disabilities or children whose parents are single or studying. Children with special educational needs enrol in the same education programme as other children, but it is adapted to their abilities. Public pre-schools charge fees to all pupils, accounting for about 30% of their operating costs. In private pre-schools, fees are usually 10%-20% higher than the fees of public schools.

- **Ireland:** Enrolment in ECEC is comparatively low at age 3 compared to the OECD average, but enrolment rates at age 4 and 5 are higher than the OECD average. The policy implemented in Ireland aims to improve performance as a priority. To respond to the challenge of improving the performance of Irish children, especially in disadvantaged communities, in 2005 the responsible government department (then called Education and Science) developed Delivering Equality of Opportunity in Schools (DEIS) as an ongoing national policy for educational inclusion. The plan consists of a standardised system to identify a school's level of socio-economic disadvantage (based on its community) and an integrated School Support Programme that provides schools and school clusters or communities with additional resources and support, depending on the level of disadvantage. The strategy aims to raise literacy and numeracy standards for pupils by: helping parents and communities to support their children, supporting teachers and early childhood education staff during pre-service and in-service education, building the skills of school leaders, setting goals and monitoring progress, clarifying curricular expectations of pupils at each level of education, and targeting learners who need additional resources the most.

- **Israel:** Enrolment in ECEC is high compared to the OECD average. Free access to ECEC has been extended to ages 3-4, and recently become compulsory from age 3. Access to education has been increased by introducing free early childhood education from age 3 to age 4 (2012/13) to ease the cost of living for young parents and allow them to actively participate in the labour market.

- **Italy:** In order to increase the ECEC participation of children under the age of 3, law 107/2015 made provision for an integrated ECEC system for children aged 0-6, under the responsibility of the Ministry of Education. Currently, further legislation is being issued to implement the new system.

- **Japan:** Japan has high enrolment rates in ECEC compared to the OECD average, mainly in private institutions. The Second Basic Plan for the Promotion of Education (2013-17) stipulates the introduction of free-of-charge and universal ECEC for all children. The Japanese government also developed the Japan Revitalisation Strategy (revised in 2014) – Japan's challenge for the future. One of the key elements of this strategy is to promote the more active participation of women in society and economic life, and to increase women's employment rate from 70% in 2013 to 73% by 2020. These policies include adding 600 000 available places in ECEC and reducing the number of children on waiting lists by the end of 2017, and increasing the benefits women can receive during childcare leave to pay 67% of their salary for six months.

- **Korea:** Coverage of ECEC is very high in Korea, and there are several policies in place to promote equity in education, most notably in the early years. In addition to the after-school childcare available to all 3-5 year-olds, the Nuri curriculum (integrated curriculum at early childhood education and nursery) has extended its daily programme time to a maximum of five hours, and the government is also providing support for additional tuition.

- **Mexico:** Enrolment in ECEC is comparatively low compared to the OECD average. To increase participation in ECEC, Mexico made pre-school education compulsory in 2002, with implementation in three different phases from 2004 to 2009. Efforts to improve quality and coverage in ECEC include the creation of care centres in urban areas for children of low-income working parents (2007), and the organisation of a national system of day care centres to enhance the quality of day care. In 2008/09, the first year of pre-school (3-4 year-olds) was made compulsory. The major positive effect has been increased enrolment rates of 4-5 year-olds.

- **New Zealand:** Enrolment in ECEC is relatively high compared to the OECD average. The government's Better Public Services programme (2011) presented ten public sector commitments to achieve within three to five years, including one related to ECEC education: by 2016, 98% of children starting school will have participated in quality early childhood education.

- **Norway:** Enrolment in ECEC is high compared to the OECD average. The Kindergarten Agreement (*Barnehageforliket*) in 2003 increased accessibility to kindergarten by providing new places, setting maximum fees for parents, and funding public and private kindergartens. Between 2004 and 2012, the participation of 1-5 year-olds increased significantly. The reform also included the revision of the Kindergarten Act in 2005, and a revised Framework for the Content and Tasks of Kindergartens in 2006. A national strategy for raising the competence of staff (2007-10) and a strategy for the recruitment of kindergarten teachers (2007-11) were also implemented. With the kindergarten reform, formal education and care has replaced informal care, even for children under 3. The number of minority-language children in ECEC has also doubled. There is a new, ongoing strategy for competence enhancement for kindergarten staff (2014-2020), and a revised Framework Plan will be introduced in 2017.

- **Poland:** Enrolment in ECEC in Poland is comparatively low compared to the OECD average. Since 2011, Poland has experienced the biggest progress in participation in ECEC. For rural areas, there has been an increase of nearly 23%. Despite growth in the number of childcare institutions and the number of children enrolled, the demand for places is still greater than the supply, particularly in rural areas. In 2014, Poland introduced compulsory foreign language instruction in pre-primary education for all 5-year-olds. Early childhood education became compulsory for 5-year-olds in 2011, although this changed to 6-year-olds in September 2016. Parliament amended the School Education Act (*Ustawa o systemie oświaty, 2013*) to provide the right to participate in pre-primary education for all 4-year-olds starting in September 2015, and in September 2017, places in early childhood education became a legal entitlement for 3-year-olds. The Ministry of Labour and Social Policy developed a nationwide *Maluch* (toddler) programme to increase the number of ECEC places for children under the age of 3.

- **The Slovak Republic:** Enrolment in ECEC is comparatively low compared to the OECD average. Evidence shows that only 28% of Roma children were enrolled in pre-primary education in 2011. The Slovak Republic has taken actions to improve access to ECEC, with a focus on expanding kindergarten capacity in high demand areas, supporting the participation of disadvantaged children, and providing childcare in the workplace. The Strategy of the Slovak Republic for Roma Integration by 2020 also aims to improve the position of vulnerable Roma communities in coming years. This support is financed from the state budget and European Union structural funds. In 2015, municipalities with the highest demand for ECEC could apply for financial support to expand their pre-school capacity (total budget allocation of EUR 15 million from the state budget). In the first round, the Ministry of Education, Science, Research and Sport will support the creation of 3 600 new ECEC places in 113 municipalities. Due to the high number of applicants, the government intends to allocate additional resources to satisfy the remaining demand.

The EU and the Slovak Government are co-financing inclusive education in kindergartens in 82 municipalities to increase the participation in ECEC of disadvantaged children, including Roma children. Additional national projects focus on raising awareness of the importance of ECEC among Roma parents, developing and implementing an inclusive kindergarten curriculum, training ECEC teachers to work with Roma children, hiring teaching assistants, and preventing the unjustified placement of Roma children in special schools.

- **Slovenia**: Enrolment rates in ECEC are above the OECD average. Nevertheless, to improve access to ECEC, the Kindergarten Act (2008) and the Exercise of Rights to Public Funds Act (2012) provide grants to parents with two or more children enrolled in pre-school education. While the supply of kindergarten institutions is increasing, according to a report by the European Commission, local authorities cannot always satisfy the demand for places for younger children in urban and suburban areas.
- **Spain** has recently implemented a plan, called Educa3, to increase the number of ECEC places for 0-3 year-olds, and promote the quality of materials and workforce in ECEC.
- **Sweden:** With the aim of giving all children the same opportunity to take part in pre-school, Sweden has taken measures to make pre-school affordable and accessible to everyone through its maximum fee policy. ECEC institutions are financed by local authorities and through subsidies received from the central government. The policy states that parents should only have to spend 1-3% of the family's income on childcare (i.e. pre-school, pedagogical care and leisure time centre), depending on how many children they have, with a discount for siblings (maximum 3% for first child, maximum 2% for second child, and maximum 1% for third child). From the autumn term when the child reaches the age of 3, and up to the time when school starts, there is a right to 525 hours free of charge per year. The fee covers most activities, including food. This means childcare costs for families in Sweden are a fraction of those in other nations. Fees make up about 8% of the total costs of a place in pre-school. Pre-school shall be granted to all children above the age of 1, to the extent that is needed regarding parents' work or studies, or to the need of the child itself. Children whose parents are unemployed

or on parental leave with a younger sibling are entitled to at least 15 hours/week (or 3 hours/day) in pre-school.

- **Turkey:** Enrolment in ECEC is comparatively low compared to the OECD average. In Turkey, most women with at least one child between 3 and 5 years-old do not participate in the labour market. ECEC initiatives to increase participation include the Tenth Development Plan (2014-18), the Mobile Classroom for children 36-66 months from low-income families, and the Summer Pre-school for Children 60-66 months. The United Nations Children's Fund (UNICEF) supported the Turkey Country Programme (2006-07) and the Pre-School Education Project (2010-13). To strengthen parent co-operation, the Childhood Development and Education Project and the pilot Pre-primary Parent-Child Education Programme Project (1999-2012) were implemented.
- **United Kingdom (England):** Enrolment in ECEC is comparatively low at age 2 compared to the OECD average, but enrolment rates at age 3 and 4 are higher than the OECD average. In England, all 3-4 year-olds continue to be entitled to 15 hours of free early childhood education a week for 38 weeks of the year. This entitlement has been extended to disadvantaged 2-year-olds (around 20% of 2-year-olds in 2013, and a total of around 40% in 2014). The objective was to increase access for children from working parents and disadvantaged children (30 hours per week, with additional GBP 50 million of support stipulated by the childcare bill).

References

Ahtola, A., et al. (2011), "Transition to formal schooling: Do transition practices matter for academic performance?", *Early Childhood Research Quarterly*, Vol. 26/3, pp. 295-302.

Bennett, J. (2011), "Introduction: Early Childhood Education and Care", *Encyclopedia on Early Childhood Development*, Centre of Excellence for Early Childhood Development and Strategic Knowledge Cluster on Early Child Development, Montreal, www.child-encyclopedia.com/pages/PDF/BennettANGxp.pdf.

Berlinski, S., S. Galiani and P. Gertler (2009), "The effect of pre-primary education on primary school, performance", *Journal of Public Economics*, Vol. 93/1, pp. 219-234, www.sciencedirect.com/science/article/pii/S0047-2727(08)00130-8.

Bertrand, J. (2007), "Preschool Programs: Effective Curriculum. Comments on Kagan and Kauerz and on Schweinhart", *Encyclopedia on Early Childhood Development*, Centre of Excellence for Early Childhood Development and Strategic Knowledge Cluster on Early Child Development, Montreal, www.child-encyclopedia.com/documents/BertrandANGxp.pdf.

Downey, D., P. Von Hippel and B. Broh (2004), "Are schools the great equalizer? Cognitive inequality over the summer months and the school year", *American Sociological Review*, Vol. 69/5, pp. 613-635, www.jstor.org/stable/3593031.

Entwisle, D., K. Alexander and L. Olson (1997), *Children, Schools and Inequality*, Westview Press, Boulder, CO.

Eurydice (2009), *Early Childhood Education and Care in Europe: Tackling Social and Cultural Inequalities*, Eurydice, Brussels.

Frede, E.C. (1998), "Preschool program quality in programs for children in poverty", in Barnett, W. S. and S. S. Boocock (eds.), *Early Care and Education for Children in Poverty: Promises, Programs, and Long-term Outcomes*, Buffalo, NY: SUNY Press, pp. 77-98.

Howes, C., et al. (2008), "Ready to learn? Children's pre-academic achievement in pre-kindergarten programs", *Early Childhood Research Quarterly,* Vol. 23, pp. 27-50, http://dx.doi.org/10.1016/j.ecresq.2007.05.002.

Kagan, S. and K. Kauerz (2006), "Preschool Programs: Effective Curricula", *Encyclopedia on Early Childhood Development, Centre of Excellence for Early Childhood Development and Strategic Knowledge Cluster on Early Child Development*, Montreal, www.child-encyclopedia.com/documents/Kagan-KauerzANGxp.pdf.

Mistry, R.S. et al. (2010), "Family and social risk, and parental investments during the early childhood years as predictors of low-income children's school readiness outcomes", *Early Childhood Research Quarterly*, Vol. 25/4, pp. 432-449, http://dx.doi.org/10.1016/j.ecresq.2010.01.002.

OECD (2017a), OECD online education database, www.oecd.org/education/database.htm.

OECD (2017ba), *OECD Family Database*, OECD, Paris, www.oecd.org/els/family/database.htm.

OECD (2017c), *Starting Strong V: Transitions from Early Childhood to Primary Education*, http://dx.doi.org/10.1787/9789264276253-en

OECD (2016a), *PISA 2015 Results (Volume II): Policies and Practices for Successful Schools*, PISA, OECD Publishing, Paris, http://dx.doi.org/10.1787/9789264267510-en.

OECD (2016b), *Education at a Glance 2016: OECD Indicators*, OECD Publishing, Paris, http://dx.doi.org/10.1787/eag-2016-en.

OECD (2016c), *Starting Strong IV: Country notes for Australia on monitoring Quality in Early Childhood Education and Care (ECEC)*, www.oecd.org/edu/school/Monitoring-Quality-in-ECEC-Australia.pdf.

OECD (2015a), OECD Education Policy Outlook 2015: Making Reforms Happen: OECD Publishing, Paris, http://dx.doi.org/10.1787/9789264225442-en.

OECD (2015b), *Starting Strong IV: Monitoring Quality in Early Childhood Education and Care (ECEC)*, OECD Publishing, Paris, http://dx.doi.org/10.1787/9789264233515-en.

OECD (2012), *Starting Strong III: A quality toolbox for Early Childhood Education and Care*, OECD Publishing, Paris, http://dx.doi.org/10.1787/9789264123564-en.

OECD (2006), *Starting Strong II: Early Childhood Education and Care*, OECD Publishing, Paris, http://dx.doi.org/10.1787/9789264035461-en.

OECD/Eurostat/UNESCO Institute for Statistics (2015), *ISCED 2011 Operational Manual: Guidelines for Classifying National Education Programmes and Related Qualifications*, OECD Publishing, Paris, http://dx.doi.org/10.1787/9789264228368-en.

Pianta, R.C. et al. (2009), "The Effects of Preschool Education: What We Know, How Public Policy Is or Is Not Aligned With the Evidence Base, and What We Need to Know", *Psychological Science in the Public Interest*, Vol.10/2, pp.49-88.

Shin, E., M. Jung and E. Park (2009), *A Survey on the Development of the Pre-school Free Service Model*, Research Report of the Korean Educational Development Institute, Seoul.

Siraj-Blatchford, I. and M. Woodhead (2009), "Effective Early Childhood Programmes", *Early Childhood in Focus 4*, Open University, United Kingdom.

Slot, P., et al. (2016), *Multiple case study in seven European countries regarding culture-sensitive classroom quality assessment*, WP2.3 Curriculum and quality analysis impact review CARE, http://ecec-care.org/fileadmin/careproject/Publications/reports/CARE_WP2_D2_3_Multiple_Case_study_FINAL_REPORT.pdf.

Tables of Chapter 4

StatLink http://dx.doi.org/10.1787/9789264276116-en

WEB Table 4.1 (Web only). Number of years 15-year-old students spent in early childhood education (ISCED 0), science performance and school characteristics (PISA 2015).

WEB Table 4.2 (Web only). Enrolment rates in formal childcare (ISCED 0 and other registered early childhood education and care settings outside ISCED 2011) of children under the age of 3, and intensity of participation in these services during a usual week (2014).

WEB Table 4.3 (Web only). Enrolment in early childhood education and primary education at ages 3, 4 and 5 (2014).

Chapter 5.

Policy outcomes of early childhood education and care: Performance at age 15, impact for disadvantaged children, effect on health and well-being, and mother employability

The brain sensitivity of highly important developmental areas, such as emotional control, social skills, language and numeracy, peak in the first three years of a child's life. Therefore, high-quality early childhood education and care (ECEC) can result in better outcomes in subsequent stages of life. For instance, the number of years spent in ECEC is a strong predictor of level of performance in and out of schools reached at later stages. In the same vein, children with an immigrant background and more globally disadvantaged children can benefit the most of attending high-quality ECEC. However, the benefits of ECEC attendance are not limited to learning outcomes. Early childhood education is also an important period for forming healthy behaviours and affordable and high-quality ECEC with an adequate number of hours per week can contribute to an increase in the participation of women in the labour force. This chapter includes indicators on the outcomes of children that are associated with both policy inputs and policy outputs. For example, it will include indicators on student performance, health, well-being and labour market outcomes.

The statistical data for Israel are supplied by and are under the responsibility of the relevant Israeli authorities. The use of such data by the OECD is without prejudice to the status of the Golan Heights, East Jerusalem and Israeli settlements in the West Bank under the terms of international law.

Key messages

The number of years spent in early childhood education and care (ISCED 0) is a strong predictor of the level of performance reached at later stages, both in and out of school

Research tells us that:

- Research in neurosciences has shown that the brain sensitivity of highly important developmental areas, such as emotional control, social skills, language and numeracy, peak in the first three years of a child's life.
- High-quality ECEC can result in better outcomes in subsequent stages of life. Children learn more quickly during their early years than at any other time in life. Children who are already falling behind in the first few years of their childhood face greater obstacles to catch up and succeed at school and beyond.
- Research shows that disadvantaged children can benefit the most from attending high-quality early childhood education. Later interventions are less efficient because they take place after children's "development window". Disadvantaged children have the greatest benefit from attending high-quality ECEC, and interventions targeted at them will have the highest returns.
- Research highlights a need for more analysis and international comparative indicators on the short-term and long-term effects of ECEC on child well-being, development and learning. Therefore, the OECD programme of work over the period 2017-2020 includes a series of projects to address this issue.

International comparisons reveal some clear trends:

- PISA 2015 data relies on retrospective self-reporting from 15-year-olds (e.g. PISA students who were in ECEC 10-15 years ago, between 2000 and 2005), however, these data show, as in previous editions of PISA, that in practically all OECD countries, 15-year-old students in 2015 who had attended ECEC settings outperformed students who had not.
- PISA data suggest that two years of early childhood education is the minimum duration needed to have a good chance of reaching a good level of performance at age 15.
- Children who attended early childhood education for at least two years perform, on average, better than others at age 15. After accounting for student socio-economic status, the difference is still statistically significant in half of the 57 countries with available data.
- The more years spent in early childhood education, the lower the chances of being among the low performers in the PISA assessment. Thus, 22% of students who attended early childhood education for less than a year performed, on average, below the baseline proficiency level in science (below level 2 on the PISA scale). In contrast, only 10% of students who attended early childhood education for more than two years scored below this level.
- PISA 2015 finds that the relationship between attending pre-primary school and better student performance at age 15 is strongest in school systems that offer pre-primary education to a larger proportion of the student population over

a longer period of time, that have smaller child-to-teacher ratios in pre-primary education, and that invest more per child at the pre-primary level of education. However, among all these variables, the strongest predictor of low or good performance at age 15 is the duration of ECEC.

- PISA 2015 data confirms that inequities persist in many countries. For instance, in 2015, an average of 72% of disadvantaged 15-year-old students and 82% of advantaged students had attended ECEC for at least two years.
- Participation in at least one year of early childhood education is beneficial for children with an immigrant background.

Early childhood education is an important period for forming healthy behaviours

Research tells us that:

- The ECEC environment provides opportunities to ensure that children understand the importance of good nutrition and physical activity, and can benefit from both. Studies show that locally focussed actions and interventions, especially those targeted at the youngest, can be effective in changing behaviours and decreasing the odds of, for example, being overweight during adolescence.

International comparisons reveal some clear trends:

- The higher the enrolment rates in formal childcare for children under the age of 3 in 2005, the lower the proportion of boys and girls who were overweight or obese at age 11 in 2014. This correlation is stronger for boys than for girls, and shows that early interventions by qualified staff can contribute to forming healthy behaviours.
- However, the potential causal nature of the link between education and health is still subject to a certain degree of scrutiny, and these data should be interpreted with caution as the conditions in which education and health are correlated are not yet fully understood.

Affordable and high-quality ECEC with an adequate number of hours per week can contribute to the increased participation of women in the labour force.

Research tells us that:

- Child development research on the benefits of full-time compared to part-time programmes is less conclusive than evidence regarding the benefits of a longer period of participation. However, from a labour market perspective, the availability of full-day ECEC services is a crucial factor that enables parents of young children, especially mothers, to take up near full-time employment and secure higher earnings.

International comparisons reveal some clear trends:

- Affordable and high-quality ECEC with an adequate number of hours per week can contribute to the increased participation of women in the labour force. In 2014, on average across OECD countries, 53% of mothers with their youngest child under the age of 3 were employed, while around 34% of children under the age of 3 were enrolled in formal childcare.

- In countries where the labour market participation rates for mothers are the highest, such as Denmark, Luxembourg, the Netherlands, Portugal, Slovenia and Switzerland (above 70% employment among women aged 15 to 64 with at least one child under the age of 3), the proportions of young children enrolled in formal childcare are also the highest.
- The usual number of hours per week that children under the age of 3 are enrolled in formal childcare is highly correlated with part-time employment among women with at least one child aged 0-14.
- In some countries (e.g. Latvia, Portugal and Slovenia), the average number of hours in formal childcare is over 35 hours during a usual week, and part-time employment is below 10% among women aged 15 to 64 with their youngest child aged 0-14. At the other extreme, in Austria, the Netherlands and the United Kingdom, children under the age of 3 spend, on average, 22 hours or less in formal childcare during a usual week, while more than 25% of women with at least one child aged 0-14 are employed part-time.

Number of years of early childhood education and care and performance at age 15

The first years of a child's life are crucial for their later development and learning.

Research in neurosciences has shown that the brain sensitivity of highly important developmental areas, such as emotional control, social skills, language and numeracy, peak in the first three years of a child's life (Gambaro et al., 2014, Naudeau, S, N. Kataoka, A. Valerio, M. J. Neuman, and L. K. Elder, 2011). These findings indicate that the first years of a child's life represent a pivotal "development window": the brain first develops rapidly, and its capacity to adapt and develop continues into adulthood, but it slows down with age. The first years are important for the development of skills as they lay the foundations for future skill development (OECD, 2015a and 2015b).

Figure 5.1. Sensitive periods in early brain development (2010)

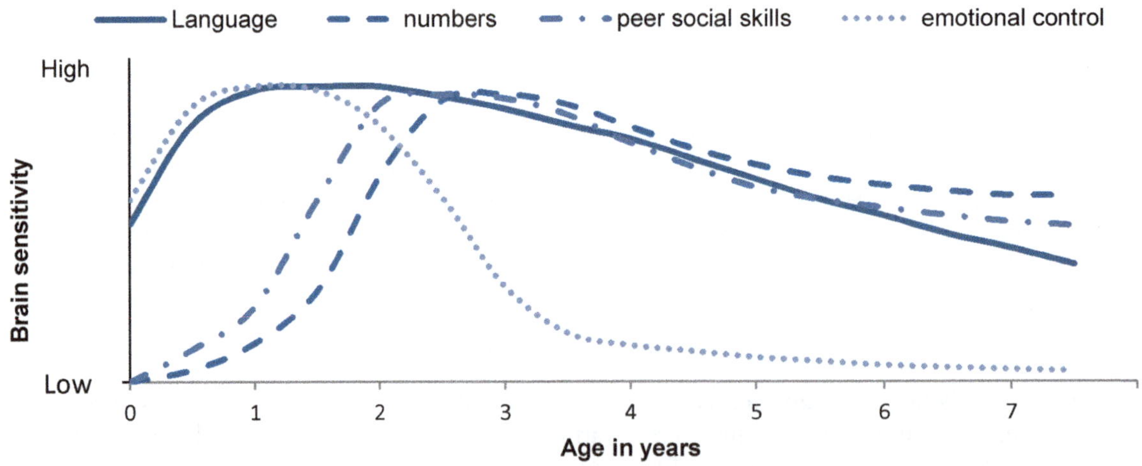

Sources: Adapted from Council for Early Childhood Development, (2010), in Naudeau S. et al. (2011). OECD (2015b), Starting Strong IV: Monitoring Quality in Early Childhood Education and Care (ECEC), http://dx.doi.org/10.1787/9789264233515-en.

StatLink http://dx.doi.org/10.1787/888933487519

The “peaks” of brain sensitivity may vary across functions/skills (Council Early Child Development, 2010). For example, brain sensitivity to the development of emotional control starts from the middle level, increases to the high level from birth to around age 1, and declines to the low level, where it stays from age 4. Peer social skills start with the low level, increase rapidly from ages 1-2, gradually decrease and remain at a medium level from age 4. Similarly, language development starts at the middle level, increases to the high level at around ages 1-2, slightly decreases towards age 4, and will continue to decrease towards the middle and low levels from then on. Numeracy starts with the low level, increases rapidly from ages 1-3, gradually decreases but will be maintained at the high level from age 4 (Figure 5.1 and OECD, 2015b).

Children learn more quickly during their early years than at any other time in life. Children who are already falling behind in the first few years of their childhood face greater obstacles to catch up and succeed at school and beyond (Naudeau et al., 2011; OECD, 2016a). Participation in early childhood education is crucial. The positive effects of participation in early childhood education include improved child well-being and early learning outcomes as a foundation for lifelong learning (OECD, 2012), as well as later student outcomes ranging from education, employment, income, health and other areas (Melhuish et al., 2014).

Data from the Programme for International Student Assessment (PISA) 2015 show a strong relationship between the number of years that 15-year-old students spent in early childhood education and their scores on the PISA science assessment.

PISA 2015 data relies on retrospective self-reporting from 15-year-olds (e.g. PISA students who were in early childhood education and care (ECEC) 10-15 years ago, between 2000 and 2005). The OECD’s PISA 2015 results, as with previous PISA editions, show that on average across OECD countries 15-year-old pupils who had attended at least one year of pre-primary school outperformed pupils who had not, at least before accounting for student and school-level socio-economic status. For instance, the difference between students who had attended more than one year of early childhood education (ISCED 0) and those who had attended one year or less of early childhood education averaged 41 score points in the PISA 2015 science assessment, with one year of formal schooling equivalent to around 30 score points.

The performance gap reduces but remains significant when comparing students from similar backgrounds. After accounting for student and school-level socio-economic status, students who had attended early childhood education for one year or more scored an average of 25 points higher in the PISA science assessment compared to those who had not. However, there are limits to the interpretation of this finding, as the proportion of those who had attended less than one year of early childhood education (ISCED 0) represents on average across OECD countries of only 8% of all 15-year-olds, and is relatively low in several OECD countries (Tables 5.1 and 5.2 on the web only).

Figure 5.2. Average score-point difference in science performance across OECD countries, by number of years spent in early childhood education (ISCED 0) by 15 year-olds pupils (PISA 2015)

Comparison made with all 15-year-olds in OECD countries having attended early childhood education for 3 years or more (e.g. >3), before and after accounting for student and school-level socio-economic status

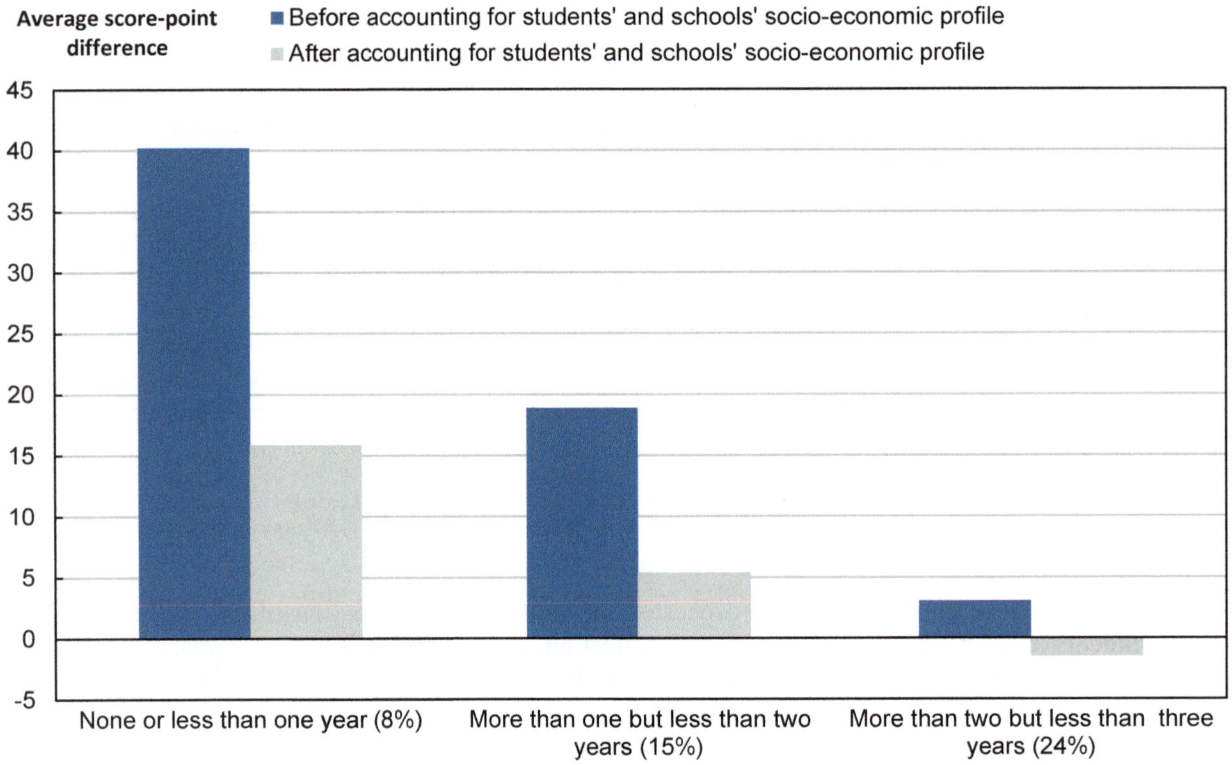

Notes: **How to read this chart?** For instance, before accounting for student and school-level socio-economic status, students who had attended early childhood education for three years or more scored an average of 40 points higher in the PISA science assessment compared to those who had attended ECEC for less than one year. The difference is still significant at 16 points after accounting for student and school-level socio-economic status.

On average among 15-year-old students who remember about early childhood education (ISCED 0), 53% of them had attended early childhood education for at least three years. The percentages of 15-year-olds who attended early childhood education (ISCED 0) in each of the other categories are added into brackets next to each category.

Source: OECD (2017a), PISA online education database, OECD, Paris, www.oecd.org/pisa/data/.

StatLink http://dx.doi.org/10.1787/888933487525

The improved PISA performance of 15-year-olds who had spent more time in ECEC is confirmed when increased duration of ECEC attendance and higher proportions of 15-year-olds are taken into account in the analyses. Figure 5.2 confirms a strong relationship between the number of years that 15-year-old students spent in early childhood education and the scores achieved on the PISA science assessment. The positive effect of ECEC attendance on performance in science at age 15 is not limited to those who benefited from more than one year of early childhood education over those who had not. In fact, 15-year-old students who had attended more than one year and less than two years of ECEC (e.g. >=1 and <2) scored an average of 21 points higher compared to those who attended less than one year (e.g. < 1), and 10 points higher after accounting for socio-economic background. This positive effect is observed in more than 80% of OECD countries with available data.

Similarly, 15-year-old students who attended more than two years and less than three years of ECEC (e.g. >=2 and <3) scored, on average, 16 points higher than those who attended more than one year and less than two years (e.g. >=1 and <2), and 7 points more after accounting for socio-economic background. This significant effect is observed in around two thirds of OECD countries. In contrast, the same statistically significant positive effect disappears when the comparison is made between 15-year-old students who had attended early childhood education for three years or more (e.g. >3) and those who had attended early childhood education for more than two years and less than three years (e.g. >=2 and <3). In this case, the difference is statistically non-significant in most countries after accounting for socio-economic status, suggesting that two years of early childhood education is the minimum duration needed to have a good chance to reach a good level of performance at age 15 (Table 5.1 on the web only, Figure 5.2). For this reason, the next sections will compare 15-year-old students who attended early childhood education (ISCED 0) for at least two years with other students.

Children who attended early childhood education for at least two years perform, on average, better than others at age 15. After accounting for the students' socio-economic status, the difference is still statistically significant in half of the 57 countries with available data.

Figure 5.3 shows the advantage in science performance among 15-year-olds who reported having attended early childhood education for at least two years or more compared to others, both before and after accounting for students' socio-economic status. On average across countries, students who had attended early childhood education for two years or more outperformed students who had attended early childhood education for less than two years in 47 out of the 57 countries with available data. After accounting for socio-economic status, this finding remains statistically significant in around half of the 57 countries with available data for both categories (Table 5.1 on the web only, Figure 5.3).

On average across OECD countries, the advantage amounts to more than 26 score points before accounting for student and school-level socio-economic status, and 15 points after accounting for socio-economic status (i.e. half a year of formal schooling). After accounting for socio-economic status, the score differences between students who had attended early childhood education for less than two years and those who had attended for two years or more are largest (i.e. at least 30 score points) in Belgium, China (Beijing, Shanghai, Jiangsu, and Guangdong), France, Germany, Hong Kong-China, Hungary, Israel, Italy, Luxembourg, Macao (China), Spain, Sweden and Singapore (Figure 5.3).

Figure 5.3. Score-point difference in science performance between 15-year-old students who attended early childhood education (ISCED 0) for two years or more and those who attended for less than two years (PISA 2015)

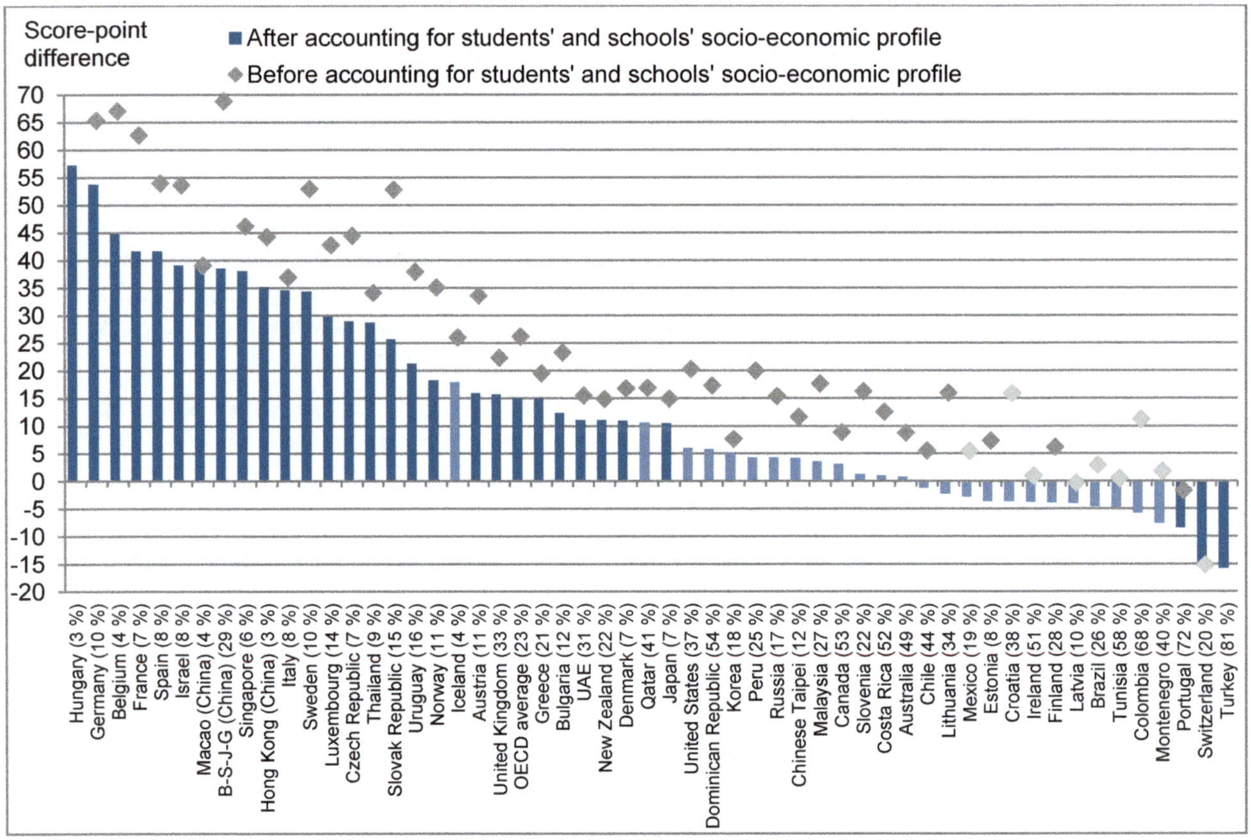

Notes: Score-point differences that are statistically significant are marked in a darker tone. The percentage of 15-year-old students who attended early childhood education (ISCED 0) for less than two years are added into brackets next to the country's name.

Countries and economies are ranked in descending order of the score-point difference in science performance between 15-year-olds who reported that they had attended early childhood education (ISCED 0) for two years or more and others, after accounting for socio-economic status.

Source: OECD (2016a), PISA 2015 Results (Volume II): Policies and Practices for Successful Schools, PISA, OECD Publishing, Paris, http://dx.doi.org/10.1787/9789264267510-en.

StatLink http://dx.doi.org/10.1787/888933487530

The more years spent in early childhood education, the lower the chance of being among the low performers in the PISA assessment.

In PISA 2015, low performers are 15-year-olds students performing below Level 2 on the assessment. Low performers may be able to use basic or everyday scientific knowledge to recognise or identify aspects of familiar or simple scientific phenomena. However, they also often confuse key features of a scientific investigation, apply incorrect scientific information and mix personal beliefs with scientific facts in support of a decision.

PISA 2015 shows that, on average across OECD countries, the more years that 15-year-old students spent in ECEC (ISCED 0), the lower their chances of being low performers. Thus, 22% of students who had attended early childhood education for less than a year performed, on average across OECD countries, below the baseline proficiency level in science (below Level 2 on the PISA scale) and are considered low performers (Figure 5.4). By comparison, 14% of 15-year-old students who had attended early childhood education for more than one year but less than two years were classified as low performers; while only 10% of students who had attended early childhood education for more than two years but less than three years scored below Level 2 on the PISA proficiency scale. When the last category is compared to students who have attended more than three years of early childhood education, the difference becomes non-significant in most countries: on average, 9.5% of students who had attended early childhood education for more than three years scored below Level 2 on the PISA proficiency scale (similar to the category "more than 2 and less than 3").

Figure 5.4. Proportion of low performers among 15-year-old students according to the number of years spent in early childhood education (PISA 2015)

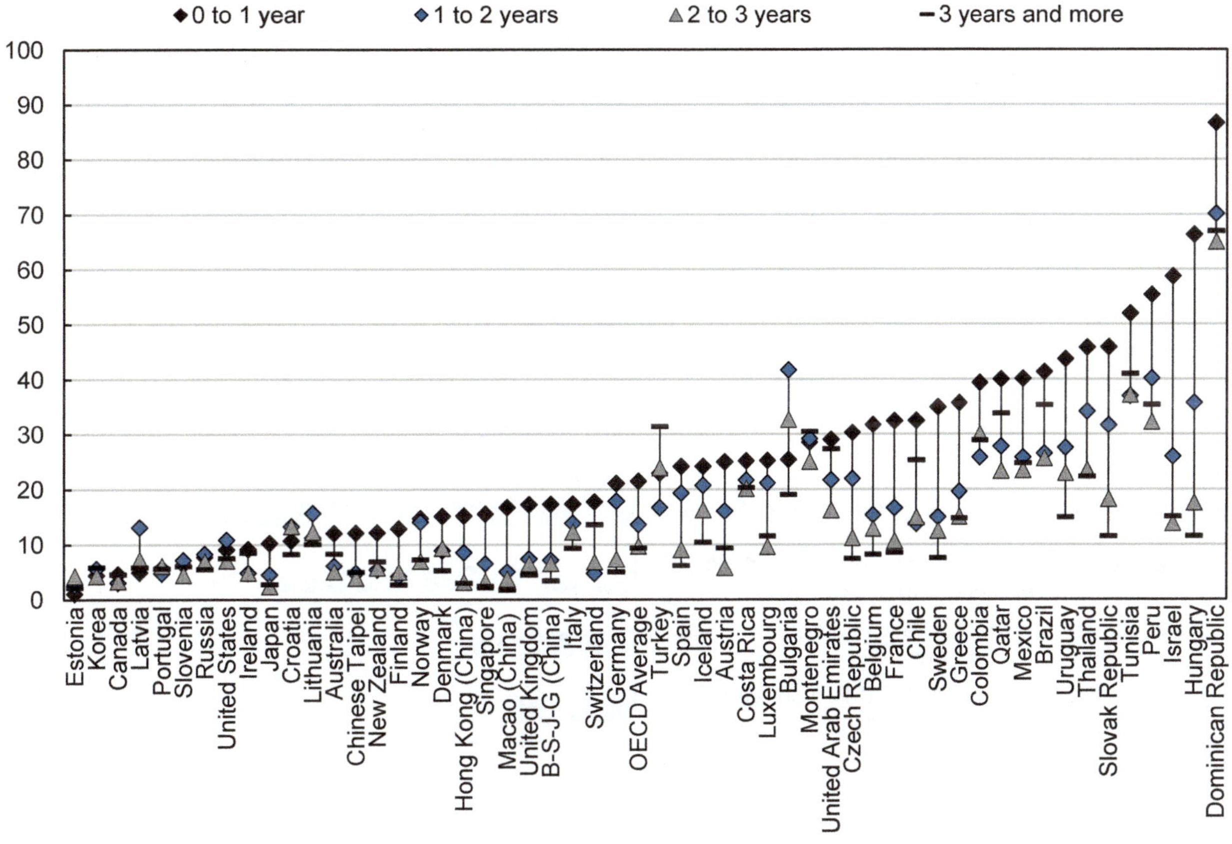

Note: Countries and economies are ranked in ascending order of the percentage of low-performing students who had not attended early childhood education (ISCED 0) or attended for "less than one year".

Source: OECD (2017a), PISA online education database, OECD, Paris, www.oecd.org/pisa/data/.

StatLink http://dx.doi.org/10.1787/888933487540

When the two extremes are compared, the difference in the share of low performers between 15-year-olds students with less than one year of early childhood education and those with three years or more is significant in most countries, and exceeds

20 percentage points in Belgium, the Czech Republic, France, Greece, Hungary, the Slovak Republic, Sweden, Thailand and Uruguay (Figure 5.4, Table 5.4 on the web only). The proportion of low performers (below Level 2) in science is small for all 15-year-old students in a small group of countries, independently of the number of years they spent in early childhood education. This is the case in Estonia, Korea, Portugal and Slovenia (left side of Figure 5.4). These four countries are recognised as being among the group of PISA countries that succeeded in making progress over the last decade in terms of performance and equity.

On average, a 15-year-old student who attended early childhood education (ISCED 0) for less than one year is 3.1 times more likely than a student who attended for one year or more to perform below the baseline level of proficiency in science (e.g. below Level 2), before accounting for student and school-level socio-economic status; and more than twice as likely (2.3 times) after accounting for socio-economic status. Across OECD countries, the odds of low performance are five times or higher in Hungary, Israel and the Slovak Republic (Table 5.4 on the web only).

The degree to which attending pre-primary school is associated with learning outcomes at age 15 also relates to how pre-primary education is provided.

Evidence of the importance of early childhood education for early childhood development and later education outcomes is convincing (e.g. Berlinski, Galiani and Gertler, 2009; Barnett, 1995; Currie, 2001), but the extent of its benefits heavily depends on the quality of ECEC services.

Figure 5.5. Structural early childhood education and care inputs improve student performance at 15-years-old (PISA 2015)

Average score point advantage associated with attending pre-primary education in school systems that:

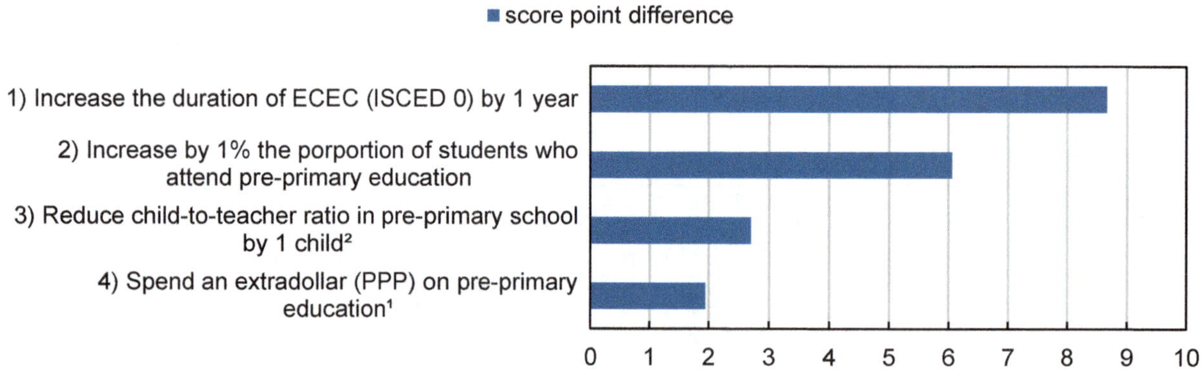

Notes: The score point difference above are statistically significant.

Series are ranked by descending "effect size".

1. Data on expenditure per child enrolled in pre-primary education are from 2013.

2. Data for child-to-teacher ratios in pre-primary education are from 2014.

Sources: OECD (2017a), PISA online education database, OECD, Paris, www.oecd.org/pisa/data/ and OECD (2016b), Education at a Glance 2016: OECD Indicators, http://dx.doi.org/10.1787/eag-2016-en.

StatLink http://dx.doi.org/10.1787/888933487556

PISA 2015 finds that the relationship between attending pre-primary school and better student performance at age 15 is strongest in school systems that offer pre-primary education to a larger proportion of the student population over a longer period of time, that have smaller child-to-teacher ratios in pre-primary education, and that invest more per child at the pre-primary level of education. In other words, input policies, such as the child-to-teacher ratio, positively affect learning outcomes. Among all these variables, the duration of ECEC is the strongest predictor of performance at age 15 (Figure 5.5).

Benefits of early childhood education and care attendance for disadvantaged children

Research shows that disadvantaged children can benefit the most from attending high-quality early childhood education.

Educational interventions during the early years have higher returns because they take full advantage of brain sensitivity peaks to develop children's skills (Figure 5.1), and because they lay the foundations for better learning at later stages. Research evidence points to high returns in early investments and interventions, and demonstrates relatively lower returns in compensatory measures at later stages in life (Carneiro, Cunha and Heckman, 2003; OECD, 2006). Later interventions are less efficient because they take place after children's "development window"; but they can have even lower returns if the student lacks the abilities needed to grasp new knowledge/succeed at later stages. Children from advantaged socio-economic backgrounds have often already developed these abilities in their families. Therefore, disadvantaged children receive the greatest benefit from attending high-quality ECEC, and interventions targeted at them will have the highest returns.

Figure 5.6. Rates of return to one Euro invested in educational interventions for disadvantaged and well-off children at different stages of the life cycle (2006)

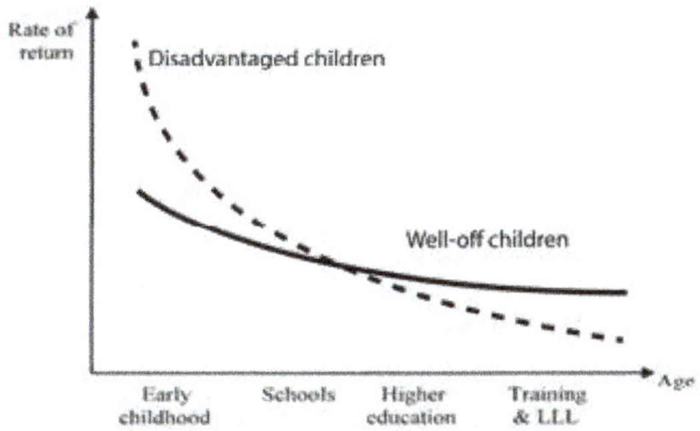

Source: Adapted from Cunha et al. (2006) in Wossmann (2008), *Efficiency and equity of European education and training policies*.

Figure 5.6 shows the rates of return to one Euro invested in educational interventions for disadvantaged and well-off children at different stages of the life cycle. Both series show a similar pattern: the rate of return decreases as age increases. However, in the first stages of life, and in particular during early childhood, the rates of returns are much higher for interventions addressed to disadvantaged children than to well-off children. On the contrary, at later stages, returns are higher when investing in education for well-off children. This illustrates the inefficiency of remedial interventions when foundations are missing, as discussed above.

These findings are from an extensive body of research, mainly based on evidence from the United States (Carneiro, Cunha and Heckman 2003, Cunha et al. 2006). However, existing evidence from European countries suggests that the pattern of relative effectiveness of educational interventions across ages and socio-economic backgrounds is the same for Europe as for the United States (Woessmann, 2008).

PISA data reveal that 15-year-old students from a lower socio-economic background or enrolled in socio-economically disadvantaged schools are less likely to have participated in early childhood education for at least two years.

Despite these findings, many of the inequities that exist within school systems are present before children enter formal schooling, and persist and even increase as students' progress through school (Downey, von Hippel and Broh, 2004). Earlier entrance into the school system may help reduce inequalities, especially if enrolment is expanded among disadvantaged children. However, although the enrolment data discussed in Chapter 4 show that enrolment has increase in recent decades, PISA 2015 data show that inequities in accessing ECEC are still persistent in many countries.

Access to at least one year of ECEC is quasi-universal in most OECD countries. On average among 15-year-old students who remember about early childhood education (ISCED 0), 92% of them declared in PISA 2015 that they had attended early childhood education for at "least one year" and, 77% for "at least two years". However, advantaged 15-year-old students had more chance than disadvantaged students of attending early childhood education when they were younger in most countries. For instance, an average of 72% of disadvantaged 15-year-old students compared to 82% of advantaged students had attended early childhood education for at least two years (Figure 5.7, Table 5.2 on the web only). Across OECD countries, the differences between percentages of socio-economic advantaged and disadvantaged students who had attended ECEC (ISCED 0) for at least two years were larger than 18 percentage points in Slovenia, the Slovak Republic, Turkey and the United States. This means that the 15-years-old students who could have benefited the most from early childhood education – those from disadvantaged backgrounds – were less likely to have participated in ECEC when they were younger (Figure 5.7).

Figure 5.7. Percentage of 15-year-old students who attended early childhood education (ISCED 0) for two years and more, by socio-economic background (PISA 2015)

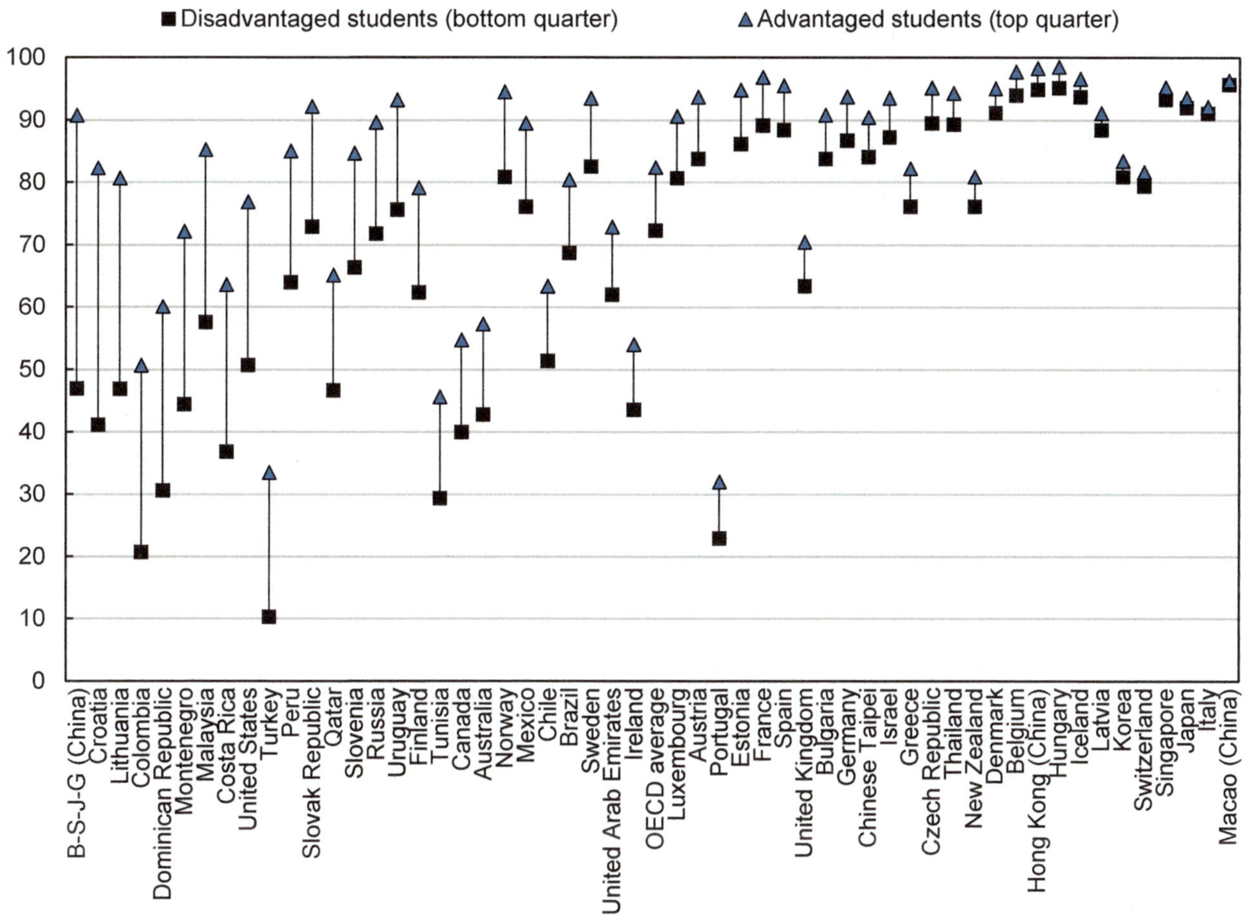

Note: Countries and economies are ranked in descending order of the differences between percentage of socio-economic advantaged and disadvantaged students who had attended early childhood school for two years and more.

Source: OECD (2017a), PISA online education database, OECD, Paris, www.oecd.org/pisa/data/.

StatLink http://dx.doi.org/10.1787/888933487575

Participation in at least one year of early childhood education is also beneficial for children with an immigrant background

Integrating young immigrant children into their new communities is of key importance in the long run, and their flexibility and the rapidity with which they can learn a local language makes the task easier. Education systems can help by encouraging their enrolment in early childhood education programmes.

Participation in ECEC programmes is, however, considerably lower among immigrant children (first and second generations) than among those without an immigrant background. Across OECD countries, an average of 88% of immigrant children had attended early childhood education for at least one year, compared to more than 95% of non-immigrant students (Tables 5.2 and 5.3 on the web only). Figure 5.8 presents information from countries where the proportion of 15-year-old students with an immigrant background (first and second generations) was above 6%. In these countries, immigrant students who reported that they had attended early childhood education (ISCED 0) for at least one year scored 36 points higher in the PISA science assessment than those who had not attended early childhood education, or attended for less than 1 year. The difference is significant, at 25 score points after accounting for socio-economic status (i.e. ten months of formal schooling). A small part of this difference is explained by socio-economic factors, given that in many countries, local and migrant children from more privileged households are more likely to attend ECEC. The benefits of ECEC for these children are related to language and integration, which are beneficial for children irrespective of their socio-economic backgrounds.

Among 15-year-old students with an immigrant background and a comparable socio-economic background, those who had attended at least one year of ECEC (ISCED 0) scored significantly better than others on the PISA science assessment in 18 out of the 31 countries with available data. The benefits of early childhood education for immigrant children is particularly significant in France, Greece, Hong Kong (China), Israel, Italy, Singapore and Sweden, where the gap exceeds 40 score points (Table 5.3 on the web only, Figure 5.8).

Figure 5.8. Change in science performance when 15-year-old pupils with an immigrant background attended early childhood education and care for at least 1 year compared to those who attended for less than 1 year (2015)

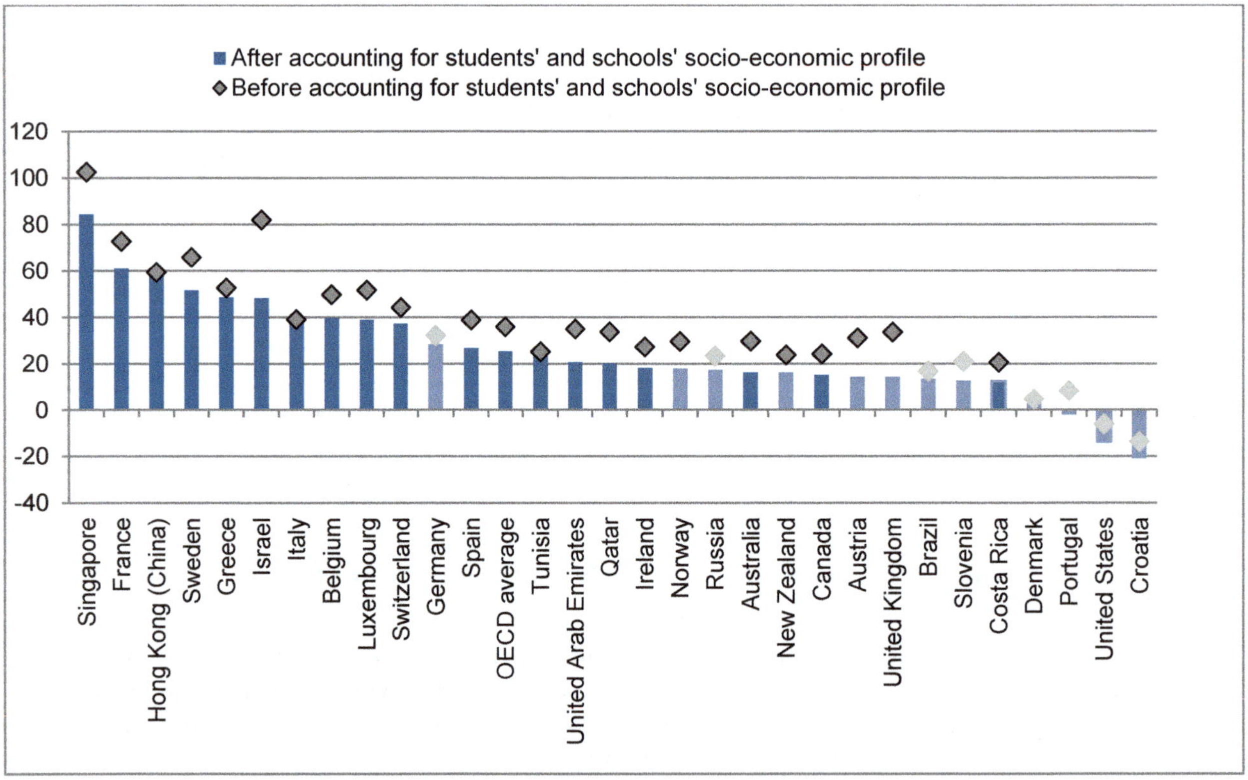

Notes: Values that are statistically significant are indicated in a darker shade.

Countries are ranked in descending order of the change in science when 15-year-old students with immigrant background had attended early childhood education at least one year, after accounting for student and school socio-economic profile.

Source: OECD (2017a), PISA online education database, OECD, Paris, www.oecd.org/pisa/data/.

StatLink http://dx.doi.org/10.1787/888933487585

In several countries (e.g. Denmark, Finland, the Netherlands, Norway and Sweden), policies to expand access to early childhood services for immigrant and ethnic minority groups have been pursued in order to expose children and families to the language and traditions of mainstream society, and provide opportunities for parents to establish social contacts and networks. Countries with indigenous populations (Australia, New Zealand and the United States) aim to preserve traditional languages and cultures, while seeking to empower families within mainstream society. The need for early childhood staff and provision to value and respond to the needs of ethnically, culturally, and linguistically diverse families remains a challenge in many countries (OECD, 2006 and more details in Chapter 3, Box 3.1).

Initiatives are not limited to these countries. Germany, for example, set a strategic goal in its National Action Plan on Integration (2011) to facilitate access to early learning, care and education in ECEC settings for children with a migrant background. A new federal programme, "Sprach-Kitas" (childcare centres that focus on language education and development) was introduced in 2016 with the aim of fostering language education and development, inclusive pedagogy and collaboration between families and ECEC centres.

In Luxembourg, recent reforms of the ECEC sector aim to reinforce language development in ECEC by offering 20 hours of free childcare to all children, with the objective of enhancing children's sense of belonging to Luxembourgish society. In the United States, many states have tried to increase immigrant enrolment in ECEC programmes as part of wider efforts to expand pre-school options among disadvantaged communities. To improve access, some states have created or expanded public pre-school systems, which supplement and complement the federal Head Start and Early Head Start programmes (Crosnoe, 2013).

Both national and municipal governments in Norway have made special efforts to support equality of participation, particularly for low-income and minority-language families. Initiatives include fee reductions or exemptions. After pilot programmes providing 20 hours per week of kindergarten free for children aged 3 to 5 in targeted areas, the scheme was extended in 2016 to all children aged 3-5 in low-income families. Although participation among minority-language children continues to be lower than for all children, the gap is closing. The biggest relative increase has been found among 2-year-olds (OECD, 2015c: *OECD Education Policy Outlook 2015, Making Reform Happen).*

Effect of early childhood education and care attendance on health

Early childhood education is also an important time for forming healthy behaviours.

Investing in early childhood education offers all children better learning outcomes at later stages, although this is not the only benefit, it is also an important period for forming healthy behaviours. The ECEC environment provides opportunities to ensure that children understand the importance of good nutrition and physical activity, and can benefit from both. Studies show that locally focussed actions and interventions, especially those targeted at the youngest, can be effective in changing behaviours, and can decrease the odds of problems such as being overweight during adolescence (Sassi, 2010; OECD, 2011a).

Research on obesity in four OECD countries – Australia, Canada, England (UK) and Korea – found that higher rates of obesity were associated with fewer years of education (Sassi et al., 2009). Similarly, recent research has also demonstrated that early intervention is important: overweight 5-year-olds were four times as likely as normal weight children to become obese by the time they were 14 (Cunningham et al., 2014). This is concerning, especially as obesity now affects more children than ever before, with 26% of boys and 16% of girls in OECD countries estimated to be overweight or obese at age 11, according to the World Health Organisation (WHO) child growth curve standards (OECD, 2017c). Among children, 11-year-old boys are more affected than girls by overweight and obesity in all the OECD countries, and more than 30% of boys are overweight or obese in Greece, Italy, Spain, Hungary and Poland.

Education and early interventions in early childhood education can play a big role in reversing the unhealthy trend of obesity. Therefore, rising enrolments in early childhood education, especially for disadvantaged families and for children under the age of 3, may provide more external opportunities for such early interventions. High-quality ECEC is linked to many positive outcomes, including improved child well-being and learning, reduction of poverty, and increased inter-generational social mobility. It may also help instil healthy eating and physical activity behaviours (OECD, 2014).

Figure 5.9 compares enrolment rates in formal childcare for children under the age of 3 in 2005, with the proportion of boys overweight or obese at age 11 in 2014. These data are not longitudinal, but show a small correlation between the two variables. Unsurprisingly, the higher the enrolment rates in formal childcare for children under the age of 3 in 2005, the lower the proportion of boys overweight or obese at age 11 in 2014. This correlation is stronger for boys than for girls, and shows that early interventions by qualified staff can contribute to forming healthy behaviours. However, the potential causal nature of the link between education and health is still subject to a certain degree of scrutiny, and these data should be interpreted with caution as the conditions through which education and health are correlated are not yet fully understood.

Figure 5.9. Relationship between early enrolment in early childhood education and care settings and rise of obesity at later stages of life (2005 and 2014)

Year 2005 is used to measure enrolment of children under the age of 3 in ECEC, while 2014 is used to measure obesity at age 11

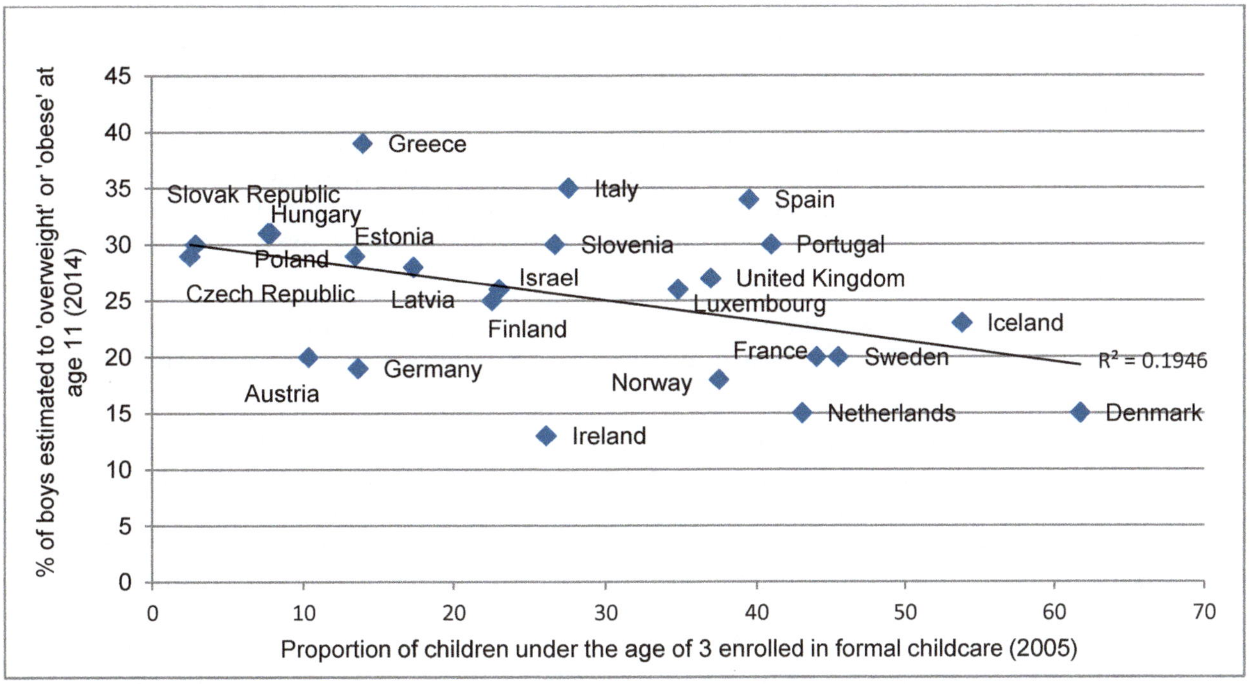

Sources: OECD (2017c), OECD Family Database, OECD, Paris, http://www.oecd.org/els/family/database.htm and OECD (2017b), OECD online education database, OECD, Paris, www.oecd.org/education/database.htm.

StatLink http://dx.doi.org/10.1787/888933487592

Relationship between access to early childhood education and care, intensity of participation and employability

Affordable and high-quality ECEC with an adequate number of hours per week can contribute to the increased participation of women in the labour force.

Investing in ECEC is not only about the benefit for children, working parents, mothers in particular, are more likely to drop out of the labour market or work fewer hours to take up childcare duties, especially when their children are young (Thévenon, 2013: Drivers of Female Labour Force Participation in the OECD). Therefore, mothers need high-quality, affordable ECEC so that they can return to work with confidence that their children are well cared for, and achieve a better work balance.

In previous years, policies implemented in most countries for children under the age of 3 emphasised the expansion of services as a necessary support for maternal employment in a strong economy, rather than as a public service that can benefit both children and parents. However, during the past decade there have been signs of convergence among OECD countries, and the concept of services for children under the age of 3 is progressively broadening to include educational, gender equality, social integration, and family support objectives. For example, an increasing number of countries has implemented an integrated curriculum in their ECEC programmes from age 1 to entry to compulsory education, which highlights that ECEC services for children under the age of 3 have expanded in most countries in response to a growing demand for better learning outcomes, as well as growing female labour force participation (OECD, 2011b).

The relationship between mothers' labour market participation and enrolment rates in formal childcare is strong, especially for mothers whose youngest child is under the age of 3.

In 2014, on average across OECD countries, 53% of all mothers whose youngest child was under the age of 3 were employed, while around 34% of children under the age of 3 were enrolled in formal childcare, e.g. in ISCED 0 or in other registered ECEC settings outside ISCED 2011 (Figure 4.2). These two averages mask wide variations across countries, but a similar pattern emerges when the two series are analysed together. In countries where mothers' labour market participation is the highest, such as Denmark, Luxembourg, the Netherlands, Portugal, Slovenia and Switzerland (above 70% employment among women aged 15 to 64 with their youngest child under the age of 3), high proportions of children are enrolled in formal childcare (ISCED 0 and other registered services).

In contrast, the enrolment rates in formal childcare for children under the age of 3 is less than 10% in the Czech Republic, the Slovak Republic and Mexico, while employment among women aged 15 to 64 with their youngest child under the age of 3 is significantly below the OECD average in these countries (Figure 5.10). This reflects deficiency in the provision of full-time ECEC services for children below 3 years of age in these countries. However, cross-national comparisons of employment rates of mothers with very young children are particularly complicated due to cross-national differences in the treatment of parents on parental leave. For example, unlike most countries, Estonia treats all parents on parental leave as economically inactive, which may contribute to the relatively low employment rate among mothers with a youngest child under the age of 3 (Figure 5.10).

In all OECD countries except Greece, Ireland, the Netherlands and Spain, maternal employment rates increase with the age of the mother's youngest child. On average, around two thirds of all mothers with their youngest child aged 3-5 years-old in OECD countries are employed. However, large variations are observed across countries. The difference in employment rates between mothers with their youngest child under the age of 3 and aged 3-5 is over 30 percentage points in a group of Eastern European countries, including the Czech Republic, Estonia, Hungary and the Slovak Republic. A relationship between enrolment rates at ages 3-5 and maternal employment among women aged 15-64 with their youngest child aged 3-5 still exist at these ages, but the correlation is weaker compared to younger ages (Figure 5.10).

Figure 5.10. Relationship between mother's employability by age of the youngest child and enrolment rates in early childhood education and care (2014)

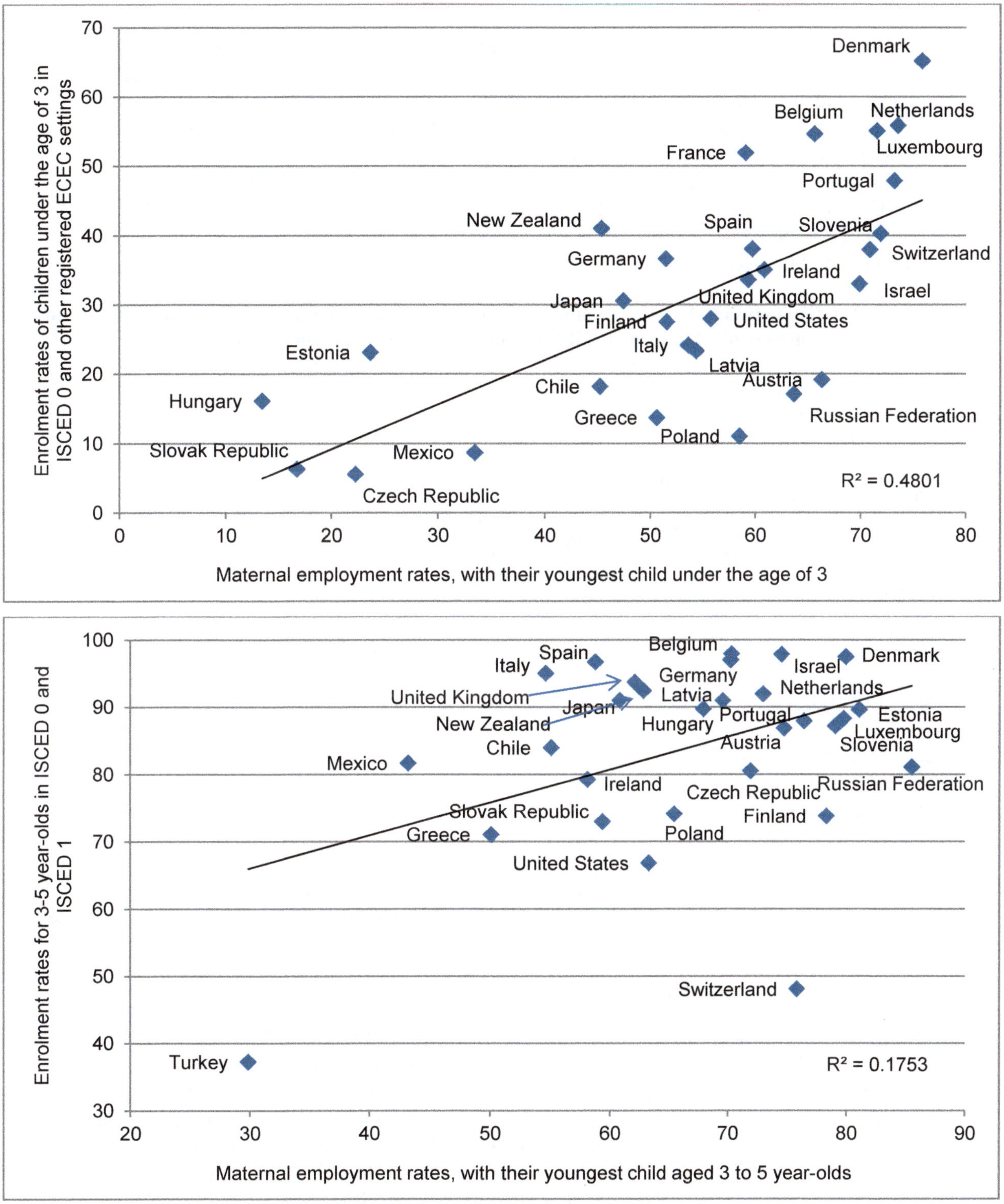

Source: OECD (2017c), OECD Family Database, OECD, Paris, www.oecd.org/els/family/database.htm and OECD (2017b), OECD online education database, OECD, Paris, www.oecd.org/education/database.htm.

StatLink http://dx.doi.org/10.1787/888933487604

Expanding access to ECEC and offering an adequate number of hours per week to ECEC services can contribute to the increased full-time participation of women in the labour force.

While high women labour force participation is becoming more common across OECD countries over the past decades (see Chapter 1, the data section), the work patterns of men and women continue to differ. Part-time employment is more frequent among women than men, and especially among women with at least one child aged 0-14 (OECD 2011b). On average, part-time employment accounts for 30% of total employment among women aged 15 to 64 with at least one child aged 0-14, and ranges from less than 10% in the Czech Republic, Denmark, Estonia, Finland, Greece, Hungary, Latvia, Poland, Portugal, the Slovak Republic, Slovenia and Turkey, to more than 35% in Austria, Germany and the Netherlands (Figure 5.11 and OECD, 2011b).

Figure 5.11. Relation between the usual number of hours per week for which children under the age of 3 are enrolled in formal childcare and part-time employment (2014)

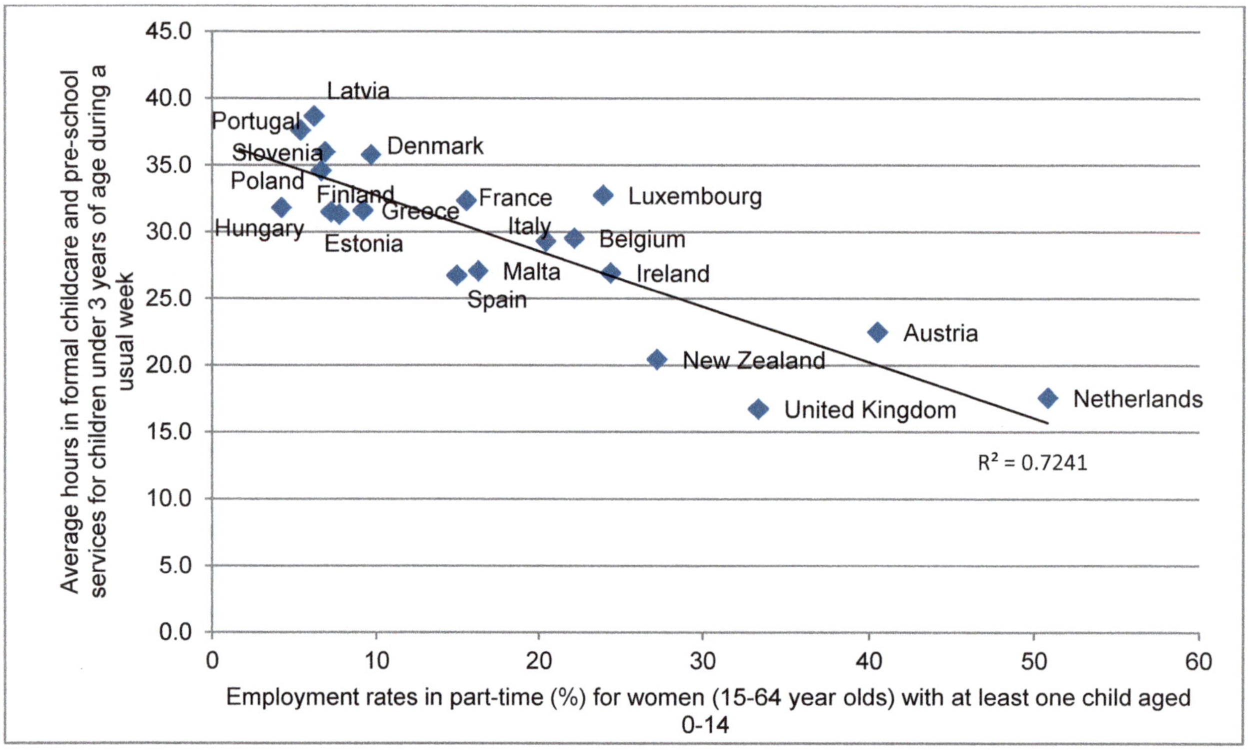

Source: OECD (2017c), OECD Family Database, OECD, Paris, www.oecd.org/els/family/database.htm.

StatLink http://dx.doi.org/10.1787/888933487612

A high level of part-time work among women may be a sign of difficulties in combining family life and a career. Therefore, affordable and high-quality ECEC, with an adequate number of hours per week, can contribute to the increased full-time participation of women in the labour force. In 2014, the average number of hours per week that children under the age of 3 were enrolled in formal childcare (ISCED 0 and other registered services) was 30 hours, and varied significantly across countries. However, a common pattern emerged. The usual number of hours per week that children aged 0-2 are enrolled in formal childcare is highly correlated (R2 of 0.72) with employment rates in part-time employment for women with at least one child aged 0-14. In some countries (e.g. Latvia, Portugal and Slovenia), the average number of hours is over 35 hours during a usual week, and part-time employment is below 10% among women aged 15-64 with their youngest child aged 0-14. At the other extreme, in Austria, the Netherlands and the United Kingdom, children under the age of 3 spend on average 22 hours or less in formal childcare during a usual week, while more than 25% of women with at least one child aged 0-14 are employed part-time (Figure 5.11).

These different patterns of part-time and full-time work have implications for society and for economic growth. The trends show that countries with a higher availability of affordable ECEC provision exhibit high maternal labour force participation rates, especially when services are accessible to the youngest child, and when they are offered full rather than half days. Therefore, the availability of affordable ECEC systems is a precondition for mothers' labour market participation.

References

Barnett, W.S. (1995), "Long-term effects of early childhood programs on cognitive and school outcomes", *The Future of Children*, Vol. 5, pp. 25-50.

Berlinski, S., S. Galiani and P. Gertler (2009), "The effect of pre-primary education on primary school, performance", *Journal of Public Economics*, Vol. 93/1, pp. 219-234, www.sciencedirect.com/science/article/pii/S0047-2727(08)00130-8.

Carneiro, P., F. Cunha and J. Heckman (2003), "Interpreting the Evidence of Family Inuence on Child Development", paper presented at conference on The Economics of Early Child Development: Lessons for Economic Policy, Federal Reserve Bank, University of Minnesota, USA.

Crosnoe, Robert (2013), "Preparing the Children of Immigrants for Early Academic Success". Washington DC, Migration Policy Institute, www.fcd-us.org/assets/2013/07/Crosnoe-FINAL.pdf.

Council Early Child Development (2010), Investing in Young Children, an Early Childhood Development Guide for Policy Dialogue and Project Preparation, 2011, from the World Bank.

Cunha, F. et al. (2006), "Interpreting the evidence on life cycle skill formation", in *Handbook of the economics of education*, Vol. 1, Amsterdam.

Cunningham, S., M. Kramer and V.M. Narayan (2014), "Incidence of Childhood Obesity in the United States", *New England Journal of Medicine*, Vol. 370, pp. 403-411.

Currie, J. (2001), "Early Childhood Education Programmes", *Journal of Economic Perspectives*, Vol. 15/2, pp. 213-238.

Downey, D., P. Von Hippel and B. Broh (2004), "Are schools the great equalizer? Cognitive inequality over the summer months and the school year", *American Sociological Review*, Vol. 69/5, pp. 613-635, www.jstor.org/stable/3593031.

L. Gambaro, K. Stewart et J. Waldfogel (eds.) (2014), *An Equal Start?: Providing Quality Early Education and Care for Disadvantaged Children*, Policy Press, Bristol.

Melhuish, E, et al. (2014), "Home, pre-school and primary school influences upon children's educational attainment at age 11", *Education Policy Analysis Archives*, Vol. 22, pp. 1-26, http://dx.doi.org/10.14507/epaa.v22.1893.

Naudeau, S., et al. (2011), "Investing in Young Children: An Early Childhood Development Guide for Policy Dialogue and Project Preparation, Directions in development; human development", Africa regional educational publications, World Bank, Washington, DC, http://documents.worldbank.org/curated/en/691411468153855017/Investing-in-young-children-an-early-childhood-development-guide-for-policy-dialogue-and-project-preparation.

OECD (2017a), *PISA online education database*, OECD, Paris, www.oecd.org/pisa/data/.

OECD (2017b), *OECD online education database*, OECD, Paris, www.oecd.org/education/database.htm.

OECD (2017c), *OECD Family Database*, OECD, Paris, www.oecd.org/els/family/database.htm.

OECD (2016a), *PISA 2015 Results (Volume II): Policies and Practices for Successful Schools*, PISA, OECD Publishing, Paris, http://dx.doi.org/10.1787/9789264267510-en.

OECD (2016b), *Education at a Glance 2016: OECD Indicators,* OECD Publishing, Paris, http://dx.doi.org/10.1787/eag-2016-en.

OECD (2015a), *Skills for Social Progress: The Power of Social and Emotional Skills*, OECD Skills Studies, OECD Publishing, Paris, http://dx.doi.org/10.1787/9789264226159-en.

OECD (2015b), *Starting Strong IV: Monitoring Quality in Early Childhood Education and Care (ECEC)*, OECD Publishing, Paris, http://dx.doi.org/10.1787/9789264233515-en.

OECD (2015c), *OECD Education Policy Outlook 2015, Making Reform Happen: Lessons from OECD Countries*, OECD, Paris, http://dx.doi.org/10.1787/9789264225442-en.

OECD (2014), Trends Shaping Education 2014, Spotlight 2: The weight of nations, OECD, Paris, http://www.oecd.org/edu/ceri/SpotlightBodyandSociety.pdf.

OECD (2012), *Starting Strong III: A Quality Toolbox for Early Childhood Education and Care*, OECD Publishing, Paris, http://dx.doi.org/10.1787/9789264123564-en.

OECD (2011a), *Health at a Glance 2011: OECD Indicators*, OECD Publishing, Paris, http://dx.doi.org/10.1787/health_glance-2011-en.

OECD (2011b), *Doing Better for Families,* OECD Publishing, Paris, www.oecd.org/els/family/doingbetterforfamilies.htm.

OECD (2006), *Starting Strong II: Early Childhood Education and Care*, OECD Publishing, Paris, http://dx.doi.org/10.1787/9789264035461-en.

Sassi, F. (2010), *Obesity and the Economics of Prevention: Fit not Fat*, OECD Publishing, Paris, http://dx.doi.org/10.1787/9789264084865-en.

Sassi, F., M. Devaux, J. Church, M. Cecchini and F. Borgonovi (2009), "Education and Obesity in Four OECD Countries", *OECD Health Working Paper*, No. 39, OECD Publishing, Paris, http://dx.doi.org/10.1787/5km4psmtn8zx-en.

Thévenon, O. (2013), "Drivers of Female Labour Force Participation in the OECD", *OECD Social, Employment and Migration Working Papers*, No. 145, OECD Publishing, Paris, http://dx.doi.org/10.1787/5k46cvrgnms6-en.

Woessmann, L. (2008), "Efficiency and equity of European education and training policies", *International Tax and Public Finance*, Vol. 15/2, pp. 199-230.

Chapter 5 Tables

StatLink http://dx.doi.org/10.1787/9789264276116-en

WEB Table 5.1 (Web only). Performance in science according to the number of years spent in early childhood education (ISCED 0) by 15-year-old pupils - before and after accounting for socio-economic status (PISA 2015).

WEB Table 5.2 (Web only). Percentage of 15-year-old pupils who had attended early childhood education and number of year they spent in early childhood education, by socio-economic background (PISA 2015).

WEB Table 5.3 (Web only). Percentage of 15-year-old pupils in Science, by immigrant background nd number of years spent in early childhood education (PISA 2015).

WEB Table 5.4 (Web only). Proportion of low performers among 15-year-old pupils according to the numbers of years spent in early childhood education and likelihood of low performance in science (PISA 2015).

Annex A.

Glossary of terms

Advisors (or counsellors)**:** professionals that work across classes and/or playgroups, providing additional guidance and support to teachers, other staff or children, generally or specific to transitions. This category only appears in a few countries.

Autonomy: The ability of a child to undertake activities, tasks etc. without the help of others (mastery of skills), to make his/her own decisions, and to express his/her own opinions or ideas, feel secure and have confidence in his/her own ability.

Appraisal: The review of a pre-school teacher's or educator's work by the centre management, an external inspector or by his or her colleagues. This appraisal can be conducted in a range of ways, from a more formal, objective approach (e.g. as part of a formal performance management system involving set procedures and criteria) to the more informal, more subjective approach (e.g. through informal discussions with the teacher).

Assessment of children: Judgement on individual progress and achievement of goals. It covers classroom/playroom-based assessments as well as large-scale, external assessments and examinations and refers to the process of documenting knowledge, skills, attitudes and beliefs. Assessment can focus on the individual learner and staff (adapted from OECD, 2013). Assessment can be direct or indirect and its use formative or summative.

- **Direct assessment:** Assessments that look at concrete outputs of learning, i.e. the measurable and demonstrated knowledge and skills of children/staff.
- **Indirect assessment:** Assessments that examine indicators of learning and gather information through feedback, e.g. in surveys or interviews (adapted from Middle States Commission on Higher Education, 2007).
- **Formative assessment:** Assessments that frequently or continuously (not at one point in time only) and interactively assess child development and progress with the purpose of understanding and identifying learning needs and adjust instruction and teaching methods accordingly (adapted from OECD, 2005; Litjens, 2013).
- **Summative assessment:** Assessments that measure learning results at the end of a certain time period to obtain summary statements. These can be used e.g. for holding staff and settings accountable for providing quality ECEC or as a method to identify whether children have learning disadvantages (adapted from OECD, 2005; Litjens, 2013).

Assistants: Assistants support the "teacher" with a group of children or class. Assistants are more common in pre-primary education than in primary education. They usually have tomeet lower qualification requirements than teachers, which may range from no formal requirements to, for instance, vocational education and training.

Career: A paid job that is likely to form a person's life's work.

Classroom/playgroup/group: A group of children who take part in supervised creative and social play or education within the ECEC setting or primary school (see also **ECEC** and **ECEC setting**).

Centre-based/school-based provision or **settings**: Publicly regulated ECEC settings provided outside the home. The services provided can be full-time or part-time and can include nurseries, day-care centres, *crèches* and kindergartens (adapted from Eurydice, 2014; OECD, 2012b).

Children: 'Children' refers to children in ISCED 2011 Level 0 and 1

Child-to-teacher ratio: The ratio of children to teacher, obtained by dividing the number of full-time equivalent children at a given level of education by the number of full-time equivalent "teachers" (see definition of teachers) at that level and in similar types of institutions (see also staff-child ratio). The child-to-teacher ratio is one of the key variables policy makers use to control spending on education. The child-to-teacher ratio is an important indicator of the resources invested in ECEC, and also of the quality of these services. Because of the difficulty of constructing direct measures of educational quality, this indicator is also often used as a proxy for quality, on the assumption that a smaller ratio of children to teacher means better access by children to teaching resources). However, a low ratio of children to teacher does not necessarily mean better access to teaching and to educational support for the individual child unless the actual pedagogical practices are developed in such a way that this is ensured. But a very high ratio of children to teacher certainly suggests insufficient professional support for learning, particularly for children from disadvantaged home backgrounds.

Counsellors: see Advisors.

Curriculum: Refers to the contents of early childhood education such as learning areas and learning goals. In a narrow sense, it describes the "what" of teaching. In a broader sense, it is often defined as "the sum of all experiences in childhood settings". Even though often simultaneously used, it is not the same as pedagogy.

Curriculum framework: It is a core policy document that includes statements about underlying values, conceptions of learning, the major aims, purposes and tasks of education. It describes a range of requirements, regulations and advice which should be respected by all stakeholders in the education system, and which should guide the work of schools, teachers and the developers of other curriculum documents (such as textbooks and teacher guides) (UNESCO IBE, 2016).

Curriculum implementation: The actual use in practice (practical application) of the curriculum or curriculum framework by ECEC staff, managers and children. This refers to the way in which the concepts of the curriculum are put into effect, and how they are used in practices and activities by staff and children, how they are interpreted, how they are used in development and learning, and how they influence teaching, caring and interactions between staff, and between staff and children.

Decentralised system: An organisation whose decision-making authority for ECEC does not reside with a central institution. Decision making on ECEC is done at a decentralised level, at the level of regions, provinces or municipalities. The central authority has little or no influence on decision making in ECEC.

Degree: An academic degree is a position and title within a college or university that is usually awarded in recognition of the recipient having either satisfactorily completed a prescribed course of study, or completed other work to show that degree requirements were met. The most common degrees awarded today are Bachelor's, Master's, and doctoral degrees. Degrees for ECEC and primary schooling include (but are not limited to) diplomas or state examinations.

ECEC: Early childhood education and care. It includes all arrangements providing care and education for children under compulsory school age, regardless of setting, funding, opening hours or programme content (see also **ECEC setting**) (OECD, 2001).

ECEC centre leader: A centre leader is defined as the person with the most responsibility for the administrative, managerial and/or pedagogical leadership at the ECEC centre. As part of the leadership role, centre leaders may be responsible for the monitoring of children, the supervision of other staff, contact with parents and guardians, and/or the planning, preparation and carrying out of the pedagogical work in the centre. Centre leaders may also spend part of their time working with the children. See also Principal.

ECEC centre (See ECEC setting below)

ECEC profession: ECEC profession refers to a vocation related to early childhood education and care, particularly working with children. The titles for this profession may vary from country to country, such as child care worker, family and day care worker, teacher (e.g. pre-primary teacher; primary teacher; kindergarten teacher; pre-school teacher), pedagogue, or other auxiliary staff. See also **ECEC staff.**

ECEC quality: A multidimensional concept covering structural characteristics and process quality. Conceptualisations cover global aspects (such as warm climate or child-appropriate behaviour) and domain-specific stimulation in learning areas such as literacy, emerging mathematics and science. Some researchers include orientation quality as an additional dimension of ECEC quality, referring to pedagogical values, beliefs and approaches of teachers and ECEC settings (see Anders, 2015) (see Structural quality, Process quality).

ECEC sector: The ECEC sector consists of multiple entities such as ECEC centres (e.g. day care centres, kindergartens, pre-schools, pre-primary schools), family day care, local educational authorities, and other institutions/services that support children's development. The sector also comprises all actors/agents on national, regional and local level that play a part in developing the practices and policies for providing ECEC. (see also **ECEC setting**).

ECEC setting: A place where ECEC is delivered. Also referred to as ECEC centre or provision. Most settings typically fall into one of the following five categories:

- **Regular centre-based ECEC:** more formalised ECEC centres typically belong to one of these three sub-categories:
  - *Centre-based ECEC for children under the age of 3*: often called "crèches", these settings may have an educational function, but are typically attached to the social or welfare sector and associated with an emphasis on care. Many of

them are part-time and provided in schools, but they can also be provided in designated ECEC centres.

- *Centre-based ECEC for children from the age of 3:* often called kindergarten or pre-school, these settings tend to be more formalised and linked to the education system.
- *Age-integrated centre-based ECEC for children from birth or one year-old, up to the beginning of primary school*: can be called kindergarten, pre-school, or pre-primary, and offers a holistic pedagogical provision of education and care (often full-day). To an increasing degree, these settings are linked to the educational system.

- **Family day-care ECEC:** licensed home-based ECEC, which is most prevalent for children under the age of 3. These settings may have an educational function and be part of the regular ECEC system, or not. The minimum requirements defined for licensed family day care services vary widely across countries. Requirements range from registration with an initial (one off) health and safety check, to registration with annual safety and health checks (the most usual form of licensing imposed on providers), to – in the most advanced cases – registration with requirements for staff and curriculum standards, annual pedagogical inspection, in-training requirements, and pedagogical supervision regularly ensured by an accredited supervisory body. Registered family day care refers to providers who are recruited, supported, and, in some cases, employed, by a public authority or publicly-funded private organisation.
- **Licenced or formalised drop-in ECEC centres:** often receiving children across the entire ECEC age bracket and even beyond, these drop-in centres often complement home-based care or services of other centre-based settings, and allow parents to complement home-based care by family members or family day care with more institutionalised services. They may also cater for children outside the opening hours of other centre-based ECEC settings, such as nursery schools. This type of ECEC setting allows children and children accompanied by caretakers (parent, guardian, relative or childminder) to attend a playgroup led by ECEC professionals on a drop-in basis (without having to apply for a place).

ECEC staff: People whose professional activity involves the transmission of knowledge, attitudes and skills to children enrolled in an ECEC setting. This definition depends neither on the qualification held by the ECEC staff nor on the delivery mechanism. ECEC staff may include teachers, educators, assistants or staff working with individual children, among other categories (see also **Teacher, Assistant**, **Staff for individual children** and **Advisors**).

ECEC systems, policies and programmes: National, regional or municipal systems, policies, and programmes for ECEC. Systems here refer to institutional, organisational entities adopted by the government. Policies refer to plans of action adopted by ECEC settings or rational courses of actions taken by governments. Programmes refer to projects or services designed for ECEC settings.

Education at a glance (EAG): Education at a Glance is an OECD annual publication containing a rich, comparable and up-to-date array of indicators that reflects a consensus among professionals on how to measure the current state of education internationally. The EAG indicators released in this publication are based on the UNESCO-UIS/OECD/EUROSTAT (UOE) data collection on education statistics administered by the OECD in 2015. The objective of the joint UOE annual data collection on education statistics is to provide internationally comparable data (mostly at national level, with some insights at the subnational level) on key aspects of formal education systems. Countries participating in the UOE data collection co-operate to gather the information, to develop and apply common definitions and criteria for the quality control and verification of the data.

Education or training: All the listed **ISCED levels** or stages of staff and leaders' learning and/or professional development represented by a structured or certified programme. This education does not need to be exclusively related to education or qualifications for working with children.

Effectiveness, effective, effectively: Effectiveness is defined as the capability of producing desired outcomes. When something or someone is "effective" it means it has produced the intended or expected results.

Employment status: Employment status refers to the type of contract agreement that an employee has with their employer. This contract agreement sets out the conditions of employment, and whether the employment is temporary or permanent.

Enrolment rates by age: Enrolment rates are expressed as net enrolment rates, which are calculated by dividing the number of children of a particular age group enrolled in the level of education by the size of the population of that age group. Generally, enrolment rates are based on head counts and do not distinguish between full-time and part-time study. Enrolment rates can be broken down by gender.

Evaluation: Refers to judgments on the quality of ECEC or primary settings or systems, policies and programmes (adapted from OECD, 2013).

Expenditure on educational institutions as a percentage of GDP: This indicator provides a measure of the relative proportion of a nation's wealth that is invested in educational institutions and of the respective role of public and private stakeholders. Expenditure on education is an investment that can help to foster economic growth, enhance productivity, contribute to personal and social development, and reduce social inequality. The proportion of total financial resources devoted to education is one of the key choices made in each country by governments, enterprises, and individual students and their families alike.

Expenditure per child: This indicator represents direct public and private expenditure on educational settings/institutions in relation to the number of full-time equivalent children enrolled in these settings/institutions. Expenditure per child on a particular level of education is calculated by dividing the total expenditure on educational settings/institutions at that level by the corresponding full-time equivalent enrolment. Only those educational settings/institutions and programmes are taken into account for which both enrolment and expenditure data are available. Expenditure in national currency is first converted into equivalent US dollars by dividing the national currency figure by the purchasing power parity (PPP) conversion factor. The children enrolment numbers used are those that are collected with a coverage aligned to that of the finance data.

Foreign-born population covers all people who have ever migrated from their country of birth to their current country of residence. The foreign-born population data shown here include people born abroad as nationals of their current country of residence. The difference across countries between the size of the foreign-born population and that of the foreign population depends on the rules governing the acquisition of citizenship in each country. This indicator is measured as a percentage of population.

Free access (to ECEC services): Use of the concerned ECEC service is free of charge for the demand side, i.e. there are no fees for children and their parents. The resulting costs for free access are typically covered by (government) subsidies.

Jobless and "complex" families: Children living in **jobless families** are children living in households where no adult is in paid work, regardless of the number of adults (and their relationship) in the household. The data is presented from the children's perspective, e.g. the indicator considers the proportion of children in jobless families rather than the share of jobless families in all households. Children in **"complex" families** include households where: i) all adults work (either full-time or part-time), ii) at least one adult works and one adult is not in paid work, and iii) no adult in paid work.

Government: The entirety of the executive at all levels of governance, at national, state-level, regional and local level.

Gross Domestic Product (GDP): Gross domestic product is an aggregate measure of production equal to the sum of the gross values added of all resident institutional units engaged in production (plus any taxes, and minus any subsidies, on products not included in the value of their outputs). The sum of the final uses of goods and services (all uses except intermediate consumption) measured in purchasers' prices, less the value of imports of goods and services, or the sum of primary incomes distributed by resident producer units (OECD, 2017a).

Head teacher: see **Principal.**

Health development: The physical health status of a child, encompassing physical well-being only (adapted from WHO definition, 2006). Mental, emotional and social development are excluded from this definition; these are included in the definition of **socio-emotional skills**.

Home-based provision: Publicly regulated ECEC provision that is delivered in the provider's home. Regulations usually require providers to meet minimum health, safety and nutrition standards. Home-based provision excludes live-in and live-out nannies and babysitters (as defined by Eurydice, 2014).

Home language: Refers to the language that a person speaks at home with his/her family. This may be the person's [first language] or may be different than the mainstream language of instruction applicable in the national context or, as applicable, in the context of the jurisdiction or region.

Induction activities: Induction activities are designed to introduce new ECEC staff or teachers into the ECEC or teaching profession, and to support experienced staff or teachers who are new to a setting. Induction activities might be presented in formal structured programmes (for example, regular supervision by the ECEC centre leader or primary school head, reduced work load, formal mentoring by experienced colleagues), or they might be informally arranged as separate activities available to support new colleagues (for example, informal peer work with other new colleagues, a welcome handbook).

Information and communications technology (ICT): The teaching and learning of technological and digital skills. Creating and developing the capacity to use digital and technological environments for development, communication and knowledge creation. Digital environments refer to computers (including laptops, tablets, iPads, netbooks, smart boards) and computer games, the Internet, television and radio, among others. The main purpose of ICT in education is to use media as a learning tool to improve learning processes. Another important goal is to teach children the thoughtful use of media for learning, education, development and to improve life quality.

Inspection: The process of assessing (inspecting, investigating) the quality and/or performance of institutions, staff, services, and programmes by those (inspectors) who are not directly involved in the ECEC settings being monitored, and who are usually specially appointed to fulfil these responsibilities.

Integrated system: When the responsibilities for ECEC services are under one (leading) authority (at the national and/or regional level), e.g. the education ministry, ministry of social welfare or another authority. Those responsibilities may stretch from curriculum development to standard-setting, monitoring or financing.

Integrated ECEC setting: An ECEC setting which, in the same physical location, provides both child care and early education in an integrated fashion.

ISCED 2011 classification: The ISCED classification was initially developed by UNESCO in the mid-1970s, and was first revised in 1997. Due to subsequent changes in education and learning systems throughout the start of the 21st century, a further review of ISCED was undertaken between 2009 and 2011 involving extensive global consultation with countries, regional experts and international organisations. The revision took into account important shifts in the structure of higher education, such as the Bologna process in Europe, expansion of education programmes for very young children, and increasing interest in statistics on the outcomes of education, such as educational attainment. The revised ISCED 2011 classification was adopted by the UNESCO General Conference at its 36th session in November 2011 and implemented in international educational statistics in 2015 (OECD/European Union/UNESCO-UIS, 2015).

- **ISCED 0 (Early childhood education):** In ISCED 2011, ISCED 0 covers early childhood education and care for all ages, including very young children. As the educational properties of ISCED 0 programmes can be difficult to assess directly, several criteria are used to come up with a technical definition. For a programme of an ECEC setting to be reported as ISCED level 0 it must have: adequate intentional educational or pedagogical properties; be delivered by qualified staff members; take place in an institutionalised setting; meet a minimum intensity/duration (an intensity of at least 2 hours per day; and a duration of at least 100 days a year) and be targeted at children from age 0 until entry into ISCED level 1. In ISCED 2011, programmes are sub-classified into two categories depending on age and the level of complexity of the educational content: early childhood educational development (ISCED 01) and pre-primary education (ISCED 02). ISCED 01 programmes are generally designed for children younger than 3. This is a new category not covered by ISCED 1997. ISCED 02 is designed for children from age 3 years to the start of primary education. It corresponds exactly to level 0 in ISCED 1997. Age-integrated ECEC are reported according to the age of the children.
- **ISCED 01 – Early childhood educational development:** Typically aimed at very young children, aged0-2. The learning environment is visually stimulating

and language rich, and fosters self-expression with an emphasis on language acquisition and the use of language for meaningful communication. There are opportunities for active play so that children can exercise their co-ordination and motor skills under supervision and in interaction with staff.

- **ISCED 02 – Pre-primary education:** Aimed at children in the years immediately prior to starting compulsory schooling, typically aged 3-5. Through interaction with peers and educators, children improve their use of language and their social skills, start to develop logical and reasoning skills, and talk through their thought processes. They are also introduced to alphabetical and mathematical concepts, understanding and use of language, and are encouraged to explore their surrounding world and environment. Supervised gross motor activities (i.e. physical exercise through games and other activities) and play-based activities can be used as learning opportunities to promote social interactions with peers and to develop skills, autonomy and school readiness.

Labour Force: The International Labour Organisation (ILO) considers people of working age to be in one (and one only) of three situations in the labour market: employed, unemployed, or inactive. The employed and unemployed together are known as the labour force. The labour force participation rates is calculated as the labour force divided by the total working-age population. The working-age population refers to people aged 15 to 64. This indicator is broken down by age group and it is measured as a percentage of each age group.

Language and literacy skills: Children's productive and receptive language skills on all levels: syntax (ability to form sentences), morphology (ability to form words), semantics (understanding the meaning of words/sentences), phonology (awareness of speech sounds), pragmatics (how language is used in different contexts), vocabulary. It also refers to children's (precursor) literacy skills, that is to say, all the skills related to reading and writing, such as recognising and writing letters and words, understanding pictures, etc.

Learning standards: Standards regarding child outcomes or child development set at a national or regional level. The standards set clear expectations that children need to meet on different developmental subjects, e.g. numeracy, reading, motor skills.

Legal entitlement to ECEC: Two types of legal entitlement to ECEC are distinguished (as defined in Eurydice, 2013):

- **Universal legal entitlement**: Statutory duty for ECEC providers to secure (publicly subsidised) ECEC provision for all children living in a catchment area whose parents, regardless of their employment, socio-economic or family status, require an ECEC place.

- **Targeted legal entitlement**: Statutory duty for ECEC providers to secure (publicly subsidised) ECEC provision for children living in a catchment area who fall under certain categories. These categories can be based on various aspects, including the employment, socio-economic or family status of their parents.

Local level or local authorities: The local level is a decentralised level of ECEC governance. It is located at city/town level in the vast majority of countries. In some countries, the municipalities take the main responsibility for ECEC.

Mean age of mothers at birth, calculated as the simple mean average age in years of women at childbirth. The mean age of mothers at birth is shown both for all births and also for first births only.

Minimum quality standards: The minimum benchmark for structural aspects of ECEC settings to ensure a minimum level of quality. These are often aspects of ECEC that can be regulated relatively easily (e.g. staff-child ratio, space, group size and qualifications of ECEC staff).

Motor skills: The ability to perform complex muscle and nerve acts that produce movements, the ability to co-ordinate the body. It refers to both fine and gross motor skills and awareness of their own body. Fine motor skills include small movements such as drawing and writing, crawling or putting shoes on. Gross motor skills are large movements like walking and kicking, running and cycling.

Monitoring: The process of systematically tracking aspects of ECEC services, staff, child development and curriculum implementation, with a view toward data collection, accountability and/or enhancing effectiveness and/or quality.

Neighbourhood: The surrounding geographical area in which the setting or school is located.

Network A group of *ECEC centre leaders* and/or *ECEC staff* who communicate together for mutual benefit, sharing experiences and practices.

Networking: Networking is defined as a possibility for (new) <ECEC staff> to interact with their peers, within or between <ECEC centres>, and could include the use of Internet. Networking with peers is based on face-to-face meetings to share experiences within or between <ECEC centres>, but could partly be based on virtual communities (see further).

Non-Immigrant and Immigrant students in PISA 2015: If the student and the Mother or/and the student and the Father are born in the country of test; or, If the student is not born in the country of test, but the mother or/and the father is, then the student is considered Non-Immigrant. If the student is born in the country of test, but none of the parents or the Data for parents are missing, the student is a Second-Generation-Immigrant. If none of the three are born in the country of test, or If the student is not born in country of test and the Data of one parent is missing, the student is a First-Generation-Immigrant.

Numeracy: The ability to reason and to apply simple numerical concepts and understand numbers. Basic numeracy skills consist of knowing and recognising space, shapes, location and direction, the basic properties of sets, quantity, order and number concepts, time and change, being able to count, to comprehending fundamental mathematics like addition, subtraction, multiplication and division.

Observation: A method to collect information on a subject from an outsider's perspective. It can be used for a specific purpose (e.g. inspection, peer review) or can be open ended (e.g. to document a child's progress for parents).

OECD Family Database: In view of the strong demand for cross-national indicators on the situation of families and children, the OECD Family Database was developed to provide cross-national indicators on family outcomes and family policies across the OECD countries, its enhanced engagement partners and EU member states. The database brings together information from various national and international databases, both within the OECD and external organisations. The database currently includes 70 indicators under four main dimensions: (i) structure of families, (ii) labour market position of families, (iii) public policies for families and children and (iv) child outcomes.

Overweight at age 11, by gender: This indicator uses data from the Health Behaviour in School-aged Children (HBSC) survey 2013/14 to provide information on the proportion of children (11-, 13- and 15-year-olds) that are considered 'overweight' or 'obese' in OECD and EU member countries. Data are presented through one primary measure: Proportion (%) of 11-, 13- and 15-year-olds with a Body Mass Index (BMI) classed as 'overweight' or 'obese' according to the World Health Organization (WHO) child growth curve standards, by gender (WHO, 2006). The BMI data are based on self-reported information from children on their weight (without clothes) and height (without shoes), with the BMI calculated as weight in kilograms divided by height in meters squared (kg/m2).

Parental/guardian associations: A formal organisation composed of parents/guardians and/or ECEC staff or teachers that is intended to facilitate parent and/or guardian participation in ECEC settings or primary schools. It may be referred as PTA (parent-teacher association) or PTO (parent-teacher organisation).

Part-time/full-time classification and conversion to full-time equivalents: Both the intensity of participation of students and the employment status of educational personnel can be classified as either ***full-time*** or ***part-time*** according to similar principles and their total numbers (headcount) can be expressed in ***full-time equivalents*** (FTEs). Students should be classified between full-time and part-time on the basis of the ***intended study load of the student*** within the reference school or academic year. Educational personnel should be classified according to their ***contractual working hours***. In order to determine whether they are full-time or part-time, their study load and working hours should be compared to those required to study or work full-time for the full reference school or academic year according to the national norms or conventions at the given level of education. A **full-time student** is one who is enrolled in an education programme whose **intended study load** amounts to at least 75% of the **normal full-time annual study load**. A **part-time student** is one who is enrolled in an education programme whose **intended study load** is less than 75% of the **normal full-time annual study lead**. **Full-time educational personnel** are employed for at least 90% of the normal or statutory working hours of educational personnel in the same job or role at the given level of education. **Part-time educational personnel** are employed for less than 90% of the normal or statutory working hours of educational personnel in the same job or role at the given level of education. The conversion of headcounts to full-time equivalents (FTE) is similar for students and educational personnel. The aim is to express study loads and working hours during the reference period in a single standard unit which equates to a full-time, full-year student or educational personnel respectively. In order to determine the FTEs of a given student or educational personnel, their intended study load or contractual working hours should be divided by the corresponding normal annual study load or normal or statutory working hours for the reference period. The concepts used to define full-time and part-time participation at other ISCED levels, such as study load, student participation and the academic value or progress which the study represents, are not easily applicable to ISCED level 0. Therefore, a consensus has not been reached on a methodology for calculating FTE for Enrolments at ISCED 0 but it is recommended in data reporting to estimate pupils enrolled in Full-time equivalents by ISCED 0 Enrolment Headcount (i.e. all enrolments counted as full-time). Headcount is not a satisfying criteria

for
full-time equivalent for indicators such as expenditure per student (even if it is accepted for enrolment comparisons).

Pedagogue: In some countries, the term "pedagogue" describes a qualified pedagogical staff member in an ECEC setting or a school who may provide either special support to some children or is the leader at the classroom or playroom level. See also **Teacher.**

Pedagogy: A set of instructional techniques and strategies to support children's learning, development, and the acquisition of skills, competencies, values and attitudes (Anders, 2015). It involves the staff's pedagogical knowledge, but also the way the knowledge is applied and the practices are implemented in interaction with children, and in response to children's requests and interests (Jensen, 2009). Curricula should provide clear and explicit pedagogical guidelines for staff to ensure that critical learning or development areas are covered (OECD, 2012).

PISA: The Programme for International Student Assessment (PISA) is an ongoing triennial survey that assesses the extent to which 15-year-olds students near the end of compulsory education have acquired key knowledge and skills that are essential for full participation in modern societies. The PISA 2015 survey focused on science, with reading, mathematics and collaborative problem-solving as minor areas of assessment. For the first time, PISA 2015 delivered the assessment of all subjects via computer. Paper-based assessments were provided for countries that chose not to test their students by computer, but the paper-based assessment was limited to questions that could measure trends in science, reading and mathematics performance. Around 540 000 students completed the assessment in 2015, representing about 29 million 15-year-olds in the schools of the 72 participating countries and economies (OECD, 2017b).

PISA Index of economic, social and cultural status (ESCS): The Programme for International Student Assessment (PISA) index of ESCS was created on the basis of the following variables: the International Socio-Economic Index of Occupational Status (ISEI); the highest level of education of the student's parents, converted into years of schooling; the PISA index of family wealth; the PISA index of home educational resources; and the PISA index of possessions related to "classical" culture in the family home. For technical information on the index please have a look at the PISA Technical Report (OECD, 2017b).

PISA index of family wealth is based on the students' responses on whether they had the following at home: a room of their own, a link to the Internet, a dishwasher (treated as a country-specific item), a DVD player, and three other country-specific items; and their responses on the number of cellular phones, televisions, computers, cars and the rooms with a bath or shower (OECD, 2017b).

PISA index of home educational resources is based on the items measuring the existence of educational resources at home including a desk and a quiet place to study, a computer that students can use for schoolwork, educational software, books to help with students' school work, technical reference books and a dictionary (OECD, 2017b).

PISA School socio-economic profile: Advantaged (disadvantaged) schools are those in the top (bottom) quarter of the distribution of the school-level PISA index of economic, social and cultural status (ESCS) within each country/economy (OECD, 2017b).

Principal (or head teacher): The person, typically a qualified teacher, responsible for the day-to-day management of a kindergarten facility or primary school (see also ECEC centre leader**).**

Pre-primary education: Refers to services for children to support early development in preparation for participation in school and society and accommodate children from age three to the start of primary education. It is also often referred to as 'pre-school' and it corresponds exactly to **ISCED Level 0.2 (see ISCED).** For international comparability purposes, the term "early childhood education" is used to label ISCED level 0 (for more details, see Indicator C2 in Education at a Glance 2015).

Pre-school: Refers to services for children to support early development in preparation for participation in school and society and accommodate children from age three to the start of primary education. It is also often referred to as 'pre-primary education' and it corresponds exactly to **ISCED Level 02 (see ISCED).**

Practical skills: Skills that involve active involvement of a child and refer to only those skills that children need in daily life such as lacing shoes, brushing teeth, etc.

Private expenditure: Private expenditure refers to expenditure funded by private sources, i.e., households and other private entities. "Households" means students and their families. "Other private entities" include private business firms and non-profit organisations, including religious organisations, charitable organisations, and business and labour associations. Private expenditure comprises school fees; materials such as textbooks and teaching equipment; transport to school (if organised by the school); meals (if provided by the school); boarding fees (OECD, 2016).

Process quality: What children actually experience in their programme – what happens within a setting, such as interactions between educators and children. It also consists of the relationships with parents, available materials and professional skills of staff.

Public and Private institutions or settings: This report distinguishes between government-dependent and independent-private settings according to the degree of dependence on government funding. ECEC settings can be classified in three categories: 1) **independent-private ECEC settings** controlled by a non-government organisation or with a governing board not selected by a government agency that receive less than 50% of their core funding from government agencies, 2) **government-dependent private ECEC settings** controlled by a non-government organisation or with a governing board not selected by a government agency that receive more than 50% of their core funding from government agencies, and 3) **public ECEC settings** controlled and managed by a public education authority or agency.

Public expenditure: Public expenditure refers to spending of public authorities at all levels. Expenditure that is not directly related to education (e.g. culture, sports, youth activities, etc.) is not included unless these services/activities are provided as ancillary services by educational institutions. Expenditure on education by other ministries or equivalent institutions, for example Health and Agriculture, is included. It includes subsidies provided to households and other private entities (often in the form of financial aid to students) which can be attributable to educational institutions (e.g. fees) or not (e.g. private living costs outside of institutions). Public expenditure on education includes expenditure by all levels of government, both education specific authorities as well as other government agencies. Thus, central government expenditure includes not only the expenditure of national education ministries, but also all expenditure on education by other central government ministries and authorities. Similarly, educational expenditure by regional and local governments includes not only the expenditure of the regional or local agencies with primary responsibility for operation of schools (e.g. provincial ministries of education; or local education authorities) but also the expenditure of other regional and local bodies that contribute to the financing of education (OECD, 2016). Public expenditure is classified by the following three levels of government:

- Central (national) government
- Regional government (province, state, Land, etc.)
- Local government (municipality, district, commune, etc.).

Purchasing Power Parities (PPPs): Purchasing power parities (PPPs) are the rates of currency conversion that equalise the purchasing power of different currencies by eliminating the differences in price levels between countries. In their simplest form, PPPs are simply price relatives which show the ratio of the prices in national currencies of the same good or service in different countries (OECD, 2017a).

Rating scale: A set of categories designed to elicit information about a quantitative or a qualitative attribute. A common example is the 1-10 rating scale, in which a person (evaluator or assessor or survey respondent) selects the number that is considered to reflect the perceived quality or performance of the subject being monitored.

Regional level/regional authorities: A decentralised level of governance. It is located at state or province level in the vast majority of countries, and can be referred to as communities, *Länder*, cantons, states, etc. Regional authorities in federal countries are often responsible for ECEC in their particular region.

Regulations/recommendations: Different kinds of official documents containing guidelines, obligations and/or recommendations for ECEC institutions. **Regulations** are laws, rules or other orders prescribed by public authority to regulate conduct. **Recommendations** are official documents proposing the use of specific tools, methods and/or strategies for teaching and learning. Their application is not mandatory (as defined in Eurydice, 2013).

Science skills: Interest and abilities in understanding the various cycles in nature, as well as in the development of scientific knowledge, the ability to question scientific phenomena and to draw conclusions about scientific subjects. Science skills also refer to the development of awareness of how science and technology shape and affect our material, intellectual and cultural environments and the ability to understand that we all are a part of nature's cycles. Those skills also enable making simple predictions, asking why, comprehending cause and effect, sorting, comprehending the common properties of living beings.

Service quality: The level of quality at setting/provision level. It is the level of quality provided by an ECEC setting, and refers to all the features that are regarded by a country/region/local authority to be of importance for quality, children's environments and experiences that are presumed to be beneficial to their well-being. This most often includes the use of a curriculum, staff characteristics, teacher or assistant behaviours and practices, and the staff-child interactions that form the core of children's ECEC experiences, referred to in the literature as process quality. In addition, quality in most countries involves structural features of the setting, such as space, group size and other standards or regulations, e.g. safety standards (NCES, 1997; OECD, 2006; OECD, 2015; OECD, 2012).

Socio-economically disadvantaged children: Children from low-income backgrounds ("economically disadvantaged"), from poor areas or regions, with poorly educated parents and/or with one or more immigrant background parent who may face learning disadvantages due to a different language spoken at home (adapted from Bennett, 2012).

Special (education) need children (or children with special needs) Special needs children cover those for whom a special learning need has been formally identified because they are mentally, physically, or emotionally disadvantaged. Often they will be those for whom additional public or private resources (personnel, material or financial) have been provided to support their education.

Split system: ECEC services are governed by different ministries or authorities at national/regional level. In many countries with a split system, policies for "care" and "early education" have developed separately and fall under the responsibility of different authorities. Childcare and early education is provided as two different services and for different age groups. For instance, "childcare" for younger children refers most commonly to children under the age of 3 and "early education" most commonly to children of 3 years or older.

Staff-child ratio: The number of children per full-time member of staff. This can be a maximum (regulated) number, which indicates the maximum number of children that one full-time member of staff is allowed to be responsible for, or an average, that is, the average number of children a full-time staff member can be responsible for. Ratios can be either for main staff only (such as teacher or caregiver), commonly reported as teacher-child ratios, but can also include auxiliary staff, such as assistants.

Standardised test: A test designed in such a way that the questions, conditions for administering, scoring procedures and interpretations are consistent and administered and scored in a predetermined, standard manner (OECD, 2012; Zucker, 2004). This means that the same test is given in the same way to all test takers. Standardised assessments are usually administered to large groups of children, and mainly for the purpose of measuring academic achievement and/or comparing members of a cohort (Rosenkvist, 2010) (see also **test**).

Structural quality: Quality aspects that consist of "inputs to process-characteristics that create the framework for the processes that children experience" (Litjens and Taguma, 2010). These characteristics are not only part of the ECEC location in which children participate, but also part of the environment that surrounds the ECEC setting, e.g. the community. They are often aspects of ECEC that can be regulated, although they may include variables that cannot be regulated.

Subsidised services: Settings that receive grants/funding from the state or other public governmental bodies (e.g. regional/local authorities or municipalities) to finance operation of the ECEC service and ensure ECEC provision at reduced fees for parents or even for free.

Teachers and comparable practitioners: Pre-primary and primary education teachers are the persons with the most responsibility for a group of children at the class- or playroom-level. They may also be called pedagogues, educators, childcare practitioner or pedagogical staff in pre-primary education, while the term teacher is almost universally used at the primary level. Data sourced from the OECD's Education at a Glance exclusively covers this category.

Staff for individual children: These staff members work with some children only, for example children with special educational needs or those who do not speak the language of the centre or school. They may be in the setting or play- /classroom every day or only for selected time slots or lessons.

Teacher salary (OECD, 2016):

- **Actual salaries for teachers:** Actual salaries for teachers aged 25-64 refer to the annual average earnings received by full-time teachers aged 25 to 64, before taxes. It is the gross salary from the employee's point of view, since it includes the part of social security contributions and pension scheme contributions that are paid by the employees (even if deducted automatically from the employees' gross salary by the employer). However, the employers' premium for social security and pension is excluded. Actual salaries also include work-related payments, such as annual bonuses, results-related bonuses, extra pay for holidays and sick-leave pay. Income from other sources, such as government social transfers, investment income and any other income that is not directly related to their profession, are not included.
- **Earnings for workers with tertiary education:** Earnings for workers with tertiary education are average earnings for full-time, full-year workers aged 25-64 with an education at ISCED5/6/7 or 8 level. The relative salary indicator is calculated for the latest year with available earnings data. For countries in which teachers' salaries and workers' earnings information are not available for the same year, the indicator is adjusted for inflation using the deflators for private consumption.
- **Statutory salary:** Statutory salaries refer to scheduled salaries according to official pay scales. The salaries reported are gross (total sum paid by the employer) less the employer's contribution to social security and pension, according to existing salary scales. Salaries are "before tax" (i.e. before deductions for income tax). Salary after 15 years of experience refers to the scheduled annual salary of a full-time classroom teacher. Statutory salaries may refer to the salaries of teachers with the minimum training necessary to be fully qualified or salaries of teachers with the typical qualifications, plus 15years of experience. Starting salary refers to the average scheduled gross salary per year for a full-time classroom teacher with the minimum training necessary to be fully qualified at the beginning of the teaching career. Maximum salary refers to the maximum scheduled annual salary (top of the salary scale) for a full-time classroom teacher with the maximum qualifications recognised for compensation.

Teaching time / Working time (OECD, 2016):

- **Actual teaching time**: Actual teaching time is the annual average number of hours that full-time teachers teach a group or class of students including all extra hours, such as overtime. The data can be from administrative registers, statistical databases, representative sample surveys or other representative sources
  - **Statutory teaching time:** Statutory teaching time is defined as the scheduled number of 60-minute hours per year that a full-time teacher per year that a full-time teacher teaches a group or class of children as set by policy, teachers' contracts of employment or other official documents.

- **Teaching time:** Teaching time can be defined on a weekly or annual basis. Annual teaching time is normally calculated as the number of teaching days per year multiplied by the number of hours a teacher teaches per day (excluding preparation time and periods of time formally allowed for breaks between lessons or groups of lessons). At the primary level, short breaks between lessons are included if the classroom teacher is responsible for the class during these breaks. The number of teaching days is the number of teaching weeks multiplied by the number of days per week a teacher teaches, less the number of days on which the school is closed for holidays. The number of teaching weeks refers to the number of weeks of instruction excluding holiday weeks a teacher teaches a group or class of students as set by policy, teachers' contracts of employment or other official documents.
- **Total statutory working time**: Total statutory working time refers to the number of hours that a full-time teacher is expected to work as set by policy. It can be defined on a weekly or annual basis. It does not include paid overtime. According to a country's formal policy, working time can refer to the time directly associated with teaching and other curricular activities for students, such as assignments and tests, the time directly associated with teaching and hours devoted to other activities related to teaching, such as preparing lessons, counselling students, correcting assignments and tests, professional development, meetings with parents, staff meetings and general school tasks.
- **Working time required at school:** Working time required at school refers to the time teachers are required to spend working at school, including teaching and non-teaching time.

Total Fertility Rate (TFR) or the average number of children born per woman over a lifetime given current age-specific fertility rates and assuming no female mortality during reproductive years. TFRs are computed as the sum of age-specific fertility rates defined over five-year intervals. Assuming no migration and that mortality rates remain unchanged, a TFR of 2.1 children per woman is generally sufficient to generate a stable population within a given country - a TFR above or below this 'population replacement rate' is likely to produce population growth and population decline, respectively.

References

Anders, Y. (2015), "Literature review on pedagogy in OECD countries", background document for the United Kingdom review on pedagogy, OECD. www.oecd.org/officialdocuments/publicdisplaydocumentpdf/?cote=EDU/EDPC/ECEC(2015)7&docLanguage=En.

Bennett, J. (2012), *Early Childhood Education and Care (ECEC) for children from Disadvantaged Backgrounds: Findings from a European literature review and two case studies,* Report Commissioned by the European Commission, Brussels, http://ec.europa.eu/dgs/education_culture/repository/education/policy/school/doc/ecec-report_en.pdf.

Eurydice/European Commission/EACEA/Eurostat (2014), *Key Data on Early Childhood Education and Care in Europe: 2014 Edition*, Eurydice and Eurostat Report, Publications Office of the European Union, Luxembourg.

Eurydice (2013), "Reference Document 2, Key Data ECEC 2014 – Questionnaire for Eurydice Figures", internal working document, Education, Audiovisual and Culture Executive Agency, Brussels

Jensen, B. (2009), "A Nordic approach to Early Childhood Education (ECE) and socially endangered children", European Early Childhood Education Research Journal, Vol. 17/1, pp. 7-21.

Litjens, I. (2013), *Literature Review on Monitoring Quality in Early Childhood Education and Care (ECEC)*, OECD, Paris.

Litjens, I. and M. Taguma (2010), *Revised Literature Overview for the 7th Meeting of the Network on Early Childhood Education and Care*, Paris: OECD.

Middle States Commission on Higher Education (2007), *Student Learning Assessment: Options and Resources,* Middle States Commission on Higher Education, Philadelphia, PA.

NCES (1997), "Measuring the quality of program environments in Head Start and other early childhood programs: a review and recommendations for future research", *Working Paper* No. 97-36, National Center for Education Statistics, Washington, DC.

OECD (2017a), *OECD Glossary of Statistical Terms,* OECD Publishing, Paris, http://stats.oecd.org/glossary/about.asp.

OECD (2017b), *PISA online education database*, OECD, Paris, www.oecd.org/pisa/data/.

OECD (2016), *Education at a Glance 2016: OECD Indicators*, OECD Publishing, Paris, http://dx.doi.org/10.1787/eag-2016-en.

OECD (2015), *Starting Strong IV: Monitoring Quality in Early Childhood Education and Care*, OECD Publishing, Paris, http://dx.doi.org/10.1787/9789264233515-en.

OECD (2013), *Synergies for Better Learning: An International Perspective on Evaluation and Assessment*, OECD Publishing, Paris, http://dx.doi.org/10.1787/9789264190658-en.

OECD (2012), *Starting Strong III: A Quality Toolbox for Early Childhood Education and Care*, OECD Publishing, Paris, http://dx.doi.org/10.1787/9789264123564-en.

OECD (2005), *Formative Assessment: Improving Learning in Secondary Classrooms*, OECD Publishing, Paris, http://dx.doi.org/10.1787/9789264007413-en.

OECD (2001), *Starting Strong: Early Childhood Education and Care*, OECD Publishing, Paris, http://dx.doi.org/10.1787/9789264192829-en.

OECD/Eurostat/UNESCO Institute for Statistics (2015), *ISCED 2011 Operational Manual: Guidelines for Classifying National Education Programmes and Related Qualifications*, OECD Publishing, Paris, http://dx.doi.org/10.1787/9789264228368-en.

Rosenkvist, M.A. (2010), "Using student test results for accountability and improvement: a literature review", *OECD Education Working Papers*, No. 54, OECD Publishing, Paris, http://dx.doi.org/10.1787/5km4htwzbv30-en.

UNESCO IBE (2016), "What Makes a Quality Curriculum?", *Current and Critical Issues in Curriculum and Learning,* In Progress Reflection No.2, UNESCO International Bureau of Education, Switzerland, http://unesdoc.unesco.org/images/0024/002439/243975e.pdf.

WHO (2006), *Constitution of the World Health Organisation,* World Health Organisation, Geneva. http://www.who.int/governance/eb/who_constitution_en.pdf.

Zucker, S. (2004), *Administration Practices for Standardized Assessments,* Pearson Assessment Report, Pearson Education, San Antonio, TX.

Annex B.

List of contributors

List of network member contributors to Starting Strong 2017: OECD key indicators on early childhood education and care

Contributors to this publication provided country data, country-specific policy information, comments on the drafts, etc. as members of the OECD Network on Early Childhood Education and Care (listed in alphabetical order).

Country	Name	Organisation
Australia	Australian Government Department of Education and Training	
Austria	Ms. Martina Stoll	Charlotte Bühler Institut
	Ms. Sandra Wimmer	Charlotte Bühler Institut
	Ms. Birgit Hartel	Charlotte Bühler Institut
	Ms. Manuela Ottowitz	Charlotte Bühler Institut
	Ms. Gabriele Bäck,	Charlotte Bühler Institut
	Mr. Wolfgang Pauli,	Statistics Austria
	Mr. Andreas Grimm	Federal Ministry for Education
	Mr. Stefan Polzer	Federal Ministry for Education
Belgium (Flanders)	Ms. Annick Denys	Policy Area Education and Training
	Ms. Isabelle Erauw	Policy Area Education and Training
	Ms. Liesbeth Hens	Policy Area Education and Training
	Ms. Elke Naessens	Policy Area Education and Training
	Mr. Guy Stoffelen	Policy Area Education and Training
	Ms. Christele Van Nieuwenhuyzen	Kind en Gezin (Child and Family), Policy Area Childcare
Canada	Mr. Kelly Hennig	Alberta Education
	Mr. Jacques Robert	Ministère de la Famille du Québec
	Mr. Christian Paradis	Employment and Social Development Canada
	Dr. Robin Liu Hopson	Council of Ministers of Education, Canada
Chile	Ms. Katherine Becker	Ministry of Education
	Mr. Rodrigo Castillo	Ministry of Education
	Ms. María Isabel Díaz	Ministry of Education
	Mr. Ignacio Fernández	Ministry of Education
	Mr. Felipe Godoy	Ministry of Education
	Ms. Victoria Parra	Ministry of Education
	Ms. Francisca Rodríguez	Ministry of Education
Czech Republic	Dr. Irena Borkovcová	Czech Scholl Inspectorate
Denmark	Undervisningsministeriet (Danish Ministry of Education) and Børne- og Socialministeriet (Danish Ministry for Children and Social Affairs)	

Country	Name	Organisation
Finland	Ms. Kirsi Alila	Ministry of Education and Culture, Councellor of Education
	Ms. Tarja Kahiluoto	Ministry of Education and Culture, special government advisor
	Ms. Petra Packalen	National Agency for Education, Councellor of education
	Mr. Mika Tuononen	Statistics Finland, project manager
France	Mr. Gilles Petreault	Ministère de l'éducation nationale
Germany	Dr. Simone Bloem	Deutsches Jugendinstitut e.V.
Hungary	Mr. László Limbacher	Ministry of Human Capacities
	Ms. Tünde Hagymásy	Ministry of Human Resources
	Mr. Tibor Könyvesi	Ministry of Human Capacities
	Ms. Andrea Pasklosz	Ministry of Human Capacities
Ireland	Mr. Michael Keenan	Department of Children and Youth Affairs
	Mr. Toby Wolfe	Department of Children and Youth Affairs
	Ms. Bevin Doyle	Department of Children and Youth Affairs
	Mr. Tony Monks	Department of Children and Youth Affairs
	Ms. Roisin O'Loughlin	Department of Children and Youth Affairs
	Ms. Aoife Conduit	Department of Education and Skills
	Ms. Antoinette Gibbs	Department of Education and Skills
Japan	Dr. Kiyomi Akita	University of Tokyo
	Dr. Riyo Kadota-Korogi	Seinan Gakuin University
	Mr. Yohei Ito	Permanent Delegation of Japan to OECD
	Mr.Takashi Kiryu	Permanent Delegation of Japan to OECD
	Mr.Takashi Murao	Permanent Delegation of Japan to OECD
	Ms. Hisayo Nomura	Permanent Delegation of Japan to OECD
	Children and Child-Rearing Administration	Cabinet Office
	Early Childhood Education Division, Elementary and Secondary Education Bureau	Ministry of Education, Culture, Sports, Science and Technology
	Early Childhood Education Division, Elementary and Secondary Education Bureau	Ministry of Health, Labour and Welfare
Korea	Dr. Yoon Kyung Choi	Korea Institute of Child Care and Education
Luxembourg	Mr. Manuel Achten	Ministry of National Education, Children and Youth
	Dr. Anne Reinstadler	Ministry of National Education, Children and Youth
	Ms. Claude Sevenig	Ministry of National Education, Children and Youth
Mexico	Mr. Carlos Tena Razo	Ministry of Education
Netherlands	Ms. Inge Bruggers	Ministry of Social Affairs and Employment
	Ms. Titia Zwarts	Ministry of Education Culture and Science
New Zealand	Mr. Siobhan Murray	Ministry of Education
	Ms. Hannah Stanfield	Ministry of Education
	Ms. Chris Harwood	Ministry of Education
	Ms. Nancy Bell	Ministry of Education
	Mr. David Scott	Ministry of Education
Norway	Ms. Maria Bakke Orvik	Norwegian Directorate for Education and Training
	Ms. Tove Mogstad Slinde	Ministry of Education and Research
	Ms. Annette Qvam	Norwegian Directorate for Education and Training

Country	Name	Organisation
Poland	Mr. Aleksander Tynelski	Ministry of National Education
	Ms. Katarzyna Malec	Ministry of National Education
Portugal	Mr. Pedro Cunha	Ministry of Education
	Mr. Helder Pais	Ministry of Education
	Ms. Liliana Marques	Ministry of Education
	Ms. Conceição Baptista	Ministry of Education
	Ms. Helena Gil	Ministry of Education
	Ms. Ana Xavier	Ministry of Education
	Ms. Olívia Soutenho	Ministry of Education
	Ms. Leonor Venâncio Duarte	Ministry of Education
Slovak Republic	Ms. Viera Hajdúková	Ministry of Education, Science, Research and Sport
	Slovak Centre of Scientific and Technical Information	
Slovenia	Ms. Barbara Kresal Sterniša	Ministry of Education, Science and Sport
	Ms. Nada Požar Matijašič	Ministry of Education, Science and Sport
	With the co-operation of the Educational Development Office	
Sweden	Ms. Åsa Källén	Ministry of Education and Research
Switzerland	Mr. Alexander Gerlings	Swiss Conference of Cantonal Ministers of Education (EDK)
Turkey		Ministry of National Education
United Kingdom (Wales)	Ms Rhiannon Davies	Foundation Phase, Welsh Government
	Mr Neil Roberts	Foundation Phase, Welsh Government
	Mr Graham Davies	Foundation Phase, Welsh Government
	Mr Steve Hughes	Schools Statistics, Welsh Government

List of the members of the "Thematic Working Group on data" who contribute to Starting Strong 2017: OECD key indicators on early childhood education and care

The Thematic Working Group on Data had for goal to provide guidance to select and develop the Indicators included in the report

Country	Name	Organisation
External expert	Dr. Cristina Stringher (Chair)	Italian National Institute for the Educational Evaluation of Instruction and Training (INVALSI) Frascati, Rome
Belgium (Flanders)	Ms. Isabelle Erauw	Policy area education and training
Canada	Mr. Janusz Zieminski	Policy Research at Alberta Education
Chile	Mr. Felipe Godoy	Ministry of Education
Denmark	Mr. Anders Holm	Department of sociology at Copenhagen University
France	Mr. Gilles Petreault	Ministère de l'éducation nationale
Korea	Dr. Yoon Kyung Choi	Korea Institute of Child Care and Education
Luxembourg	Dr. Anne Reinstadler	Ministry of National Education, Children and Youth

ORGANISATION FOR ECONOMIC CO-OPERATION AND DEVELOPMENT

The OECD is a unique forum where governments work together to address the economic, social and environmental challenges of globalisation. The OECD is also at the forefront of efforts to understand and to help governments respond to new developments and concerns, such as corporate governance, the information economy and the challenges of an ageing population. The Organisation provides a setting where governments can compare policy experiences, seek answers to common problems, identify good practice and work to co-ordinate domestic and international policies.

The OECD member countries are: Australia, Austria, Belgium, Canada, Chile, the Czech Republic, Denmark, Estonia, Finland, France, Germany, Greece, Hungary, Iceland, Ireland, Israel, Italy, Japan, Korea, Latvia, Luxembourg, Mexico, the Netherlands, New Zealand, Norway, Poland, Portugal, the Slovak Republic, Slovenia, Spain, Sweden, Switzerland, Turkey, the United Kingdom and the United States. The European Union takes part in the work of the OECD.

OECD Publishing disseminates widely the results of the Organisation's statistics gathering and research on economic, social and environmental issues, as well as the conventions, guidelines and standards agreed by its members.

OECD PUBLISHING, 2, rue André-Pascal, 75775 PARIS CEDEX 16
(91 2017 05 1 P) ISBN 978-92-64-27610-9 – 2017